"Artful . . . f recent
bereavement and the lingering pain of older memories . . . [She] evokes
the Montana landscape in lyrical, vivid prose." —*Boston Globe*

"Lovely rhythms, spare language, tenderness, and flashes of rage . . .
There is a deep spiritual landscape explored in *Black River* . . . This in-
teriority and consideration of faith reminds one of Marilynne Robin-
son's books . . . Hulse aims high in her realistic exploration of an indi-
vidual mind, a wronged man. The novel evokes consideration of life
and faith. It does not debate right and wrong but aims higher: at the
possibility of salvation." —*Los Angeles Review of Books*

"A promising debut . . . The lyrical landscapes and the emotional
weather are in place." —*New York Times*

"Impressive . . . *Black River* offers a carefully controlled burn . . . This
is a novel about people's lives closely hitched to the past by law or
trauma or sorrow. As the narrative gracefully dips back in time, we
hear of fiery conflicts long after the fact . . . Hulse is one of the few
novelists working today who seem capable of portraying religion as
a natural, integral element of characters' lives—the way it is for most
Americans . . . The possibility of solace, if not redemption, hangs tan-
talizingly close in this tough, honest novel by a surprisingly wise young
writer." —*Washington Post*

"[Hulse] writes with carefully meted-out nuance . . . This novel is an
intricate work that layers faith with broken promises, broken bones,
broken hearts . . . A complex and powerful story—put *Black River* on
the must-read list." —*Seattle Times*

"Ultimately a novel about legacy and whether redemption by faith is possible, or whether the sins of the past generation live on as a twisted, fated inheritance ... Hulse believes that grace happens in a look between two people, or a moment of holding back. It's a powerful elegy to the knowledges we bear and the silences we hold."

— *Guardian*

"[*Black River*'s] questions of faith lead us to ponder; Hulse's empathy for her characters gets us to care ... *Black River* is surely about the everyday heroism of people, not larger than, but the actual size of life."

— *Oregonian*

"This striking debut novel by Spokane writer S. M. Hulse is a contemporary western that has earned critical comparisons to the work of Larry McMurtry, Annie Proulx and Wallace Stegner — and deservedly so. Hulse uses spare language to craft a rich portrait of inland Northwest ... Brimming with grief, guilt and the glorious relief music can provide."

— *Seattle Magazine*

"This first novel pulses with dramatic tension and emotional resonance ... Hulse's story is lyrical, elegiac and authentic. Watch for it on best-of-the-year lists."

— *BBC Culture*

"One of the best debut novels I've read in a long time. S. M. Hulse is a smart and sensitive writer, utilizing strong, clean and evocative prose to tell us of Wes Carver, a man who is wrestling with the world and himself, haunted by an old horror, tattered family bonds, a wife who is dead but not gone."

— Daniel Woodrell

"*Black River* is such a vivid, compelling debut novel. S. M. Hulse is an astute guide to an implacable western landscape of grief, violence and redemption."

— Jess Walter

"The prose in S. M. Hulse's debut novel *Black River* mirrors the Montana land in which it's set: spare, powerful, and dangerous . . . Like Kent Haruf and Larry McMurtry, S. M. Hulse knows the landscape about which she writes, and she understands the hearts of those who live there."
— Wiley Cash

"*Black River* tackles themes of Old Testament proportion — the inheritance of sin, deliverance and damnation, good and evil . . . With an empathic touch, this sophisticated debut illuminates how fine a line there can be between vengeance and redemption. This is a story you won't forget."
— Siobhan Fallon

"Hulse writes with great clarity and precision, her language a celebration of rigor and intensity, and with such awareness of human rage and love — and fear of love — that her novel *Black River* feels like a river itself, teeming and unexpected and driven . . . One of the great joys of reading this novel is watching how she manages this — and how her perfect balance allows her deeper and deeper insights into the ways that people, especially men, negotiate their love for, and their fear of, each other and themselves."
— Kent Meyers

"Like her forbears Kittredge, Proulx, Carlson, Hulse examines the mountains and rivers of the West, its implacable beauty, and makes the landscape her own . . . A wonderful debut by a welcome new voice."
— Ehud Havazelet

"Hulse is a wise and compassionate writer who understands the tricky and heartbreaking borders between principle and rigidity, justice and revenge. Her debut novel is provoking and memorable."
— Deirdre McNamer

"Richly evocative of its Montana setting, an impressively drawn debut about faith and redemption." —*Largehearted Boy*

"Hulse's crisp prose matches the solemn, economical speech of her reluctant main character . . . The narrative of *Black River* is not a straight shot; it uses interesting flashbacks to further highlight character construction and development. The flashbacks humanize Wes, peeling back layers of his tough exterior . . . Hulse takes the road less traveled, hinting at the rebirth of fatherly love and the transformative blessing of forgiveness." —*Bookslut*

"This top-of-the-line modern American western debut explores the themes of violence, revenge, and forgiveness with a sure hand . . . From the bluegrass theme to the western rural setting, Hulse handles [this] story like a pro." —*Publishers Weekly,* starred review

"Comparing [Hulse] to Annie Proulx, Wallace Stegner, or Kent Haruf is no exaggeration. Her debut is bound to turn readers' hearts inside out and leave them yearning for some sweet, mournful fiddle music." —*Library Journal,* starred review

"Hulse clearly loves Montana, and her own fiddle playing and knowledge of horses shine through the novel." —*Booklist,* starred review

"A stark, tender tale . . . Profound issues addressed with a delicate touch and folded into a strong story populated by wrenchingly human characters: impressive work from a gifted young artist." —*Kirkus Reviews,* starred review

BLACK
River

S. M. HULSE

MARINER BOOKS

HOUGHTON MIFFLIN HARCOURT

Boston • New York

For my mother and father

First Mariner Books edition 2016
Copyright © 2015 by Sarah M. Hulse

For information about permission to reproduce selections from this book, write to trade
.permissions@hmhco.com or to Permissions, Houghton Mifflin Harcourt Publishing
Company, 3 Park Avenue, 19th Floor, New York, New York 10016.

www.hmhco.com

Library of Congress Cataloging-in-Publication Data
Hulse, S. M.
Black River / S. M. Hulse.
pages cm
ISBN 978-0-544-30987-6 (hardback)   ISBN 978-0-544-57023-8 (pbk.)
1. Widowers—Fiction. 2. Correctional personnel—Fiction.
3. Stepfamilies—Fiction. 4. Prisoners—Fiction. 5. Parole—Fiction.
6. Loss (Psychology)—Fiction. 7. Montana—Fiction. 8. Psychological fiction.
I. Title.
PS3608.U436B53 2015
813'.6—dc23
2014027025

Book design by Greta D. Sibley

Printed in the United States of America
DOC 10 9 8 7 6 5 4 3 2 1

PART I

White Light

WITHDRAWN

The music, she thinks, is supposed to comfort. It's meant as a kindness; they are relentlessly kind here. It comes from a small plastic stereo the nurse switches on after helping Claire onto the bed. Claire thinks she recognizes the melody, and feels mildly ashamed for not being able to put a name to it. Wesley would know.

He's outside, in the waiting room. Not reading. Not watching the endlessly looping cable news. Certainly not placing pieces in the unchanging, half-completed jigsaw puzzle near the registration desk. No, Wesley goes still at hard moments. Sets his jaw, lets his features stiffen into an impassive mask, quiets his hands. If some well-meaning person who isn't wearing scrubs or a white coat tries to say hello or offer a commiserating smile, he either won't notice or will pretend he hasn't. But he'll be watching the comings and goings of every nurse, every doctor. Every opening of the door leading to where she is.

The music isn't comforting. Too many violins and horns and drums going all at once. Cacophony.

Years ago they didn't offer sedation for bone marrow biopsies, only lidocaine. Her first time, while Claire lay face-down on the bed waiting for numbness to replace the stinging in her skin, a nurse who looked like a child placed the four-inch trephine needle on a tray in Claire's line of sight.

Maria, Claire's doctor had said, we try not to let the patients see those.

Like a meat skewer, Claire decided. Or a knitting needle.

Afterward Wesley asked her if the pain had been bad, and she lied and said not really. He has never liked to be told even gentle untruths, so he doesn't ask anymore.

She likes simple melodies. A series of single notes that leave a trail she can follow.

Afterward they help her to one of the reclining chairs in the infusion suite and get Wesley. Without asking, he takes a chair from the nurses' station and rolls it to her side. His hair is backlit by the blue light of a fish tank behind him. He asks how long they have to wait before the nurses will let them leave—it's a question he asks just for the sake of speech; he knows this routine as well as she does—and she says twenty minutes. She is about to tell him she's cold, but he's already standing, moving across the room to the heated cupboard with the warmed blankets folded inside.

Wesley hates coming here, but he now occupies this place as though it is their home, with none of the deference he showed the staff in those first days and weeks. They have become used to the hospital in different ways, she and her husband. Claire feels less like herself here. Meeker. She lets people usher her from room to room, guide her through the stages of her illness. Wesley treats the hospital as territory to be conquered. He is impatient, uninterested—for the first time in his life—in policies or procedures. Wesley is one of those Montana men whose mouths hardly move when they speak, for whom words are precious things they are loath to give up. Here, though, she has heard him raise his voice at the nurses' station loud enough that she can hear him in her room down the hall. Here he has interrogated and threatened and—once—even begged. Sometimes, when he thinks she is asleep, he prays aloud. He is confrontational with God.

One of the nurses breezes by, depositing two cans of orange juice on the table. More of that maddening courtesy: snacks for the spouse as well as the patient, unasked. For a moment neither Claire nor Wesley moves, and then she begins to unwrap herself from the blanket.

Don't, he says. I'll get them.

Wesley, she says. The cans have pull rings on top. He can't manage pull rings. He fumbles with one anyway, his skewed fingers unable to get enough purchase on the ring to lift it. His face doesn't betray him — sometimes Claire thinks he trained all the expressions out of his face when he was working at the prison — but she watches the skin over his swollen knuckles blanch and knows it hurts him.

Wesley, please.

The can slips from between his fingers and clatters against the tile, rolls under her chair. He leans forward to pick it up, but stops halfway, bent, eyes in shadow. Claire reaches from beneath the blanket and puts her hand on his bowed head, brushes his hair back from his forehead. It's reddish blond, a color more suited to a little boy than a grown man.

Leave it, she tells him. It tastes tinny anyway.

Claire hopes that when Wesley dies, it will be quick. Heart attack. Stroke. Aneurysm. She cannot imagine him with a lingering illness like this one, cannot imagine him subjecting himself to the doctors and nurses, bearing whatever necessary pain they might inflict. Not after the riot.

It is always the two of them waiting. Waiting for the lab results to come back, for Claire's name to be called, for the drugs to drip into her veins. Waiting for remission. Waiting for news, good or bad. Now they are waiting in one of the exam rooms in her oncologist's office, on the bench beside the empty countertop where he will plunk down his laptop, open the lid, tilt the screen toward them. Wesley is sitting nearest the counter, so his body will be between hers and the doctor's numbers. The verdict.

She aims her eyes out the window. The September light has just begun its slow fade from summer-bright, and its gentle cast gilds the edges of the buildings downtown. Claire has never grown to love Spokane, has never come to think of it as her home. It is too obviously fallen from grace, a city with grand but dilapidated architecture and residents who speak fondly of a golden age none of them remember. And the mountains in the distance are so small. Claire misses the mountains in Black River, their immediacy and immensity. These hills are shades of what she left behind.

I hate this fucking clock, Wesley says quietly. The first time she's heard him swear in thirty years of marriage. Claire looks. An ugly red plastic rim, a pharmaceutical logo emblazoned across the face.

I suppose it was free, she says, but she knows what he means. It's a loud clock. The hand moves audibly, every second sounded. Gone.

She doesn't worry about him. He knows how to endure.

They could be wrong, Wesley says in the truck on the way home. They're at a red light, and the engine idles so loudly she has to strain to hear him. He says, There are other doctors. Better, maybe.

We've seen them, Claire says. Seattle. A bigger hospital, more doctors with more letters after their names. More treatments that weren't quite effective enough. We knew this was coming, Wesley.

We might find someone still willing to try a second transplant.

I'm not, she says. Willing.

Her doctor was kind but honest. He used words like *terminal, palliative, hospice*. Claire can almost see Wesley turning the conversation over in his mind, looking for the loophole. The sun is on his side of the car, and it slices through the window, bright on his skin. Sweat beads above his upper lip, darkens the hair above his ears. She is cold all the time now, but she says, It's getting a little warm in here, and he cracks the window.

The light turns green, but there is still a man in the road, crossing the street with a slow, swaggering gait. Wesley sinks his foot against the accelerator, cuts close behind the man, who turns just before the curb and gestures with one hand, his mouth opening, the syllables obliterated by the rush of air past the window.

No. She does worry. His father was a suicide.

Wesley turns onto their street. His fingers hang over the edge of the steering wheel, neither curved nor straight, but caught in their permanent seize. He slows the truck, eases the tires over the wide, weed-split cracks in the asphalt. Each time the truck hits one of the cracks, Claire feels it. She feels it everywhere her blood goes. When the doctors first told her there was something wrong, she lay very still at night and tried to feel the disease, the cells building up in her marrow, thickening her blood, coursing through her veins. Now there's nothing but the pain of the illness and its treatments, always there, under and above everything else.

The house, a postwar bungalow of yellow brick, is small, though it had seemed large when they signed the papers. They put a new roof on it after the first winter, two fresh coats of paint on the trim since. A cherry tree in the yard blossoms once a year and drops sour fruit on the lawn months later. The cherries are past ripe now, black and full but still clinging to the branches.

Wesley kills the ignition, and the engine ticks. He brings his hands together, rubs one over the other. He must have clenched his fists while her doctor was talking; she should have noticed and stopped him. Claire reaches across the seat, takes his right hand in both of hers. She moves her fingertips over his knuckles, down the healed bones of his fingers, around each outsized joint. Coaxes his pain away.

I want to go to Black River, she says. She looks at him, and he stares through the windshield at the fence. The muscle in front of his ear jumps once, twice.

All right.

She lets go of his right hand, holds her palms out for his left. I don't mean for a trip, she says.

The bench seat's springs creak as he twists to give her his other hand.

I know.

She will miss the cherry tree.

Wesley doesn't look at her the way he used to. Now it's all half glances, stolen looks when her own eyes are directed elsewhere. When he does look at her directly, he maintains absolute eye contact. Looks for her soul, avoids her body. Claire understands. When she goes into the bathroom now, she leaves the light off. In the truck, she doesn't pull the sunshade down even if the sun burns right in her eyes, because the mirror set into it finds the worst of her: the white glare of her scalp through tufted hair, the taut patch of scar tissue below her collarbone, where her port sits beneath the skin. When her older sister, Madeline, was feeling cruel when they were girls, she would tell Claire that she looked like a German milkmaid, all rounded curves and thick blond hair. Claire, eleven or twelve and oblivious to the sensuous potential of such an image, would suck in her cheeks and make a futile effort to comb her hair straight and sleek. Now she must work to find the milkmaid in her reflection, and even then it's mostly imagination.

Claire leaves most of the chores to Wesley, but she calls her son herself.

Of course you can come, Dennis says. For as long as you want.

She can hear the boy in him then, the wishful thinking. As if what she wants has anything to do with it. Wesley's coming, too, she tells him.

He hardly pauses, but she hears the edge come into his voice. That's fine, he says.

He's my husband, Denny. I love him.

I know, Mom. I said it's fine. He's angry now, talking through his teeth.

I want to be with you, she says. You and Wesley both. When it's time.

She wishes she had said, *When I die. When my heart stops beating. When this disease takes the little I have left and kills me.* He needs to hear it. He needs to understand. But even Wesley still says *if something happens. If.* Never *when.*

Something she has never told Wesley: when they left Black River eighteen years ago, without Dennis — when Wesley made her choose — Claire didn't go because she needed him. She didn't go because she thought he was right. She went because she knew her son, even at sixteen, would be all right without her. She couldn't say the same about her husband.

Wesley is glad to have tasks. Over the next days, he approaches each with single-minded purpose: calling her doctors here, calling the hospice there, arranging time off work (Claire suspects this is harder than he reports; he has already taken so much). He counts out her medications, checks labels, calls in refills. Lays out more clothes than she'll ever wear. Sorts through photographs and mementos, wraps everything she could possibly want in layers of newsprint and bubble wrap. He stacks the things he packs in their bedroom, against the far wall. Two suitcases, one duffel, three boxes. He is packing for the time he hopes she will have. For more time than the doctors have suggested she will have. Is this delusion, she wonders, or denial?

He sits on the edge of the bed. We can go tomorrow, he says.

I'm glad.

They're predicting sun the whole way. Ought to be a pretty drive.

Where's your fiddle?

A sharp look. What?

You haven't put your fiddle with the other things. You have to take your fiddle.

Claire.

Get it.

He stands, slowly. Goes to the closet and reaches to the top shelf, pulls the worn chipboard case down and sets it on the foot of the bed. His fingers leave clean black streaks in the dust on the lid, linger over the tarnished brass clasps at either end of the case. He speaks without looking at her. Ain't no reason to bring this.

Don't leave it behind, she says. He won't come back after.

Something else she has never told him: she still wonders if she made the right choice.

Sometimes she can't put it out of her mind. She's dying. Not *Hey, we're all dying from the day we're born,* but really dying. Here. Now. When she can't stop the panic in time, when it threatens to take hold and overwhelm her, there's one way to hold it at bay: she thinks about her last moments. About what will happen when death arrives. People see things. Loved ones. A tunnel. White light. Science thinks it's explained all this. Electrical impulses. Firing synapses. Chemical reactions.

Claire doesn't care. She's never been a believer, and if it is only science, isn't that wonderful, too? A built-in safety net, an evolutionary shield to protect a person at her most desperate moment. It doesn't matter if what she experiences as she dies is real or not; what matters is that she experiences something. Claire already knows what it will be. Sound. Song. Wesley's song. "Black River." He first played it the day they met, at Harvest. It came to be his most well-known tune, though it wasn't fast, didn't end with impossible cascades of notes and broken strands of horsehair dangling from his bow. It was slower, wistful. Bittersweet.

Everyone loved it. Claire loved it. Wesley, though, was never quite satisfied. Every day it was the last tune he played before his fiddle went back in its case, and every day it changed. Just a bit. The changes became smaller and subtler over the years: adding a grace note, dropping a double-stop, digging his bow more deeply into a string. Each time he played it, Claire knew she was one day closer to hearing a masterpiece. And then the riot. Bobby Williams. Dust on a chipboard case.

Claire got the musical terms mixed up, always called it a lament. Wesley would shake his head. It's an air, he'd tell her. Laments are for the dead.

Claire is the first to know that they won't be going to Black River. She wakes in the dark with a pressure building in her chest, a hand closing on her throat. Wesley is asleep beside her, his teeth clenched tightly, the line of muscle along his jaw taut. He is never peaceful when he sleeps, and this lets her wake him without guilt.

Sit up with me, she says. The words come out more quietly than she intends, but he is awake.

You're burning, he says, and goes to stand.

Stay, Claire says. With me. She wonders if he will. If he'll be able to let this be.

He stays at her side all day, sits with her in bed so she can lean her body against his. He is very still. A nurse comes, one Claire doesn't know. She is kind, and does less to Claire than she is accustomed to nurses doing. Wesley goes to the hall to talk with her. Claire cannot hear them, though they are near enough she should be able to. Wesley keeps his hand on the doorframe, and she watches it until he comes back to her. Something is wrong with his fingers.

Time becomes untrustworthy. It is day, the only one Claire remembers since waking Wesley. But her fastidious husband has more than a few hours' worth of stubble on his face. (It is gray, not blond, and this makes her feel peculiarly sad.) And this is not the gown she wore to bed. Is it? She's angry; if time has ever mattered, it matters now.

Breathing becomes a conscious, messy act; she is choking on her own saliva, on the mucus in her nose and mouth and lungs. There's a strange sound in the room, a wet rattle, and at some point she realizes it is her. She's afraid Wesley will be disgusted by these things her body is doing, but he wipes her face and strokes her hair and rests her head on his chest.

I can hear your heart, she tells him.

That's good, he says.

For a long time the light in the room is a slow, sweet gold. And then it is dark, and Claire cannot understand how a day has gone by. (One day? More?) She wishes the window were nearer, so she could look out and see the mountains, black against black. She has always loved the mountains here.

Play for me, she says.

Wesley's body stiffens beneath her cheek. What?

Play, she says again. Play your fiddle for me.

He sighs. A long breath like she will never have again.

Not for long, she tells him. One tune is all.

Claire . . .

Please?

A lament.

He sits on the edge of the bed and rests his fiddle on his knee, cradling the neck in his left hand. Golden varnish, unblemished ebony, the bright lines of the strings. He holds the bow loosely in his right hand, the stick lying across the bed. The horsehair leaves a fine white line of rosin on the blanket. Wesley passes his thumb lightly over the fiddle's strings, and even Claire can hear the discordant notes, knows it isn't in tune.

Wesley looks over his shoulder at her. What do you want to hear? he asks.

You know, she says.

"Black River."

Yes.

He watches her for a long time, and it's been thirty years—thirty years—but she cannot read his expression. She wants to tell him that the color of his fiddle is like the color of his hair, which is like the color of summer evening sun, but the thought of forming the words overwhelms her, so she closes her eyes and waits. The bed moves as Wesley shifts his weight, and Claire wants to look at him again so she can see the fiddle under his chin—he looks almost haughty when he plays, and she has always loved this about him—but she is so tired. She hears the brush of his skin against wood, the light touch of the bow as horsehair comes to rest on wound steel. The breath before the note.

She listens.

Wes Carver was sixty years old and had been a widower five days. He was in his truck, struggling up the Idaho side of Lookout Pass, not quite two hours into a four-hour trip. His fiddle was in its case on the floor, the DOC letter and his revolver in the glove compartment. And Claire's ashes there beside him on the bench seat, in a small box wrapped with brown parcel paper and labeled with a bar code sticker. They'd warned him the package would be small, but he'd still been surprised when he signed the papers and they handed it to him.

Tractor-trailers eased into the left lane and passed him, their haz-ards flashing. Years ago, when Wes was still living in Black River, he'd come through here in January. Couldn't say why anymore. The storm had been bad enough he shouldn't have been driving — the left lane impassable, the right invisible against a snow-filled sky — but by the time he realized, it was too dangerous to pull off. At the top of the pass, at the Montana state line, he'd come upon an accident in which a little sedan had thrust itself beneath the trailer of a semi. Never saw it, most likely. Wes must've arrived just after the state patrol, no ambulance yet. The patrolmen were standing on the side of the road with the driver of the truck, collars turned up against the blowing snow. The way the car had folded under the trailer, there was no doubt. When he drove by at five miles an hour, Wes saw blood melting the snow beneath the union of twisted metal, illuminated by the chemical glare of the nearest flare.

Now the truck badly needed the long coasting down the Montana side of the pass. Wes took the curves a little too fast, riding close to the white line. The sun was low, streaming through the passenger window, burning at the corner of his eye. The mountains crumpled up around him, ravines and canyons everywhere, all a uniform green. A few brief moments here near the summit to see it all before descending back into the deep valleys that blinded a man to all but the path ahead or behind. (The day before she died, Claire opened her eyes just as the sun went down. A softness to her gaze. Maybe the morphine. Maybe the first haze of death. Are we still going to Black River? she'd asked. He'd put his hand over hers. Yes, he said. Of course we are.)

So easy to go sailing off this road. A wonder more folks didn't. All that space, waiting. Wes never could've planned a suicide, couldn't have swallowed the pills or loaded the gun or climbed the trestle. But this would take only a single moment of conviction, an instant of courage that could be abandoned almost as soon as it had been summoned. The briefest contraction of the muscles in the arms, a short jerk of the wheel to the right—a few inches would do it—and then: through the low guardrail and into the air. The truck, the fiddle, the ashes, the letter. Him. Falling like flying.

He'd waited there a long time, fiddle on his collarbone, bow touched to string. Poised beside his dying and then dead wife in a mockery of something he could no longer do. His arms must have begun to ache, but he didn't notice. In the dark it had seemed possible to stay there like that: Claire just a moment from breath; he just a moment from music.

Hearing was the last sense to go. The last filament connection to life. Dr. Harmon had told him that, and it was knowledge Wes didn't want, knowledge he'd have given anything to refuse. Why not sight? Why not touch? A reassuring gaze, a comforting hand. Those things he could've offered her. But she wanted his music. So he'd taken his fiddle and brought it to his body and laid horsehair down and then could do no more. Even if he'd drawn the bow across an open string, the pegs had slipped long ago, the strings gone flat.

How long had she waited?

Her eyes had closed, and the rattle of her breath crescendoed and dwindled and still he held his fiddle and his bow. Suppose she wasn't gone yet. Suppose she still waited to hear him play. Suppose she thought he was unwilling, not unable. He waited. Prayed. Considered trying to tune and rosin and play, knew he could do none of those things because he'd tried so long and so hard so many times before.

When dawn began to edge out night, he lowered the fiddle. Lowered the bow. Thought about smashing both against the wall. But instead he smoothed the blanket over her body. Laid the fiddle back in its case. Closed the lid. Fastened the latches.

It was impossible to be lost in western Montana. The mountains were always there against the sky, their unchanging silhouettes as sure as any map. Wes felt them closing in as he followed the interstate into the Elk Fork valley: the Sapphires melting into the Bitterroot Range to the south, the Sawtooths behind him, the Whitecaps, Missions and Swans to the north. The Garnets still ahead, to the east. Peaks appeared he could put a name to, some distant and dusted with snow, picturesque, others closer, immediate, covered with dry brown grasses or green pine or black slashes of basalt. Mount Sentinel, Blood Summit, Squaw Peak (he thought they'd changed the name of that one, the Indians upset or some such, but he couldn't remember what folks were supposed to call it instead). Elk Fork—a city in Montana, a town in any other state—was nestled in the shallowest part of the valley's bowl, sharing space with three different rivers that laced together and parted again at regular intervals. On the east side of the city the mountains began to draw together, and the valley narrowed, a single strand of water winding through. Black River lay thirty miles into the canyon. Wes remembered one of his grade school teachers telling them how this landscape had come to be—one of those geological phenomena involving ancient, vanished glaciers and lakes—but as a child he had thought the slopes of the mountain ranges looked like the hands of giants, or maybe of God, each ravine and peak delineating fingers and knuckles, just visible above the edges of the earth. A person in Elk Fork's wide valley felt like he was cradled in the palms of those giant hands. In Black River he was between two clenched fists about to collide.

Elk Fork was still in the midst of a long autumn twilight, a golden stretch of hours between the time the sun dipped below the mountain peaks and when darkness truly fell. The canyon had already succumbed to shadow, though, and Wes turned on the headlights as he steered around the first curve. He was starting to feel the tension high in his back, between his shoulder blades. The joints in his hands were aching, too, though he'd been careful to drive mostly with the heels of his hands, tucking his wrist over the crosspiece of the steering wheel on the curves and gripping with his fingers only when absolutely necessary. He opened and closed each hand a couple times, did his best to put the pain out of his mind. Plenty of practice.

Just before the Black River exit was the familiar large sign: *Montana State Prison, 6 Miles.* Then the smaller signs, every couple hundred yards: *Do Not Pick Up Hitchhikers.* The house was west of town, and Wes was glad. Meant he didn't have to drive through Black River yet, didn't have to confront all that had changed and all that hadn't. Didn't have to set eyes on the prison. He took the exit, drove three miles down the frontage road. Long strands of barbed wire sagged along the periphery of the fields, tattered white ghosts of plastic bags fluttering where they'd snagged. A pair of ribby horses swished their tails in a grazed-down pasture. Crumpled cans glinted amid the weeds in the ditch, and the speed limit signs bore round silver dents where kids or drunkards had used them for target practice. The final cutting of alfalfa stood in the few cultivated fields, and the heavy, sweet scent filled the cab of the truck. Seemed to Wes it ought to have smelled strongest at midday, beneath a hot sun, but it was always evenings, when the grasses began to cool.

He knew he was approaching the house even before he saw the welded pipe gate across the drive. Something about the pitch and roll of the mountains, the cant of the trees. There was a clasp on the gate's chain, but it was unfastened. Wes wondered if Dennis had done that on purpose, if he knew the clasp would've been too much for his hands. Maybe he always left it like that. Another six-tenths of a mile to the house, through evergreen woods. The weave of the forest was just different enough—trees missing, new deadfall on the ground, trunks leaning at steeper angles—that looking too closely was unsettling. Through a lattice of pine, Wes saw the mercury-vapor lamp at the house blazing against the coming dark.

Dennis was waiting on the front steps. Already not like him. The Dennis Wes remembered would've been watching from behind a parted curtain, or while pretending to be absorbed in some task, fixing a fence or working on his truck. Not just sitting there, watching steadily with those familiar wary dark eyes. Here, suddenly, was the face Wes had searched for so many years, looked for in the features of every inmate on his tier. His stepson, no longer a teenager but an adult. Same taut features, skin skimming close over muscle and bone. New lines at the edge of his mouth that ran so deep they looked like cuts. He was just thirty-four, but his dark hair was already going steadily gray at his temples, and he'd cut it short, shorter even than Wes wore his. He stood when Wes pulled up, but didn't move off the porch.

What to do. No hug. Not after so many years, and not after the kind of leave they'd taken from each other. And no handshake, either. Dennis almost forgot, offered his hand before awkwardly dropping it back to his side. Claire had come back to Black River for two weeks every spring. And Dennis had come to Spokane when she fell ill, of course, and to Seattle after the transplant. But in the hospitals, Dennis always phoned Claire's room before he visited, and Wes made sure he was gone. He'd called Dennis a few times, when Claire was too sick to do it herself. And last week, after she died. Maybe ten minutes of conversation in eighteen years, all of it on Claire's behalf. And now Wes stood on the porch that had once been his, with a stepson who used to be his to care for, and he had no words.

Dennis hooked his thumbs behind his belt, cocked his weight onto one hip. "Trip all right?" he asked.

"Yeah."

"Lot of tourists?"

"A few RVs. Not so many as I thought there'd be."

"Season's kind of winding down."

He should've rented a room at a motel. There was a decent one in town, a dozen cottage-like buildings with peeling gray paint spaced evenly around a gravel horseshoe. Wes had no idea what'd possessed Dennis to offer to put him up at the house, even less what'd made him agree. (He'd lived here with her.)

"You want a beer?" Dennis asked finally.

The house still smelled the same. Lemon, linen, smoke. Would've figured it'd have a different scent after all this time. Wes found himself anticipating each squeak of the floorboards. Dennis went to the kitchen, and Wes set Claire's ashes on the dining table, near where she used to sit. It seemed somehow wrong, so he moved them to the floor; that was worse. Decided, at last, on the wicker chair next to the front door. When he turned, Dennis was in the doorway, watching, two opened bottles in one hand.

Wes sat on the couch. Dennis settled on the hearth, one wrist balanced on a bent knee, the other leg straight out ahead. His casual sprawl was a little too conspicuous, the effort of it showing.

"You look good," Dennis said.

"So do you." Wes turned the beer bottle in his hand, the condensation wetting his palm. Dripping off his wrist like blood. (No. Not like blood.)

Dennis glanced down, smiled briefly at some unshared thought. He set his bottle on the brick of the hearth, got to his feet and meandered around the perimeter of the room, glancing sidelong at Wes every few steps. He stopped beside the dining table, his back to Wes. Put one hand on the fiddle case. "You've kept it all this time."

Wes said nothing.

Dennis moved his fingertips over the pebbled surface of the case, over the yellow line of stitching that chased itself around the contours of the lid. And then his hands went to either end, positioned over the brass clasps, and Wes saw tendon push against skin as his fingers flexed, and Wes said, "Don't."

Dennis looked down at his hands. They stayed taut for a long moment. Then he sighed, and his hands fell away from the case. He turned around but didn't look at Wes. "I made up the guest bedroom for you."

It was the same twin bed Dennis had slept in when he was a boy. Wes's old bedroom — his and Claire's — was across the hall. Dennis's now, of course. All of this was his, the house, the land, all of it signed over to Dennis on his eighteenth birthday. A far more generous gift than the boy had deserved, but one that had pleased Claire, eased the anxiety she'd felt since leaving Dennis behind in Black River. Wes lowered himself onto the edge of the bed, the creak of the springs so sharp as to be almost tangible. A palm out to touch the quilt. Claire had made it. Pieced and quilted it all by hand. She started it when Dennis was a toddler, finally finished it for his twelfth birthday. He remembered her in the front room in the evenings, red and blue scraps of calico joining in small strips and squares, slowly working into a bigger pattern that covered her lap and then most of her body. The hoop and thimble and needle. So nimble with that needle. She'd seemed reluctant to work in front of him after the riot, sewed mostly in the mornings before he got up.

The quilt was soft beneath his hand, the fabric gentled by repeated washings. Touching it was almost like touching her. The stitches like writing. Or scars. After the riot, Wes wore long sleeves, hid what he could. Late at night, he and Claire together on the couch in winter or the porch swing in summer, she would take first one, then the other of his hands into hers — her skin always cooler than his — and she would move her fingers across skin and tendon and bone, soothing his most persistent aches in a way doctors and pills never could. Then she would unfasten the buttons at his cuff, and she would feel him try not to pull away, feel his muscles go hard under his skin, and she would wait but not draw back. She moved her hands over his wrists, his forearms, touching skin and scar tissue he let no one else set eyes on. Claire could make the ugly, hated letters on his left arm disappear. She never traced them, never avoided them. Moved across them like they were any other flesh. She did touch the six smooth rises on the soft underside of his right forearm, hid each beneath the pad of a fingertip. When she stretched her hand to its widest span she could cover five of the scars, obliterate them from existence. But there was always one left, stubbornly visible.

He drifted into sleep, woke to the moan of a train whistle. Dark still. It took him a moment to remember where he was—still a shock at every waking to realize Claire was gone—and another moment to recognize the whistle for what it was. Long and low, an animal sound. They were all freight trains here in the canyon; the Amtrak only ran up north on the Hi-Line. Freights didn't look like they moved fast, but when you stood right next to the tracks you saw they barreled along pretty good. There was a trestle over the river not far from the house, and when the trains crossed it the river ran beneath at matched speed. Silent, though.

The whistle sounded again, more distant this time. Across the hall, Wes heard a sigh, the sound of shifting weight on bedsprings. Then a long stillness. He'd never been a good sleeper, not even before the riot. He used to get up in the middle of the night and take his fiddle outside, unless it was cold enough to throw it out of tune. He'd walk halfway across the field toward the river and the mountain slopes, hearing the shifting steps of Arthur Farmer's horses in the pasture across the fenceline, and when he was far enough away not to wake Claire or Dennis he'd play. Music for the moon and stars. Claire would still be asleep when he returned to bed, but in the mornings she hummed what he'd played.

〜

When Wes woke a second time, the sun was already high over the mountains and Dennis was gone. In her last weeks, Claire had slept more and more, going to bed early and rising late, naps throughout the day. The doctors said it was normal, that she'd be harder to wake as they got closer to the end. Wes had slept less and less himself, staying up to watch the rise and fall of her chest, deluding himself into believing vigilance might make a difference. It'd been all he could do not to constantly bring her out of sleep, and sometimes he found himself shifting heavily in bed beside her, just enough to rouse her but pretend it was an accident. A little too easy to sleep long and deep now.

There was coffee in the pot on the kitchen counter, a clean mug beside it. Dennis feeling civil this morning. Wes poured, added a little sugar but no milk. Outside the night chill lingered despite the sun, and the wooden seat of the porch swing felt damp through his jeans. Wes waited for his coffee to cool, enjoying the heat of the mug on his palms. The property looked good. It wasn't much—twelve acres in all—but it'd always been plenty for Wes's family, the land narrow east to west but stretching south toward where the river hugged the bottom of the mountain slopes. The foothills rose abruptly here, as though the earth had suddenly run aground of something much stronger and sturdier and been left with nowhere to go but skyward. Old logging roads crossed the bare slopes like neat surgical scars. North of the house it was all wooded, but this side was pasture. Dennis had mowed it, replaced the old barbed wire with white rope, built a metal run-in shed. There were three horses in the field. No—two horses and a mule. They stood a few yards from one another, muzzles buried in separate piles of faded green hay. Wes watched the steady working of their jaws, the absent swishing of tails and twitching of ears.

The letter was still in the glove compartment. Still in its envelope. It had arrived the day of Claire's last biopsy, sandwiched between a medical bill and an insurance statement. He'd left it alone then. Overwhelmed. Other things to attend to. Truth was, Wes had a pretty good idea what was inside that envelope, and he thought he might put off opening it until it'd be too late to do anything about it. Probably not too late yet. Probably ought to leave it alone for a few more weeks.

In the pasture, the red horse began eating the mule's hay. The mule pinned his long ears, squealed and brayed, but the red horse ignored him and after a minute the mule walked to the vacant hay pile, swishing his meager tail hard against his flanks.

Wes set his coffee on the porch, crossed the yard to the truck. One of the horses, the black one, raised his head to watch. The envelope was made of cheap paper, had lost its crispness after a night in the glove compartment. There was a familiar black ink-stamped return address in the corner, not straight: *The State of Montana Department of Corrections*. Been a long while since Wes got a letter with that mark. He settled back on the porch and took his pocketknife off his belt. Twice he got his thumbnail against the groove in the blade, and twice the knife slipped from his fingers. He tried once more, forcing his grip until the deep ache flared in his joints and the knife clattered to the porch, skittering across the wooden boards and over the edge into the grass. The simplest fucking things. The black horse was still watching.

Wes stood, retrieved the knife. Finally got it open, slipped the blade beneath the envelope's flap and sliced. One sheet inside, the message short and to the point: The State of Montana Department of Corrections inmate Robert F. Williams had come eligible for parole. He, Wesley J. Carver, had the right to deliver a statement at the hearing. No acknowledgment there that he'd given twenty-one years of his life, and then some, to the service of the state. Just the same duty-done letter Victim Services sent to everyone, impersonal enough it took a more generous man than Wes not to think they were hoping folks would stay out of it altogether. It was dated three weeks ago. Still relevant for another five.

So there it was. Bobby Williams, getting another chance. Wes waited for shock, disbelief, but he'd kept a tally of the months and years going in his head, and he knew the math was right. He wasn't naïve. Money played a role in parole decisions, and space, and manpower, and politics. All sorts of things that had nothing to do with justice. He could accept that. What made him angriest, then, wasn't anything to do with the DOC or the state or the parole board, but the fact that Williams's name still brought with it the memory of the sloppy crunch of breaking bone, that it still sent Wes's gut into spasm and set his heart racing. That the mere memory of the man still brought forth these symptoms of fear.

He heard the grind of gravel and looked up. Arthur Farmer—once Wes's friend and neighbor, widower to Claire's sister—was only a few yards away, scuffing his boot heels in the driveway so Wes would hear him coming. His horse stood on the other side of the property fenceline, stock-still, its reins dropped to the ground. Farmer stopped when he was still a little farther away than most folks would've come. He nodded. Knew better than to offer his hand. "Wesley."

He looked older, of course—Wes so plainly saw age on everyone but himself—but in no way frail. Be like an ox till the day he died. A wide white mustache hid his upper lip, and a dusty bone-colored felt hat covered what had to be a balding head. Farmer was almost seventy now, and his blue eyes were rheumy and seemed to have faded in the years since Wes had last seen him, like paint exposed to years of sun and wind and snow. Looked right at you, so damned sincere.

Wes stood, took one step down from the porch. "Arthur."

"I'm so sorry about Claire."

Wes didn't do well with sympathy. Never had. There would be cards piling up back at home, well-meaning but trite condolences, and he'd toss them all unopened. "Well." He took another step down to the gravel, rocked a stone against the sole of his boot. "Known for a long time she might not make it."

Farmer looked sideways, like Wes had done something it wasn't polite to stare at. "Shame a lady like her should have to go through that."

"Deserved better," Wes agreed. He listened to his own voice critically, made an adjustment as he spoke. He knew how to do that, control tone and note. Music, really.

"Will there be a service?"

"No. Claire didn't really believe in all that."

"I remember."

"She wants to be buried near her sister."

Farmer smiled, an infuriating sort of smile, sad and content all at once. "Maddie would like that," he said.

Wes was starting to feel his own pulse. "Nice-looking horse you got there."

Farmer looked back over his shoulder. Wes didn't care a whit about horses, and Farmer knew it. "Yeah," he said. "Brought her over from Billings last fall."

"You still rodeo?"

"Here and there. I been roping some with a fellow over in Drummond."

"And your guitar?" Steady the voice. "Still play?"

Farmer glanced down quick. "Not really." He put his hands in his pockets, casual-like, but Wes had already seen the calluses on his fingers. That was Farmer. Thought Wes was fragile, thought he had to be lied to. Pitied.

"Not really," Wes repeated.

Farmer squinted at the ground.

"Well," Wes said, "good of you to stop by."

"Wesley," Farmer said quietly, "can I ask you something?"

"Guess I can't stop you."

"Are you here just for Claire, or are you here about the hearing, too?"

The man never did know how to mind his own business. Thought the fact that they'd been close once meant they still were. "Why? You all got a pool going down at the bar?"

"Christ, Wesley." Taking the Lord's name in vain. Most folks wouldn't expect that of Farmer, his being a deacon of the church. "I heard about it from Sara, and I figured the timing couldn't be worse. Just asking after you is all."

Sara Gregory. Lane's widow. "Is she giving a statement?"

Farmer looked at the sky. "Can't. They never did connect Williams to Lane."

"How about Bill's people?"

"He's only got a sister, and she's down south somewhere. Florida, Georgia."

"Long way."

"Yeah."

Farmer had been the first one into the control room after the riot. The one to kneel next to Wes, to put a hand on his shoulder and tell him it was all right and just hang on, Wesley, we're gonna get you out of here now. He knew what was under Wes's sleeves.

"Williams ought to be a lifer."

"Ought to be," Farmer agreed.

"Think they're going to let him go?"

Farmer winced, but didn't look away. "They might. Two of the board used to be police, and they ain't gonna like it. But they might. Money," he added apologetically, as though Wes didn't know why anyone ever got paroled. Sure as hell wasn't because they were model prisoners. No such thing.

~

It was too hard to stay at the house. Wes kept seeing Claire at the periphery of his vision: there at the stove, apron strings dangling over her rump; at the end of the couch, her legs tucked under her and a book on her lap; standing at the window in the bedroom. Not quite hallucinations. Not quite ghosts. Normal, he'd been told. The social workers, the hospice folks, they'd given Wes a handful of brochures in Spokane. All pastels and italics. He'd tried not to look at them, tossed them in the garbage as soon as he was home. Dug them out later, damp, smelling like coffee grounds. It was all there: the shock of grief; the anxiety; the anger; the heart that beat out of rhythm, shallow and fluttery like bird wings. Wes hadn't been able to decide if he resented fitting so neatly into some psychological profile or if he was relieved to know he wasn't flat-out crazy.

Black River, though, was no less fraught with memory than the house. It'd changed, yeah; he saw that the moment he drove down Main Street. The town stretched a good five, six blocks longer than it used to, inching eastward, toward where the new prison waited beyond the curve of the canyon. Modern glass and concrete buildings picked up where the old brick storefronts left off. A new high school — windowless and solid, with *Black River Wardens* painted on the exterior wall — stood where cows had once grazed. But it'd avoided the boom so many other towns in Montana had experienced: the Californians weren't moving here; the movie stars weren't building luxury ranches on the outskirts. The prison spared the town that much, at least.

Despite the changes, Black River remained more familiar than Wes liked. It had been a logging town before it was a prison town, and the railyards were still there on the north side of the interstate, piles of raw logs waiting beside empty track. The bulk of the town was south of the freeway, longer than it was wide because it butted up against the mountains. Half the residents lived in houses or trailers on the crosshatching of streets here in town; the other half lived on swatches of land up and down the canyon. Having land didn't mean you had more money than those who didn't; it just meant at some point you'd had a daddy or a granddaddy who bought up acreage when it was cheap. A few folks, like Farmer, still lived on a piece of their families' homesteads.

The buildings on Main Street were mostly brick, standing since the twenties at least. Chipped painted advertisements for products that no longer existed were barely visible above sagging awnings. There were two cafés, their signs topped by warring cola logos. A Back to School poster hung in the window of Jameson's Mercantile, its colors starting to fade. Old streetlamps lined the curbs, ensconced beneath generations of paint, and the streets themselves were lined with pickups, a few sedans and station wagons sprinkled in. A single traffic light hung at the center of town, a four-way flasher caught in a perpetual sway up on its wires.

The old prison stood on Main Street at the corner of First, occupied the whole oversized city block. It was a peculiarly Gothic structure, its stone façade something like an ancient European fortress. The walls rose straight up from the street, and when Wes was a boy he and his friends used to come here after school to stand at the base of the wall, arch their necks back and watch the guards pace from tower to tower with their rifles. It was dark inside, the stone eternally damp. The kind of place that made you expect claps of thunder and flashes of lightning. Wes had spent his entire career here; it had been the state penitentiary right up through 1995, when everything had moved to the new campus four miles east. It was a museum now, and the legislature had granted it some kind of historical designation that ensured it would always lord itself over Black River.

Claire had asked him once, when she was in one of her playful moods, what he'd wanted to be when he was a boy. The question brought him up short. Truth was, he'd always known he'd be a CO. That was the way it worked. Most of the sons of Black River did what their daddies and their daddies' daddies did, and that meant they went to the academy and got a uniform and spent their days inside the gate. Wasn't really a pride thing—plenty of the COs Wes had worked with prayed their children would find another way to make a living—but prison work paid better than retail or ranching, and neither of those offered government benefits. Doing something else meant leaving town, and the canyon had a way of holding on to its people.

He'd lied to Claire. A firefighter, he said. Or maybe a construction worker. He'd turned the question back on her quickly, and she'd catalogued a whole host of careers that weren't meant to be: ballerina, veterinarian, chef, painter, stewardess. It seemed there was no fantasy so fleeting it'd escaped her memory; they were all there, preserved as alternate versions of herself. Claires that might have been. He liked hearing her talk about them, and wondered only briefly if wife and mother were ever a disappointment to her.

She'd stopped suddenly, as though he'd spoken aloud. Ask me again, she said.

What?

Ask me again what I wanted to be when I was a girl.

He'd smiled, puzzled. What about you, he'd asked again. What did you want to be?

This, she said. I wanted this.

The cemetery was midway between Black River and the new prison, a sprawling acreage settled on one of the low gold hills below the mountains, far enough from the road that folks only had to set eyes on it when they'd prepared themselves to do so. Wes wore his good shirt, the crisp white one. The office was by the front gate, a squat little building with worn red carpeting and a cloying floral smell that must've come from a can. The man sitting behind the desk was much younger than him—it constantly surprised Wes that so many people in

the world were now younger than him—and he repeated his rote condolences too many times.

The man squinted at his computer screen when Wes told him he
wanted to bury Claire's remains beside her sister's. "I'm sorry," he said
yet again. "I'm afraid that sector of the cemetery is closed. All the plots
have been sold. I do have some very nice—"

"I just got ashes," Wes said. "Not a coffin."

"I understand, sir. I do have some very nice plots in the newest part
of the cemetery."

Wes pressed his palms against the wooden armrests of his chair.
The varnish was worn off from years of touch, like on the neck of a
fiddle. "She's in a little box," he said. "Like this." He let his right hand
hover eight inches above the glossy surface of the desk. The man stared
at Wes's crooked fingers, and Wes jerked his hand back down.

He let the man lead him to the open section of the cemetery. He
thought they would walk, but the man showed him to a green-can-
opied golf cart, and they drove along the asphalt paths with a feeble
hum. The stones there were flush to the ground. Easy to mow over.
Convenient. No trees overhead, just a few spindly maples bound to
support stakes with rubber loops. The sound of traffic rose from the interstate. It was a glorified potter's field, not so different from the patch
of grass behind the old prison where they'd buried the unclaimed remains of inmates.

Wes had the man leave him there, and waited until the sickly
drone of the golf cart had disappeared. He walked back through the
older part of the cemetery. The trees there were aged, maples and
oaks whose leaves were just beginning to turn, and sturdy pines with
trunks bleached white where the automatic sprinklers soaked them
every day. Wes's father was buried here, but he didn't try to find the
grave. He stopped instead in front of a white stone angel whose hair
and wings were turning black with lichen as she stared into the distance and pointed one finger toward the sky. Wes remembered Madeline's funeral. A lot of the officers were there—Farmer was a lieuten-
ant then, respected and liked—but Wes stood at the graveside with

Claire. He remembered her silent tears he couldn't coax away. The way she wouldn't look at Farmer, who wouldn't look at anyone. It was an accident, a moose on the road. But Farmer had been driving.

There was space here, beside the white angel. Claire didn't need a whole plot. Just room enough for the box, and a small marker. Used to be you could bury your dead on your own property. Way back on Farmer's land there were three graves; the grass and weeds were wild that far out, but there was a little wire fence and a patch of grass Farmer kept mowed, and three weathered wooden crosses. His grandparents, a child of theirs who had died without a name. Rules against that kind of thing nowadays.

Wes used to like rules. He liked knowing what to do, when to do it, how. He'd always felt that folks on the whole didn't know what was best for themselves, and what he did for a living didn't change his mind any. Believed rules helped. But then there were the rules the doctors had when Claire was sick. Visiting hours, when anyone could see a dying woman needed family with her. Rules the insurance company had about which treatments could be tried, and tried again. And now rules against burying a dead woman beside her sister.

A curled brown leaf spiraled down through the air and landed on the angel's hair, obscuring one eye. Wes watched it for a moment, fluttering like paper in the light breeze, caught there on the marble. He thought about brushing it away, but in the end he left it, and went back to his truck.

~

Dennis was still gone when Wes returned to the house, but a steady metallic ringing echoed off the hills, and when Wes squinted through the trees he saw Dennis's truck parked at Farmer's place. Wes walked slowly down the access lane that ran between the two properties. He stayed in one of the tire ruts; the grass on the centerline to his left was broken close to the ground, but on the verge to his right it brushed almost knee-high. Used to be Farmer kept it all mowed. Dennis's truck was butted up to one of the barns, a brown horse just visible in the shadows of the aisle. There was a small propane forge swung out to one side of the dropped tailgate, and when Wes got close he could hear it blowing. He hadn't noticed the lettering on the side of the truck before. *Black River Horseshoeing* was stenciled on the door in white, *Dennis Boxer, CJF* in smaller letters below. Wes studied the name for a good minute. Boxer was Claire's maiden name. After she married Wes she'd taken his name, and given it to Dennis, too. He'd been Dennis Carver growing up.

Dennis stood to one side of the barn door, his back half turned to Wes, eyes on the anvil before him. He had a hammer in his right hand, tongs in the other, a blazing orange horseshoe at one end. The strike of metal on metal was gentler than Wes would've expected, each note almost musical in its pitch and cadence. He could see the taut flex of Dennis's muscles beneath skin, though, and wings of sweat had bloomed over his back. Dennis used the tongs to turn the horseshoe on its side every few strikes, the duller sound metered in with the hammering. Wes watched carefully, but whatever Dennis looked for when he turned the shoe, Wes couldn't see it. A few more minutes of hammering and turning, and then Dennis disappeared into the darkness of the barn; a moment later Wes heard a hiss, and a cloud of acrid smoke spilled lazily from the aisle. He fought the urge to cough. Dennis came back out and dropped the shoe into a bucket of water. Steam rose from the bucket as he straightened and passed the back of his wrist across his forehead, and if he was surprised to see Wes, it didn't show in the easy, half-lidded glance he gave him. Dennis crossed to the forge and switched it off. Silence hit hard. He met Wes's eyes again. "Everything all right?"

"Just got back from the cemetery."

"Something wrong?"

"We ain't burying her there."

For a moment Dennis just watched him, and Wes looked back and saw the way the interior of the forge still glowed behind Dennis, the way the heat rising from it made the air over his head shudder. "All right," Dennis said finally. "Hang on." He turned and called, "Scott!"

A teenage boy appeared in the barn doorway. He was probably fifteen or sixteen, though Wes was too distant from that stage of his own life to be sure of his guess. A slight kid, with freckles bridging his nose and black hair that might've been dyed that color. He wore the same sullen look Wes had seen on the faces of kids at the mall where he'd worked security in Spokane, an expression that plainly announced to the world how much he resented it. "What?"

Dennis nodded toward the barn. "I'm almost done with Beau. Go bring Caesar in for me, will you? Big gray in the far pasture."

The boy picked up a halter and lead rope off the hood of the truck, but stopped short of the pasture gate and gave Wes a suspicious up-and-down glance. "Who are you?"

Dennis spoke before Wes could. "This is my stepfather, Mr. Carver. Wes, this is Scott Bannon."

The kid's expression didn't change, but he shifted the halter and lead to his left hand and mechanically offered his right, like an obedient dog performing a trick. Wes took it cautiously and stilled his own features against the pressure on his hand. "Good to meet you, Scott," he said.

Scott couldn't play his half of the charade, though, and his mask broke. "What the hell happened to your fingers?"

"Scott," Dennis warned.

"Someone broke them," Wes said. "Long time ago."

"On purpose?"

"Yep."

Scott waited, but Wes didn't elaborate. The boy studied him with the slightly bemused expression people wore when they hadn't yet decided if you were smarter than them, or if they were smarter than you. Inmates did it all the time.

"Well, shit," the kid finally said.

"Scott." Dennis's voice carried the gently admonishing edge of a parent's. "Caesar. Big gray."

"Right." Scott disappeared through the gate with a final backward glance.

Wes waited until he was out of earshot. "He work for you?"

"Sort of. He's a kid I'm . . . mentoring, I guess they call it."

"You sign up for a program or something?"

"Nah. I did this career day thing at the high school last spring." He smirked. "Not sure anyone told them my education tops out at halfway through eleventh grade. Anyway, Scott said he was interested in horses." Something in the way Dennis phrased that. "His father's in prison and his mother moved them to Black River to be near him. He doesn't exactly fit in real well."

"Lady ought to have known better." Black River was a CO town, full stop.

"No shit." Dennis shrugged. "But she didn't want him to lose touch with his father, and they come from Miles City." Well. Not exactly a short trip.

"What's his father convicted of?"

A long moment before Dennis answered. Thinking again. Deciding how much to tell. Wes always noticed hands, and his stepson's were tanned and sinewy, the right still gripping the hammer hard enough for tendon to rise and bone to blanch the skin over his knuckles. "He says armed robbery. Don't know if that's the truth."

"You better be careful with him around your things."

Dennis smacked his hand hard against the tailgate, and Wes heard the rattle of chains from the barn as the brown horse tossed its head. "Jesus, Wes!" He laughed, but his eyes stayed hard. "Don't tell me you still buy into that bad-seed shit."

"I'm just saying."

Dennis fished the cold shoe out of the water bucket, shook it hard. "Whatever happened to that scripture you like so much? The sins of the father and all that. Thought you were supposed to treat everyone as his own man."

Amazing how quick anger could tighten up a man's chest, like it was a physical thing pressing down on his heart. "Bible argues both sides of that one, Dennis."

"And didn't God say something about free will? Seem to remember that being in there somewhere."

Wes's hands were starting to throb, and he quieted the impulse to rub them. "Just told you to be careful is all. You're doing a good thing for that kid, but it's hard for a person to fight his own blood."

The muscles at Dennis's temples bulged and hollowed as he worked his jaw, and the way he kept his palms pressed against the tailgate suggested he was deliberately keeping himself corralled behind it. "Yeah? That mean you're still waiting for me to go out and start forcing myself on women?"

Wes stepped straight to him. "Don't you dare bring your momma into this."

"Thought you came here to talk about her," Dennis said, his voice flat and careless and exactly the way Wes remembered it.

"Don't you dare," he repeated, feeling the words drop to a growl in his throat. His voice carried authority, and people listened to him, even when they didn't want to. It was a gift Wes had put to good use all his life. He'd had to learn the rest of it when he started work at the prison: how to walk and carry himself, how to keep his face from betraying any trace of fear or intimidation, how to let his body show he was not afraid. But he'd never had to train his voice.

Dennis knew better than to fight that voice. But he didn't look away, and Wes matched his gaze and wondered if it was true, if he was, in fact, still waiting for the poisonous half of Dennis's blood to show itself. He'd done all he could to keep that from happening, to raise Dennis right and teach him discipline and values. And he'd succeeded, at least in that Dennis was living in Black River by choice and not because someone had locked him in a cell behind coils of razor wire. But in doing the job, Wes had cast a wide gulf between them, and it seemed the years hadn't begun to mend it. Shouldn't have surprised him. The only thing he and Dennis had in common was that they both loved Claire, and now that she was gone, so too was the fragile, frayed thread that tied them together. Still, Wes had loved Dennis once, when his own straight fingers had been fast on the strings, when Dennis was a child who danced while Wes played. Felt like he was carrying that memory for someone else, though, for another man who had lived in his body before him.

"Well, you haven't changed one fucking bit," Dennis finally said, biting off each word almost before it left his mouth. No different than as a boy, everything just barely controlled, just waiting to crack. "And I sure as hell don't know why Mom wasted her life on you."

"That's it," Wes said. His tone was even; he almost wished it weren't. "Had enough of this." He backed away from the truck a few steps, and when he turned hard he just missed the black-haired kid, gray horse in tow.

His name was Shane, Claire had told him once. And for a while, she said, when I was sixteen, I thought I was in love with him.

That was it. His name was Shane. Claire thought she was in love with him. The phrase stuck in Wes's ear, a wrong note. *Thought* she was in love with him. Why not just *was?* (Claire looked at the floor when she said his name.) At the time, Wes had known little of Claire's life before she and Dennis arrived in Black River, and he might have put aside his misgivings about Shane—assumed the man was simply a run-of-the-mill deadbeat—if it weren't for Claire's sister. Farmer and Madeline never had any children—couldn't, was the impression Wes had, though no one ever said as much—and Madeline doted on other people's. She taught fifth grade at the elementary school and worked in the church nursery on Sunday mornings. Always kind, always gracious. It made the fact that she didn't love her own nephew that much more obvious. Even when Dennis was just four, five years old, she could barely stand to look at him, and when she spoke to him her voice took on an oddly rigid quality. Once Wes caught her eyeing the boy with an expression of what could only be called disgust.

One night—after the engagement but before the wedding—Wes went to see Madeline when Farmer was at work. They sat in the kitchen. Condensation beaded the untouched glasses of lemonade Madeline put before them. A fly buzzed around the daisies in the center of the table, alighting for a fraction of a second before going airborne again. Madeline, who was six years older and six inches taller than Claire, but shared her sister's face, sat staring at her folded hands.

"She won't call it rape," she said.

It was merely a confirmation of his suspicions, but the word charged his blood. Hard not to stand up and rage right there.

"She was his girlfriend," Madeline continued. "Your typical high school infatuation. Puppy love, you know? Talked my ear off about him for a time. But she didn't want that. What happened, I mean. I know she didn't." Madeline batted the fly away with the back of her hand. "She called me afterward. There was no real ambiguity about it, Wes. Not the way she told it to me. But I think it hurts her more to think of it as rape, so she invents excuses for him. Says he was confused, that she led him on. That sort of thing."

"Where is he now?"

Madeline looked up sharply, and Wes was afraid he'd frightened her. But Madeline wasn't fragile, and her expression was bitter. "He's gone. After it happened, our father went looking for Shane with his shotgun over his shoulder. He left town. Probably the state."

But Wes never quit searching for the name on the inmate rosters, never quit studying faces for one that looked like Dennis. A man who would force himself on a woman once would do it again.

If Claire knew Wes had talked to Madeline, she didn't say so. Wes tried to bring the subject up a few times, but she had a quiet way of refusing to answer his questions, of redirecting the conversation with a delicate absoluteness. At some point, around the time Dennis quit being a child and started being a teenager, Wes became gradually aware that the boy knew the truth about his father. Wes certainly hadn't told him, but maybe Dennis had picked up on the same things Wes had. If he had gone to his mother, Wes knew, she would have told him the truth. She held things back from Wes sometimes, even lied to him on occasion—always lightly, always gently—but she had never seemed able or willing to do the same to her son. There was a bond between them as mother and child that allowed, or demanded, the frank discussion that he as husband wasn't entitled to. There were other things over the thirty years of their marriage that Wes and Claire didn't talk much about, that they avoided: the riot; that last night at the house; the decision to leave Black River. But Shane and what he had done was a forbidden subject the way nothing else was. There were just those few words, just that once: *His name was Shane. And for a while, when I was sixteen, I thought I was in love with him.*

~~~

During the riot, Bobby Williams took his wedding ring. Slid it off Wes's blood-slicked finger, raised it to the light, squinted one eye shut. "Is your wife pretty?" he asked. The ring palmed, gone. "I bet she is." His breath hot and moist on Wes's ear. "I bet she's real pretty." The words parceled out slow: "I wish she were here."

~~~

Most of the folks in Black River who owned land ignored it. Maybe they kept a few chickens or goats, or grew a little hay, but most just let the land go to seed or used it as a repository for rusted, beaten cars and appliances that had long since stopped working. Wes had expected to see more of the same at Dennis's, but if anything, his stepson had bettered the place. He'd replaced the siding on the house, painted the porch swing, graded the road, expanded the workshop, improved the pasture. When Wes went back to the house a few hours after his argument with Dennis, he found the other man on one knee beside a fence-post near the pasture gate, toolbox open at his side. He looked up when Wes pulled his truck into view, but turned his eyes straight back to his work. An Indian summer was beating down on the canyon, and Dennis worked bare-chested, yellow work gloves with dirt-blacked palms on his hands. He had the same body he'd had as a teenager, small but strong, all lean muscle, skin that looked tanned even in winter. Wes noticed a couple of tattoos: a ring of barbed wire around his biceps—the Montana special—and some kind of bird on his shoulder blade, a barn swallow, maybe. Wes tried not to judge. Lots of folks had tattoos these days. More did than didn't, he'd read somewhere.

Wes walked to the fence and waited, waving away a hardy late-season fly that buzzed around his head. Dennis had replaced the old barbed wire with three lines of braided white rope shot through with coppery threads, studded at each post with yellow plastic insulators. The red horse and the mule were at the far end of the pasture, heads down to the grass, but the black horse who had watched Wes so closely this morning stood easily a few feet beyond Dennis's crouched figure, one hind hoof resting so the toe just touched soil.

After a few pointedly silent minutes, during the last of which it looked to Wes like Dennis wasn't doing anything but running thoughts through his head, Dennis stood, shut his fencing pliers into the battered toolbox and started toward Wes with a careless, loose-jointed stride. On the other side of the fence, the black horse followed at a pace's distance. There was something awkward in the way the animal moved, a deliberateness to each step that Wes recognized.

"Wait here," Dennis said, walking past Wes without even glancing at him. About enough to make Wes turn around and leave. *You're here for Claire,* he reminded himself.

Dennis headed for the outbuilding near the house, where Wes's father used to have his workshop. The black horse raised his head over the fence and swiveled his ears toward Wes. It was an old horse, he saw now. A smattering of colorless wiry strands tarnished his black mane, and short white hairs edged the long angles of his face. The hollows over his eyes were deep enough for a man to sink his thumbs into.

"You hear that fence now?" Dennis called from inside the shed.

Abruptly the horse stepped back from the rope, lifting his head high, and a short ticking noise sounded every couple seconds, regular as a metronome. "It's going."

Dennis ambled back, pulling a T-shirt over his head. Wes felt Dennis's eyes on his long sleeves, on the sheen of sweat Wes knew must show on his face. He pushed his hands into his pockets. "Listen," Dennis said. "Sorry about all that shit I said earlier. Should've kept my mouth shut." He forced the words out like a nauseated man who just wanted to vomit already and be done with it.

Wes accepted the apology with a short nod. "These your animals?"

"This one is," Dennis said, reaching a hand over the fence to gently slap the side of the black horse's neck. The horse turned, and Wes saw that while the near eye was normal, a deep syrupy brown, the far one had a white around it, like a human eye. It was unnerving, robbed him of the vaguely benevolent gaze most horses had. "His name's Rio."

"You get him from Farmer?"

"Years back. That sorrel and the mule are his."

Wes watched Dennis rub Rio's face, and thought it was a small miracle that a man who'd loved something so much as a child still loved that same thing so many years later. Most folks were mercurial in their passions, changing quick from one to the next, or they cultivated a whole slew of interests, parceling out a little time and energy to each in turn. Maybe to really love something you had to be born with it, had it pressed into your soul before you even took a breath, so that it was something you could neither explain nor deny. The fiddle was like that for Wes. For Dennis it was horses. When he was a kid he'd spend entire afternoons watching the broodmares slowly meander around Farmer's pastures, and his favorite toys were his plastic horses. He'd had dozens of them, and increased his herd every Christmas and birthday. All of them, Wes remembered, had names and complicated made-up histories that Dennis could recite on the spot and never varied. Once, he dropped one on the floor and its front leg snapped in two. Cried so hard you would've thought they'd had to shoot the thing in the head. Wes spent the night in his father's workshop, measuring and drilling tiny holes into each half of the broken leg and setting it with a pin and glue. Took three tries to get right, and he finished four hours before he had to go back to the prison. Put an end to the tears, though.

Wes wondered if Dennis remembered that. It had been a gray horse. Dappled gray. "We didn't talk about your momma yet," he said instead.

"Right." Dennis started walking back toward the house, didn't check to see if Wes followed. "Didn't take us long to revert back to form this morning, did it?"

"Guess not."

Dennis reached the porch and turned. One corner of his mouth tugged into an ironic smile. "At least I didn't pull a gun on you this time."

"Don't think I'm ready to joke about that, Dennis."

His stepson sighed, a short exhalation like a bull's snort. He sat on one end of the top step, and Wes took the other. Yeah, the place looked good. Not much to criticize. It still felt like his house, though. Still felt like it belonged to him, like he might hear the creak of the screen door any moment now, like Claire might step out onto the porch and smile down at them, call them *my boys*. Like that last night and the gun and the eighteen years since hadn't happened at all.

"Got a cigarette?"

Dennis glanced sideways.

"You got nicotine stains on your fingers," Wes said. "Probably ought to cut back, you're smoking that much."

Dennis frowned, but he pulled a pack of cigarettes from his tool-box—Wes's old brand—and shook one out. He held it out to Wes without looking at him, like he'd just as soon let it drop into the dirt. "Mom said you quit."

"I did." Wes had to use both hands on the lighter.

"Want me to get that?"

"No," he said around the cigarette, "I don't." And finally the flame did catch and he pulled the smoke into his lungs. Didn't bring him the same easing of tension it used to. "I went to the cemetery this morning."

"You said."

"They can't bury her near Madeline. Full up or something."

"They got spaces in the rest of the place, right?"

"It ain't nice enough." Wes's fingers twisted over one another when he closed them—the doctors had a fancy name for that—so he held his cigarette with an open hand. Gave him a showy style that didn't suit him. "I thought instead we might scatter her ashes somewhere pretty."

Dennis didn't say anything right off, and Wes took that for acceptance. He was glad of it. Didn't know if he could argue about this and keep his head.

The end of Dennis's cigarette glowed as he drew on it. He spoke without exhaling, so a bit of smoke escaped between his lips with each word. "There's a good spot up in the mountains," he said. "It'll be best if we go up in the evening. Around this time."

"Tomorrow, then."

It rained hard during the night, though, and was still pouring the next morning. A good twenty degrees cooler than it had been, too. Happened like that sometimes. Summer one day, autumn the next. Winter not too far off. Dennis and Wes drank their coffee standing silent in the kitchen, and Dennis left for his first shoeing appointment.

After Dennis was gone, Wes made the drive to Elk Fork. They'd remodeled the hospital since he'd been there last—new tile on the floors, prettier colors on the walls—but it still assaulted the senses like any other medical facility. The disinfectant smell everyone liked to complain about didn't bother Wes much, but the sounds did: the rattle of metal casters as carts were pushed across tile; the dispassionate voices of the doctors and nurses; the breath-holding silences between the electronic beeps of monitors. Wes scanned the wide felt readerboard mounted near the elevator bank. Found "Oncology" out of habit, though Claire had never been admitted here. Fourth floor in this hospital. "Donation Center" was on the second.

He'd called ahead, and the staff seemed pleased to see him. In Spokane they knew him by name, but here he had to go through the full screening again. The paperwork took him a long while, and by the time he finished his joints were aching. They weighed him, took his temperature, gauged his blood pressure, pricked his finger and finally guided him back to the donation area, where a woman in pale violet scrubs appeared at his side.

"How are you this morning, Mr. Carver?"

"Just fine," he told her, because that's what you said.

She sat on a padded stool beside him, and he watched her eyes move back and forth over the sheet on her clipboard. Two years ago he would have called her a nurse, but he knew better now, knew she was a phlebotomist or a medical assistant. She was half his age, with curly black hair she'd piled on top of her head and fixed in place with a slew of bobby pins. The tag pinned to her scrub top said her name was Molly. She'd stuck a glittery sunflower sticker in the corner; it covered part of the *y*. "So," she said, "it looks like you're a regular platelet donor over in Spokane."

"Yes, ma'am." He shifted, couldn't get comfortable. The chair was too like those in the infusion suite where Claire had taken her chemotherapy. In Spokane, Oncology was way up on the seventh floor, and he and Claire would sit facing the wide windows and watch the city journey through its day below, and she would hold one of his hands between both of her own as though he were the one who was sick. "You do single-needle apheresis here?"

The phlebotomist—Molly—looked up from her clipboard. Tried and failed to hide her alarm. "No. But—"

"It's all right," Wes told her. "Just curious."

"I'll be very quick with the needles," she promised. "I'm gentle."

Wes nodded. Let her think a phobia was the reason he'd rather not have a needle in each arm.

"It's wonderful you're here," Molly was saying. She'd forced an incredible amount of enthusiasm into her voice, apparently still concerned he might bolt. "We always need platelets."

"My wife had leukemia," Wes said, without meaning to.

Molly stopped fussing with her tray of equipment and found his eyes for the first time. "I'm sorry to hear that."

"She passed last week."

Molly sat back down on the stool and touched his hand. "I'm so sorry," she said. He could tell she meant it, and felt the sudden horror of tears forming in his eyes. Molly turned away, and Wes hated her for that small kindness, because in granting it she betrayed the fact that she'd seen his grief.

"She had a transplant, but she relapsed," he said, forcing himself to talk through it, waiting for the constriction in his throat to ease. "We couldn't get her in remission again. She needed a lot of transfusions. I wasn't her blood type, but I figured if she was gonna be dependent on strangers, then I ought to do my part for someone else."

"It's a wonderful gift," Molly said, and Wes was relieved she'd re-treated back to the usual banalities. She was ready, so he raised his right arm a few inches.

"Could use a little help with the buttons," he said. "My hands ain't what they used to be."

She seemed thankful to be faced with a concrete task, a physical task, and Wes watched her unfasten the small plastic buttons at his wrists. Nurses and other medical types were the only people he didn't much mind asking for help. They weren't squeamish about disability or deformity, and most of them knew what was their business and what wasn't. "I got it from here," he said, once the buttons were free. "Mind getting the curtain?"

Wes waited until the green cloth was drawn around them. He hoped Molly might turn away to prep lines or needles, but she didn't, so while she watched he pushed his right sleeve up over his elbow and revealed the scars on the underside of his forearm. Six of them, spaced evenly from wrist to elbow, and impossible to mistake for anything but the cigarette burns they were. The left arm was worse, and Wes was careful not to look at Molly when he rolled up his other sleeve. Five letters carved into the flesh from elbow to wrist, each line thick and raised, lighter in color than the surrounding skin. The name still legible despite a crosshatching of newer scars defacing the letters. Impossible to see the muscle, the bone, the structure made strong and lean by a lifetime of fiddling. Impossible to see anything but that fucking mess of scar tissue.

To her credit, Molly didn't say anything. They usually didn't. Wes was long used to his scars, but he always felt an odd guilt for exposing them to the donation center employees, as though he were foisting knowledge upon them they hadn't asked for and would rather have done without. He waited in silence while Molly tied the tourniquet around his right arm and ran her fingertips over the skin at the inside of his elbow. He held his breath at the rough, cool touch of the alcohol swab. Acknowledged the warning of "Here comes the poke" with a brief nod. Waited while she repeated it all on the left arm.

It was hard for him. The riot had done a number on his body, but Wes liked to think he'd come through it with his mind relatively intact. He hadn't had a breakdown. Hadn't been reduced to a nervous wreck. Hell, he'd even gone back to work at the prison for two more years. But there were things. Small things, mostly, almost embarrassing in their predictability. He liked his back to the wall, always. He'd taken to carrying his father's old pocketwatch because he could no longer tolerate the feel of anything tight around his wrists. And sitting in a chair and letting people lay their hands on him—that was damned near impossible. He'd never minded the dentist before the riot, but afterward he'd dreaded each appointment and finally quit going altogether. Asked Claire to cut his hair so he could avoid the barber. Even these platelet donations, strictly voluntary, were difficult; sometimes he was turned away for the day, his blood pressure having rocketed the moment he sat in the chair. He'd hoped, at first, that forcing himself to face this particular fear so often would ease its hold on him, but so far it hadn't happened. His palms still sweated. His stomach still churned. His heart still raced.

Molly arranged the lines and started up the machine. She offered him magazines and movies, which he declined, and she left him alone with promises to check on him frequently. Wes listened to the mechanical rhythm of the machine and looked where the reclining chair pointed his eyes, at the join between the green curtain and the ceiling. The fabric was pale, a sickly sea green, the same color as the U.S. Forest Service trucks that barreled down Montana's back roads, the same color as the corridors leading to the warden's office in the old prison.

Almost two hours he sat there, while the machine beside him whirred and clunked, spinning his blood into different components and giving some of them back to his body. The gentle weight of the plastic tubing on his skin reminded him his arms were bare, but he didn't look. He tried to be still. He tried not to think. Should've gotten easier, but it got harder, so by the time Molly sat back down on her stool Wes was just barely holding back from tearing the needles out of his arms. But he nodded, and thanked her when she buttoned his shirt cuffs, and made another appointment.

"If it could be with you again," he said.

It was early afternoon when Wes left the hospital, but seemed like twilight because the clouds that still spilled rain rode low over the valley, settling like slow-churning froth onto the peaks surrounding the city. The sun was so well hidden behind them Wes couldn't say where in the sky it hung.

He saw the kid on the interstate ramp. Leaning there against the guardrail, thumb over his shoulder, a sodden, overloaded bookbag at his feet. Wes took a few seconds to decide to take his foot off the accelerator, pulled over well ahead of the kid. He turned to see the boy slinking toward the truck. Stopped a few feet shy. Wes leaned across and unrolled the passenger window, and the kid stepped forward, ducked his head partway into the cab. His sweatshirt had a hood, but it hung limp down his back, and raindrops nested in his hair before soaking in. "Hey, Mr. Carver, you remember me?"

"Wouldn't have stopped if I didn't."

The kid didn't smile, but his features relaxed. "Right. Scott," he added, tapping his chest, and Wes was irritated to think the kid might've realized he couldn't remember his name.

"Help you with something, Scott?"

The boy looked at the ground, shrugged the bookbag higher onto his shoulder. He had two metal rods jammed through one eyebrow; Wes tried not to stare, but the glint drew his eye. "Think you could give me a ride to Black River? If you're going there."

"I don't suppose I got to tell you that hitching a ride ain't the smartest thing in the world."

"I have a car," Scott said, with a vehemence only a teenager could muster. "But it's a piece of shit."

"You really gotta talk like that?"

"Sorry," Scott said, without conviction. "It got me out here but now it's dead. The mechanic says it needs a new starter, and that's, like, three hundred bucks I don't have." Rain dripped from his hair into his eyes, but he didn't wipe it away, just blinked hard. Wes felt a little sorry for making the kid stand out there while he interrogated him. A little.

"Can't your momma pick you up?"

"She's at work."

"All right. Get in." Wes didn't trust the kid—he had no illusions about what a kid who wanted to lie could do to an honest man's reputation—but you did what you could for your fellow man, especially if it didn't put you out any. Even if your fellow man was a teenager who shoved sharp objects through his own face for recreation.

Scott plunked his bookbag down on the seat between them, and Wes waited until the kid had buckled up before pulling back onto the ramp. Scott slouched against the window, staring out as they drove through Elk Fork and into the canyon. This close, Wes could see his eyelashes were dark red. Hair was dyed, then. Earbuds dangled against his chest on a white cord that sprouted from the collar of his sweatshirt, and he pulled his sleeves down over his knuckles. The laces of his boots were untied and clotted with mud where they'd dragged on the ground. A button pinned to his bookbag read, *If I were you, I'd hate me too.*

For a good ten minutes neither of them said anything. At Milltown, the rain poured down so hard Wes had to turn the wipers to their highest speed just to see the taillights of the semi up ahead. A deer dashed into the road, its legs skittering every which way, and Wes hit the brakes hard. The deer flung its head high and spun back the way it had come.

Wes accelerated again and cleared his throat. "So I hear you like horses."

Scott didn't turn away from the window. "They're all right, I guess."

"You been working for Dennis long?"

"Since June."

"He said you were from out of town. Originally."

"Yeah. Miles City."

"My wife was from out that direction."

Scott straightened in his seat. "Dennis said she died."

Hands tight on the wheel till they hurt. "That's right."

"Sorry."

Not much as condolences went, but it sounded genuine enough, and Wes had to admit that surprised him. He nodded his thanks, didn't look to see if the kid saw.

More rain. More road. A silence more awkward than the last.

This time Scott broke it. "Did Dennis tell you why my mom and I moved here?"

"Might've mentioned it."

"That's good he told you, 'cause you were probably the only person in the whole town who didn't know."

Wes glanced sideways. The kid was staring right at him, arms crossed over his chest. "You get to see your father much?"

"My mom makes me visit him every week. I wouldn't call it a 'get to' kind of thing."

Wes could believe that. They'd tried, in a halfhearted sort of way, to make the visiting room at the old prison somewhat welcoming. There was a mural on one wall—a flat, childlike painting of the landscape that lay outside the gate—and a soda machine that dispensed off-brand cola. But no two ways about it, the place had been depressing as hell, and he doubted the new prison was any better. Wes never could decide what was worse: the visits where the inmate and his visitor sat stiffly, barely talking, or the ones where they held hands across the table and stared into each other's eyes until you had to just about drag one or the other of them out. Scott, Wes guessed, was one of the former. The barely-talkers. But you could never tell.

"So what do you do?" Scott asked. "For a job."

"I'm retired."

"From what?"

Wes steered around a flattened, sodden piece of cardboard in the road. "I was a musician," he said. Sounded like a lie.

The kid raised his metallic eyebrows. "Seriously?"

"Yeah." He could feel Scott's eyes on him and felt oddly nervous. Wondered if the kid could tell he'd been a CO, if it was apparent somehow in the way he moved, the way he talked. Sometimes it seemed that criminals could sense a cop a long way off; maybe it was hereditary.

Scott leaned forward—for a moment Wes thought he was going for the glove compartment; he remembered the revolver and his heart seized—and punched the power button on the radio. Music filled the cab, accompanied by grating static. Never could get a clear signal in the canyon. "Country, huh?"

"Not your cup of tea, I'd guess."

The kid surprised him. "A lot of it sucks. But some of it's all right. The older stuff."

"I played the fiddle."

"Yeah?"

"Old-time, mostly. Some bluegrass."

"I hear strings are hard."

"Hard to do right," Wes agreed.

"I'm a singer."

Wes thought about that. Maybe the kid was a singer the way every kid thought he was a singer. They all wanted to be famous, stand at center stage with folks screaming their name and begging for autographs. Thought they could do it, too, with all the shows on TV now promising instant celebrity. Most of them had no idea how talentless they were. But something in the way Scott said it—plain, confident, no mitigating "kind of" or "pretty good" or even "want to be"—made Wes think there might be something to it.

They came around a curve, and Black River spilled along the canyon before them. Not raining quite as hard here. The sun occupied a horizontal gap between cloud and mountain over the south slopes, and light glared off the wet asphalt. "I always thought if I was going to learn to play something it would be the guitar," Scott said. "But maybe fiddle would be cool, too."

Wes didn't say anything.

"Can you still play?"

He looked at Scott. The kid rubbed a thumb over his nose, across his freckles, and looked about five years younger than he had when he got into the truck. His eyes were on Wes's hands, hooked over the yoke of the steering wheel.

Wes didn't answer him.

He and Dennis shared dinner that night, the first time they'd sat down together rather than stood over the counter in the kitchen. The table was a small cherry wood square, set against one wall of the living room. Tonight Dennis sat on the side nearest the kitchen, where Wes always used to sit, and Wes sat opposite, in Claire's old place. It put his back to the door, but that was better than sitting the way they used to, the way they had on that last night.

Dennis spoke while Wes's head was still bowed, grace running silently in his head. "I hear you gave Scott a ride into town today."

Wes thought his *Amen,* looked up. "Seemed like he needed it."

"Didn't rip off your truck's stereo or anything, did he?"

"Do you really got to do this tonight, Dennis?"

Dennis held up a hand. "Fine, sorry."

Wes watched his stepson push a single pea back and forth with his fork, a millimeter one way, a millimeter the other. Wes wasn't sure if this edginess was because of his presence or because that was just who Dennis was. Everything he did, every move he made, it was like he was trying to hold back, keep from exploding. It gave him an odd aura of stillness, but with a great deal of force behind each minute movement. "Seriously," Dennis said finally. "What'd you think of him?"

"Why ask me? Ain't like you've ever bothered with my opinion before." Hell. *Hell.* Why say that? Must be this house. This damned table.

Dennis dropped his fork onto his plate. "Jesus, Wes. Do *you* have to do this?"

"Sorry. I didn't mean nothing by it. Let it go." He took a long swallow of water, set the glass down harder than he meant to. "Scott. I don't know. Seems like a nice enough kid, I guess. Not real happy to be here."

"You blame him?"

"No." Wes set his fork down, pushed his plate away, most of the food still on it. No appetite since Claire died. "I'll tell you one thing, though: that kid don't seem especially interested in horses." Dennis looked up, and Wes saw he wasn't saying anything his stepson didn't already know. "Which I suppose means he must really like you."

Dennis smiled, not at Wes. "And you find that hard to believe?"

He noticed Dennis's nose all of a sudden, the way it ruined his profile. Wes broke it eighteen years ago, at this table, the one and only time he'd ever laid a hand on him in anger. Hadn't strictly meant to, but he still wasn't sorry for it; Dennis had deserved that and more. What he thought he might be sorry for was the afterward. The leaving. It was a new idea, that he might be sorry for that. And he thought again about Scott, the anger that poured out of the kid so you could almost smell it on him, sharp and sour. "Dennis," Wes said, looking back across the table, "I don't think I know you well enough anymore to say."

He stayed up late that night, later than Dennis, though he had church in the morning. He walked around the silent house, treading close to the walls to keep the floorboards from creaking. Still a house he could move through in the dark. Still a house whose shadows he knew, the cast of moonlight through the uncurtained windows familiar as it fell.

The walls were most different. Gone, of course, were the things he and Claire had taken with them when they'd left: the cross Wes's father had carved from a knotted piece of deadfall; the wooden calendar with a painting of a goose Claire ordered another year's worth of pages for every November; the small poster from the last time the band played Harvest, a few weeks before the riot. Gone, too, were the things they had left behind: a handful of pleasant but generic art prints, a collection of haphazardly framed family photographs. The walls of the house now were nearly bare, cool white almost everywhere he looked.

The exception was the space over the mantel, where Claire's wide mirror used to be. When he was fifteen and in the midst of one of his rages, Dennis threw a book at the mirror and cracked it. All the way across, from one corner of the frame to the other, a finer spiderweb of fractures at the point of impact. Now there were a handful of photographs in its place, each carefully matted and framed. A yellow stand of aspens in low sun; a distant image of a broad-antlered bull moose; a horse running blurred, scattered sharp catches of image standing out: the glint of a steel shoe nailed to a hoof, the bristly texture of a tangled mane, a taut line of muscle powering a stride.

And his wife. A photograph Wes had never seen before. Dennis must have taken it during one of Claire's last visits before she became ill. She had never liked having her picture taken, and Wes was suffering the consequences of her aversion now; he had so few photographs of her. Soft light on her skin, highlighting her profile as she turned from the camera, her hair in a thick, heavy braid over her shoulder, a shy close-mouthed smile curving her lips. A beautiful portrait. But her eyes were aimed a few degrees away from the viewer, and no matter where Wes stood, he couldn't pretend she was looking at him.

～

The Black River Presbyterian Church was a block off Main Street, in a wide building whose geometric shape had probably seemed innovative (rather than ugly) when it was built. The sign by the road had been replaced, but that was the only obvious change Wes could see. Same kinds of trucks in the lot. Same kinds of people walking in.

He waited until three minutes to nine before he went inside. The usher looked distantly familiar, but he smiled through Wes and handed him a program with a rote greeting. The town had grown in the last eighteen years, but the sanctuary was emptier than he remembered it, no more than half full, and the sign outside listed this as the only service of the week. Wes took a seat in the second-to-last pew, near the windows, dotted today with a scattering of raindrops making a slow descent toward the ground outside. The stained glass spanned the entire left wall of the sanctuary and reflected a typical Presbyterian austerity: no figures of Christ or saints, just thin bars of color: pink, gold, blue, green. As a young child, Wes thought the windows looked like they were made of sheets of hard candy. Knew it was mere fantasy even then, but as he and his father filed out of the pew one morning, he'd leaned close and touched the tip of his tongue to the cool glass.

When Wes was a boy, church was for him and his father alone. His mother bowed her head at the dinner table, and on the bookshelf at home there was a small Bible with her name in script on the dedication page, but she stayed home Sundays. Later, when he was an adult, Claire stayed home, too. She had never come with him to church, not in Black River and not in Spokane. Not even to the chapel in the hospital. But she never laughed at him, never belittled his commitment, though she knew the strength of his doubts.

The pastor today was new to him, a younger man with a voice that was stronger than his thin face and slight frame suggested. Wes passed judgment on him over the course of the hour and decided he was a good pastor for a town of corrections officers, hitting the Old Testament heavily, making plentiful references to justice and duty. During the litany of sorrows and misfortunes that made up the weekly prayer list, Wes heard Claire's name. It rang in his head, seemed a strange convergence of his own thoughts and the outside world. Claire Carver, Claire Carver. Claire Carver, dead and gone, pitied and prayed for. It took Wes a minute to find Arthur Farmer in a pew near the front; he'd gone bald beneath his hat. He'd have put her name on the list. He'd have thought it was his business. The ringing of her name died, the service went on. Wes bowed his head for the prayers and recited words that were good by virtue of their familiarity, offered up notes in a low voice for the hymns. He put a twenty in the collection plate when it passed. Didn't take communion. Never did.

When Wes was fourteen, his father switched from evening watch to day watch at the prison. It was a change he had waited years for, but it meant he was now inside the gate Sunday mornings. They began attending evening service, and it was a habit Wes held to as an adult; he was sorry to see it had been done away with. At evening service, the sanctuary was peopled mostly by men who sat alone, wide gaps between them in the pews. The pastor's voice was tired but unyielding, and the hymns took on an appealing strangeness when sung only in low men's voices. It was during that spare, solemn hour, in the largely empty sanctuary, the bright candy windows dark, that Wes came closest to believing.

His father died on a Sunday. It was autumn, but the long arctic summer evenings lingered, and the sun was just beginning its slow sink below the mountains when the service let out. His father sent him to walk home alone, said he had an errand to run in town. When he thought back on it later, Wes realized this was a mere veneer of a lie; everything in town was closed on Sunday evenings. He hadn't recognized it then, though, and for years he felt guilty, wondered if his father had been intentionally clumsy with this untruth, hoping his son would catch him in it. But Wes had accepted it easily, and his father had smiled and said, "Help your mother." Another warning there, maybe, a deeper meaning, but Wes missed it, too, and when he arrived home, he didn't go straight for his fiddle as usual but went instead to the kitchen and helped his mother chop carrots and peel potatoes.

They said later that his father didn't jump from the trestle before the train hit him. How they knew this with such certainty went unsaid, but Wes was old enough to imagine. He took a macabre pride in the knowledge. Wondered if he, too, would have the fortitude to stand his ground with a freight train bearing down on him, no railings restraining him and the river black and heavy far below, the water offering a chance, however distant, of rescue, reversal.

Wes had been up on the trestle twice. Once was days afterward, when he made a white-knuckled climb of the iron scaffolding and walked between the rails in a frightened crouch. At the midpoint, the river evenly split below, he found a dark stain on one of the wooden ties that might have been blood or might have been grease. The other time was years later, the night his relationship with Dennis had shattered. A harder climb, not for age but because even then his hands were halfway to useless. There was a chill breeze blowing on the trestle that he'd been sheltered from at the bottom of the canyon. It lifted his short hair and cooled his skin almost to the point of pain. Wes walked straight that night, his arms held slightly out from his sides, maybe for balance, maybe to better feel the movement of the air around and against him. The height was seductive, and he didn't stay long.

—

Late Sunday afternoon the storm broke into pieces and drifted apart, and Wes and Dennis decided to go up the mountain. The suit he'd brought stayed on its hanger in the closet, and he wore his good jeans and a green shirt instead, the one Claire bought for him because she said it matched his eyes.

He found Dennis outside, tying the black horse to a heavy hitching rack beside the shed. The red horse was tied too, already saddled. Wes crossed the yard, mud pushing up from beneath the gravel and squelching over the sides of his boots. The red horse skittered sideways at his approach, jerking its head up and startling itself all over again when it hit the end of its rope. Dennis reached out to the animal, laid his palm flat on its neck. "Easy, Serrano," he said, voice low.

"The hell is this?"

"It's a long way up," Dennis said, without looking at him. "We'll ride."

"You couldn't have told me this before?"

"Didn't see any reason to." Dennis ran a bristle brush over the black horse's back and laid his free hand over its withers. "I'll put you on Rio. He's a good horse."

Wes didn't say anything. He could ride. Didn't especially like to, but his father had kept a couple horses, chunky animals with coats that never shed all the way out and hooves that chipped on the rocks in the pasture. He'd used them to pack elk out of the mountains, and for a few seasons Wes went along. Fine. He'd do it Dennis's way, this once. For Claire.

He watched Dennis smooth the blanket over Rio's back and swing the saddle up so it settled easy. His stepson moved with the kind of speed and confidence a person exhibited only when he didn't have to think about what he was doing. Wes watched his hands. They expertly tightened the cinch and knotted the latigo, moving swiftly over leather and metal and still finding time for a gentle glide over muscle and hair. "Let's get Mom's ashes set up here," he said.

Dennis's hands crowded each other when he held the small box. The brown paper wrapping was still on, and it rustled as Dennis gently settled the box into the bottom of a leather bag. He tied it to the skirt of Rio's saddle so it lay against the horse's flank and rose and fell slightly with the animal's breath.

Dennis turned away from the saddlebag too quickly. "Ready?"
Wes nodded.

Rio took the bit readily when Dennis offered it, closing his eyes as Dennis guided the leather straps of the bridle over his ears and fixed the buckles. The reins were split, and without so much as a glance at Wes, Dennis balanced them out in his hands and knotted them together. He started to lead the horse toward a bale of hay near the fence, but Wes stopped him. "I'm good." He took hold of the saddle horn, set his foot in the near stirrup and hauled himself into the saddle. He could often force his way through a single action—mind over matter lasted that long, at least—but his hand punished him good when he tightened his grip on the horn. A sweet pain on a day like this. Tangible.

"Can you hold those reins all right?"

"They're fine." He cradled the knot in his palm and let the reins drape over his fingers. He wondered if Dennis had thought it out beforehand.

"Sit back on your pockets a little more," Dennis said, then turned away to bridle the red horse.

They started up through the access lane that ran between Dennis's land and Farmer's, Dennis in front. The red horse was a firecracker, but Dennis rode him with a natural calm. His spine was absolutely straight, and Wes suddenly remembered this about him, this perfect posture he'd always had, even as a teenager, when most boys slouched like they'd slipped a few notches back on the evolutionary scale. Rio settled easily into step behind the red horse, his head and neck swaying slightly. Wes drove his heels toward the ground, remembering that single piece of advice from his father, and tried to let his body follow

the rhythmic movement of Rio's. It was a strange sensation, made so by
the distance of time, but strange in another way, too, a way that made
him recall the hitch he'd seen when he watched the horse in the pasture
a few days back. Rio's hind legs moved stiffly, with an up-and-down
jerkiness, like pistons short on grease. "This horse has got arthritis,"
Wes said.

Dennis turned in the saddle, and Serrano started jigging. He
watched Rio for a minute, and the muscles at the sides of his mouth
tautened. "He's old," he said, the words like a sigh.

"This ride going to be too much for him?"

"No," Dennis said, but he didn't sound sure. Wes reached forward
and grazed the knuckles of his free hand against Rio's neck, received a
backward flick of a single ear in return.

At the base of the slope they reached the end of the access lane and
turned onto an old logging road. A handful of aspens, their leaves
winking gold to white in the breeze, stretched their branches past the
pines. The incline was gradual, but the waterlogged ground slowed
their progress. The road was wide enough to ride abreast, but Wes and
Dennis made their way single file instead so they could ride down the
center, where grass tall enough to brush the soles of Wes's boots held
the soil more or less in place. Even so, the horses' hooves sucked at
mud, and the rain had carved deep rivulets that crossed the road and
interrupted their gaits.

Twice during the ride Wes reached back to touch the leather bag
that held his wife's ashes. Still didn't sit right with him, Claire reduced
to a few handfuls of coarse powder. Seemed disrespectful somehow.
He wanted her to have a casket, flowers, her favorite clothes, a restored
body. He wanted the embalming, the prayers, a service in a church and
another at a graveside. She would have done those things for him.

Dust to dust, love, she'd said.

He would do this thing for her.

And then they were there, and Dennis was stepping off the red
horse. "Just bring the reins over his head and drop them," he said.
"These two ground-tie."

Wes had to give Dennis this much: the man had an eye for beauty.

The place they'd stopped was less a clearing than a space where the road ran too close to the edge of the mountain to support trees. Roots burst from the earth and dangled in open air, and fallen forms of trees lay scattered on the slope below. They faced west, looking out over the join of canyon and valley. Below, the Wounded Elk flowed black through the shadowed corridor of the canyon and then curved into the open plain of the valley, where it greeted the setting sun and turned to quicksilver. The black grid of the train trestle spanned the border between light and shade. Across the valley, a lone rain shower was making its way across the Bitterroots, the outline of the mountain behind softened at the edges, like the face of an actress in an old movie, made gentler and flawless with the aid of a blur lens. The sun, dimmed by the clouds, was about to touch the highest crest. Wes glanced back over the other side of the ridge, east, and though Black River was still in plain sight—he could just make out the gray roof of the house—the new prison was hidden beyond the slow curve of the canyon. And ahead, behind, surrounding: endless folds of forested mountain, then white-dusted peaks rising up beyond, too distant to seem entirely real.

Dennis took Claire's ashes from the saddlebag and pulled the brown paper off, real careful, the way a person might unwrap a Christmas present if he wanted to reuse the paper next year. The urn was smooth brushed metal, and it had her name on it. Wes hadn't thought about the screws. Dennis had a jackknife on his belt, though, and he used its blade to coax the screws from their homes. And then he held it like that, lidless, in cupped hands, looking like a little boy with a robin's egg in his palms who's just realized he can't put it back into its nest.

"Should we say something?"

Wes walked to the edge of the ridge, felt a clump of damp soil give way under his feet. "Can if you want to."

But neither of them did. Didn't move, either, and they stood together for a long moment, Wes noticing Dennis's eyes getting a sheen to them. His own eyes were dry, but his heart beat hard in his chest, drumming against his breastbone in irregular bursts of impossible speed. Normal, he reminded himself. Normal for the permanent absence of a person to derail his heart from its rhythm, as though his

PART II

Grace

Dear Lord, he says.

She finds herself wanting to believe it didn't start to fall apart until after the riot. That would make it simpler. That would make it Bobby Williams's fault, and it would be so easy to lay it all at his feet. But Claire has always been cursed with honesty, and she cannot forget that it started long before.

What she wants is baseball. Dennis is four when they come to Black River—old enough to realize his own fatherlessness—and Claire wants a man who will buy her son a glove, who will teach him to catch and throw and hit, who can pass on all the arcane rules and rites, the etiquette, the folklore. (Shane played shortstop. Claire spent a season's worth of afternoons cheering from the bleachers, his letter jacket draped over her shoulders. But she tries not to remember that.)

As it turns out, Wesley doesn't like baseball, and neither does Dennis. Claire adapts. Hunting, she thinks. That's something fathers and sons do. Stalk an animal together, kill it, eat it. A little more primal than she might've hoped for, but it'll do. But Wesley doesn't hunt, though the trophy mount of an eight-point buck in the back of the hall closet proves he knows how. Dull, he tells her. A waste of time. Claire thinks he doesn't like the killing. The blood. Maybe that's mere hope.

What Wesley does have to offer is the ritual of afternoons.

He comes home from the prison still dressed in his blue uniform, his boots polished to a high shine (though the sergeants, he's told her, don't really care). The creases in his shirt and slacks could be sharper, but he irons his uniforms himself. Doesn't like her to touch them. He keeps them separate from the other clothes in their closet, empty inches of space between fabrics. When he comes through the door, Claire doesn't try to talk to him until he's showered, shaved, changed. He comes out of the bathroom with his hair still dripping and his cuffs un-buttoned and rolled up two turns each, to just above the knobs of his wrists. Then she can ask, How was work? And he will say, It's over.

He looks at her for a moment after he says it, apology for not saying more, plea for her not to ask. And she never does, because this is when he takes his fiddle down from the mantel. Dennis puts down his cray-ons and watches, and Claire sits beside him. Dennis will let her touch him at this moment—he squirms away from her hand at other times—and she is always struck by the coolness of his skin, tries to send him warmth from her own body.

Wesley takes his bow out of the case first, tightens the hair. Some-times he rosins it, more often he doesn't. Then he lifts the fiddle to his collarbone, settles his jaw over it. When he tunes, Claire has noticed, the D string gives him the most trouble. He warms up with scales and arpeggios, but they don't sound like exercises or drills; they sound like music. He knows how to lean on a note, make it just a bit fuller than the brother notes that come before and after, to coax sound into song. Then it's straight into whatever tunes he's been playing with Lane and Arthur. Sometimes Claire doesn't recognize the melodies, but more often she does. He plays some tunes more than others: she rarely hears "Whiskey Before Breakfast" or "Red-Haired Boy," so she has to lis-ten a few seconds to know what she's hearing; they're near strangers. Others—"Lost Girl" and "Blackberry Blossom" and "Hell Among the Yearlings"—he plays almost every day, and Claire knows them even before he's finished drawing the first note; they are familiar guests in her home.

Then, when Wesley has practiced to his satisfaction (he is so rigid in this, work before play, the band's tunes before anything else, though she doubts her husband considers anything he does with his fiddle to be work): a hymn. These are for her. She's Claire the heathen, Claire the agnostic, and she loves hymns. Her favorite is "Blest Be the Tie That Binds." She thinks Wesley's must be "Nearer My God to Thee," because he plays it almost as often, though she's never asked him to.

When he's pulled the last note from the hymn, Claire goes to the kitchen and slices vegetables, boils water, puts glass casserole dishes in the oven. She listens while Wesley plays Dennis's favorite tunes: "Flop-Eared Mule" and "Angelina Baker" and "Spotted Pony." She feels the thumps through the hardwood floor as her son spins and whirls around the living room, but she pointedly doesn't watch, afraid she'll see him crash into the furniture or send something shattering to the floor. (He never does.) Sometimes she hears Dennis's voice—it's thin and high and goes right to her heart—as he asks a question. How do you make it sound like that, he wants to know, or, Why do you move the bow that way? Wesley's voice is always too low for Claire to make out, but then he will demonstrate, a slow scale first on single strings and then with drones, or a slide, one shuffle and then another. From the kitchen, it sounds as though he answers her son with song.

After the casserole has come out of the oven and the bread has been put in, after the vegetables have been drained and the jam transferred from jar to dish, Claire sets the table. She sends Dennis to wash up, and Wesley plays "Black River." She waits by the table and listens. Sometimes she can hear how he has changed it from the day before, and sometimes she can't. Always it sounds different from all his other tunes. He is a gifted musician no matter what he plays, but he is a master of this one piece.

Beautiful, she tells him, when he's done.

He lowers the fiddle, loosens the bow hair. Better, he allows.

Wesley puts his fiddle away, and Dennis comes back from the bathroom, and Claire brings the food from the kitchen. Then they sit down to dinner and Wesley says grace.

Bless this family as we share in Your bounty.

When they are first married, Claire closes her eyes for grace. Her family never prayed, so she studies her husband and does as he does:

eyes closed, head bowed, fingers intertwined. Though Claire does not believe in God, she loves her husband's efforts at faith. He keeps a Bible on their bedside table and reads from it most nights before turning out the light; he told her once, while they were lying beside each other in the dark, that the stories in its pages never seem quite the way he remembers them from church.

One Friday when Dennis is six, Wesley gets up with the sun and drives to Elk Fork. When he comes back, it is with a fiddle small as a toy. Dennis is delighted—so delighted Wesley has to hold the tiny fiddle on his lap until Dennis stops bouncing around the living room and can be trusted not to break his new acquisition. The sounds he produces are truly blood-curdling. He wraps one hand around the fiddle's neck, another over the bow, and he pulls the horsehair indiscriminately over the strings—on the wrong side of the bridge, or halfway up the fingerboard—beaming as the instrument shrieks.

Wesley grins at her, and it's the rarest of grins, wide enough she can see the glint of a silver molar, true enough his eyes brighten with it. He squats down beside Dennis and guides his arm into position, loosens his grip on the neck. Dennis doesn't shrink from his touch, leans toward him when he speaks. He shows Dennis how to hold the bow, folding his own hand into a rabbit shape, bouncing it across the space between them. Dennis happily follows suit. Remember, Wesley tells him, wrapping his fingers around the bit of ebony at the end of the bow, the rabbit holds the frog. He puts his hand gently over Dennis's and draws the bow smoothly over the string, a small but clear sound filling the room.

By the time he is ten, Dennis knows dozens of tunes by heart, but he is not a musician. This is clear even to Claire. It isn't that he's bad—he plays more or less in tune, and produces a decent tone—but he can only mimic, and there's a mechanical quality to his playing. It is as though her son is a wind-up toy that plays a tune whenever fiddle and bow are placed in his hands.

Wesley doesn't seem to mind. He sits knee-to-knee with Dennis in

the afternoons and practices with what must seem to be an almost painful deliberateness. A single tune, repeated and repeated and repeated.
Wesley plays harmony, mirrors the melody above or below Dennis,
taps his foot when her son loses the rhythm, crosses his bow over the
strings lightly to let Dennis's hesitant playing come to the fore.

And yet. They never talk during practice anymore. They used to.
Perhaps, Claire thinks, Dennis has reached a level of such proficiency
that they are able to communicate with music rather than words. Perhaps there is something in those notes, those pauses, that she cannot
hear or understand, a hidden language known to her husband and son
from which she is excluded. Perhaps there is more to it than she can see.
(This is what she sees: tune after tune after tune, and then an abrupt
end to it at five o'clock sharp, Dennis shutting his fiddle in its case,
Wesley retuning and continuing with his own practice.)

I know he isn't as good as you, Claire says one evening. They are
outside on the steps; Dennis is at the fence, watching Arthur's horses
graze.

That ain't important, Wesley tells her.

I'm sure it's a little disappointing to you.

It's front-porch music, he says. You don't got to be a prodigy to
enjoy it.

I know he does, Claire says. Enjoy it, I mean.

Wesley takes her hand but doesn't say anything.

One day — it is a Tuesday — Wesley comes home and changes out
of his uniform and gets his fiddle, and Dennis does not come. He isn't
in his room, or the yard. Arthur has been letting him groom the horses
after school; Claire calls his house, but no one answers.

I'm sure he'll be along, she says.

Wesley gives her one of those looks, a little too sharp. It's gone in
an instant, hidden again — a slip, an expression he didn't mean to bring
home with him — but she's already seen it.

He plays alone, and though Claire listens carefully, she can hear
nothing different in his music today. He doesn't stop playing when
Dennis comes in the door at half past four, doesn't quit until she has

placed the last dish on the table and called him to dinner. He says the same grace he says every night, and she waits through the whole meal for him to say something to Dennis about the broken ritual, for Dennis to offer excuse or apology. She waits.

Shield us from those who would tempt or harm us.

When he is twelve, Dennis comes to her and asks about Shane. It's not the kind of asking that can be deflected, or answered with omissions. Claire has thought of crafting a gentler story—a loving father-to-be, a tragic accident before Dennis was born—but too many people know the truth for it to remain a secret forever, and already Claire knows her son will never learn to see the loving intent behind a revealed lie. And he knows even before he asks—not details, not facts, but he knows there is something she doesn't want to tell, something he doesn't truly want to hear. (How does he know? No one said anything; Claire is sure of it. Instead, it's in the way they treated him, the way they looked at him, or didn't. Wesley, maybe. Madeline, certainly. And her? Surely not her.) Wesley, she thinks, would never ask a question he didn't want an answer to. But Dennis is different.

She says, Your father was not a good person.

She says, I didn't want to . . . be with him, but he forced me. Do you understand what I'm telling you?

She says, But I love you.

Again: I love you.

When she thinks about the conversation in the years that follow, she will remember Dennis listening in silence. But she can't swear to the memory. Her own words so fill the space in the room, in her mind—they are so clear and sharp-edged—that everything else fades.

Years pass before Claire starts opening her eyes during grace. She sees then that Dennis doesn't close his eyes, either, doesn't fold his hands. Did he do those things as a younger child, or has he always waited like this? He is watching her, and Claire immediately feels that she has been caught in an embarrassing act. She looks away, to Wesley. Beneath the fragile skin of his eyelids his eyes jerk back and forth, as though he reads the words as he speaks them. Even in the midst of prayer he seems too alert, too cautious, as though a single slip will bring ruin.

To be clear: she doesn't believe in God. The devil is another matter entirely.

Let us rejoice in Your gifts of sound and song.

Before Wesley comes home from the hospital after the riot, Claire puts his fiddle away. Nestles it in its red velvet, pulls the lid of the case shut, closes the brass clasps. She puts the case in the closet and leaves it there for an hour, then takes it out again and puts it back above the hearth, lid open, light pooling on the fiddle's worn varnish. When Wesley comes home he looks straight at it, and she doesn't know if she was right to move it or right to put it back.

For months afterward Wesley doesn't touch his fiddle. Even after the splints and bandages come off, he leaves it to gather dust on the mantel. No new routine replaces the old. He comes home and changes out of his uniform, and then he sits on the couch and watches television, or comes to the kitchen and stands uneasily beside the counter and listens to her talk while she cooks. Sometimes he leaves the house and is gone for hours. Every afternoon is different.

And then one day he goes to his chair beside the hearth and takes his fiddle out of its case. He winces when he tightens the screw on the bow, and he takes a long time to tune, tweaks the pegs and fine tuners even after the fiddle sounds good to Claire. He looks up, sees her in the doorway.

Goes out when it's left like this, he says, and she nods.

He crosses his bow over the strings, nudges one of the pegs again. Again. Claire goes to the kitchen to give him privacy, and there she stands beside the range with her hands on the edge of the counter and the refrigerator buzzing in her ear and she begs his God not to take this from him.

She has never heard him play slowly, Claire realizes. He always plays at speed, and she has wondered if he ever had to play slowly, even as a child, or if all his music was always inside him, waiting to be called. But now he begins to play so slowly she has to listen for several long seconds before she recognizes the familiar melody of "Over the Waterfall." (She is both sorry and grateful he doesn't begin with "Black River.") He hits the first wrong note just a few bars into the A part, a sharp that shouldn't be there. Another a couple notes later, this one flat. He's out of practice, Claire tells herself. Rusty is all.

Still. "Over the Waterfall" is a simple tune. One of the first he taught Dennis. It has always surprised her that he likes it so much, because it cannot possibly challenge him. It reminds her that what Wesley likes most is the music. He has so much talent, so much skill, that she sometimes falls into the trap of thinking it's all about the virtuosity. But he, too, can like a melody simply because the notes sound good together.

Another wrong note. He's stiff, then. Nine broken fingers, after all, two surgeries. He's gone to his physical therapy appointments religiously, but the fiddle is different. It will take time. Then he gets to the B part, the faster half of the tune. When he plays this in public, this is where people quit chatting with each other and set back and really listen, where they start whooping and stamping their feet. One missed note. Two, three. His bow slips and squeals against a string.

When Claire goes to the doorway, she finds Dennis in the hall. He is half hidden in the shadows, pressed against the wall, his teenage face young with bewilderment. And Wesley, in his chair beside the hearth, jaw set against the chinrest, eyes resolutely *not* on hers, *not* on his fiddle and the fingers that can't play it. The worst of it is that the familiar melody is still recognizable, just close enough to right that Claire still finds herself listening for it, each wrong note jarring the ear all over again.

And he won't quit. Tries to force it, plays faster, leaves "Over the Waterfall" behind and aims for something else, anything else. Claire almost recognizes a few measures of any of a half-dozen tunes, but the notes tumble over one another in a grating cacophony.

Dennis moves to go into the living room, and Claire stops him with an arm across his chest. She looks at him, and suddenly she misses the bewilderment, because it has been replaced with a resignation he isn't old enough for, an expression that says this is no less than he expected, that this fits right in with what he knows of the world. Claire wants to lie to him, tell him everything will be all right, but she goes to Wesley instead, kneels beside him and puts a hand on his thigh. Wesley, she says.

He ignores her. His eyes are on his strings now, his bow, his fingers that won't obey.

Wesley.

The bow sawing desperately, the motion hardly intentional anymore, nearly a seizure. A sound to set your teeth on edge.

Wesley, please.

He makes an awful sort of pained sound deep in his throat, and Claire reaches forward and curls her hand over the scroll of his fiddle and pulls it down, away, and finally he relinquishes its weight to her and quits. Half drops and half throws his bow to the floor. It clatters dully on the hardwood, a blunt coda to his ruined song.

We thank You for our sorrows and trials, for they make our joys shine ever brighter.

What happens first? Does Dennis start to act like his father, or does Wesley begin to fear he will?

The third time Dennis runs away he is fifteen, and he stays gone two days. He has always come back by dark before. Wesley spends every moment of those two days scouring the hills, trawling the streets of Black River and Elk Fork in his pickup, walking the banks of the river and reluctantly searching its currents. (He denies the last when she asks, but Claire has seen him from the porch, hands in his pockets, head bowed to the water.)

He's okay, Wesley tells her again and again.

She nods. Again and again.

He's a smart kid. Knows how to look after himself.

Dennis turns up Wednesday evening, dirty and smelly and looking a little frightened but a lot pleased. Wesley is home for a brief supper, his truck keys waiting beside his dinner plate, coat unzipped but still on. Claire meets her son at the door and folds him into the tightest embrace she can muster, is relieved to feel him squeeze her back. Wesley stands with her, waits until she lets Dennis go.

You all right, boy?

Yeah.

You ain't hurt?

No.

Then you apologize to your momma, and you apologize to me.

She sees her son's mouth twitch—she can't tell if he's angry or amused, and oh, it's an unpleasant sight—but he pulls himself straighter yet, dutifully meets her eyes and says, I'm sorry if I scared you, Mom.

She's almost glad he doesn't sound like he means it. Shane always sounded like he meant it when he told her he was sorry.

I'm just glad you're safe, she says.

Wesley waits long enough to be sure Dennis isn't going to say anything else.

Apologize to me, he says again.

Dennis looks at him.

Wesley's been looking for you, Denny.

Didn't ask him to.

He had to trade two shifts.

Didn't ask him to do that, either.

Wesley steps carefully around her and pushes Dennis against the wall. It's a controlled movement—the heel of one hand against Dennis's breastbone, just enough pressure to put him against the wall and keep him there—but Dennis grunts and the back of his head connects solidly with plaster. Claire can't decide if this is something she should object to, if this is violence she is seeing. Later, when she plays the moment back in her head, she still won't be able to decide.

You're going to stand here, Wesley says, until you apologize. Dennis tries to force his way off the wall, but Wesley leans into him—he only moves an inch or two—and Dennis stays where he is. He puts his hands around Wesley's wrist, and Claire sees fingernails digging into flesh, but Wesley doesn't flinch and doesn't move.

So Dennis stands against the wall. Wesley sits back down, inches of space between his spine and the back of the chair. Thank you for dinner, Claire, he says, without looking away from Dennis. I'm finished.

They are still there when she has washed and dried the dishes. Wesley stares at Dennis; Dennis stares at the empty space over Wesley's head. Dennis's hands are in fists against the wall, and there's a worrisome smudge of something on his wrist, mud or blood. Wesley's hands are resting on the tabletop, loose and open, the kind of casual that can only be dangerous. The skin over his knuckles is flushed, and Claire can imagine the heat of the pain he never mentions but is always etched on the periphery of his expressions, evident behind the careful modulation of his voice. She rests a hand at the place where his neck joins his shoulder, leans close to his ear. Maybe it would be best to deal with this tomorrow, she says. When you've both had—

Good night, Claire. I'll be in as soon as I can.

She goes to bed. She does not sleep. She listens to the silence in the living room, to her husband not moving, to her son not speaking.

Dennis never does apologize. Sometime after three, Wesley will tell her, Dennis's eyes roll to the whites. It's not the standing. It's not; he'd skipped meals in the two days he'd been gone. Claire scrambles out of bed when she hears him begin to fall, but when she gets to the living room Wesley has already caught Dennis in his arms.

And we thank You, Lord, for the certitude that You are with us as we walk through this life . . .

Wesley is a good man.
Dennis is a good boy.
Why is this not enough?

. . . and for the knowledge that You will never abandon nor forsake us.

Her son is sixteen. He has been suspended from school four times this year—for fighting each time—but still has straight A's. He never plays his fiddle anymore (Wesley sold it last year, for two hundred dollars, and gave the cash to Dennis), but he spends weekends working at Arthur's. He's good with the horses, Arthur says. Has a natural affinity.

Her husband is forty-two, and for the first time in his life he is beginning to look old. He's working day watch again, and when he comes home now it is an hour before Claire dares talk to him. Not because she is afraid of him—he has never given her cause to fear—but because the sound of her voice, too soon, seems to pain him. He tries so hard to show her that he is fine. He hasn't sold his own fiddle, but he doesn't touch it, either.

That night—the last night—Wesley says grace, and Claire and Dennis watch each other while they listen. When Wesley is finished, Claire immediately starts talking. (During the day she plans what she will say, careful to choose topics neither of the boys in her life will care about: gardening, what Hallie Christiansen told her at Jameson's that morning, a story from the radio program she has taken to listening to while she cooks.) Dinner has become performance art, a one-woman show in which she must provide all the conversation while also consuming a meal and guarding against dangerous silences that might tempt Dennis or Wesley to fill them. It's going well until Wesley interrupts her.

What happened to your face?

There is a bruise at Dennis's hairline, faint enough that Claire had hoped Wesley wouldn't notice. (What doesn't he notice?)

Nothing.

You been fighting again?

Wesley, let's—

No.

No? Wesley catches Dennis's wrist, turns it so the light falls on the blackening scabs over his knuckles. If I call up the school tomorrow and talk to your principal, he gonna tell me "no," too?

Do whatever the fuck you want. See if I care.

Claire puts her hands to her face.

What did you just say, boy?

Fuck, Wes. I said fuck. F-u-c-k, fuck. Want me to say it again?

And Wesley is standing, and he is not Wesley her husband, he is

Wesley the officer (abruptly, Claire realizes she has always thought of them as separate people; just as abruptly, she understands they are one and the same), and his voice is suddenly hard and sharp and much deeper than usual. Get up, he barks. Up!

(*He is not his father,* she has told Wesley.)

Dennis doesn't answer, and he doesn't move, but Claire can see the bravado bleeding away. His hands are in his lap, his shoulders hunched. He is trembling, just slightly.

(*He is not your father,* she has told Dennis.)

Get up, Wesley commands again, and he grabs the back of Dennis's shirt collar. And then — it is as though time jumps forward a few seconds, as though Claire doesn't see it happen at all — Dennis is on his feet and Wesley still has hold of his collar and there is a gun in her son's hand and a gun aimed at her husband's face.

Claire just has time to see that Dennis's eyes are black with fury, that he has both hands on the grip of the revolver and that it's shaking anyway. Just has time to see Wesley's features go blank, the anger that was there a moment ago gone, gone, gone, replaced with nothing at all. Then Wesley moves, so fast, and he grabs Dennis's wrist and hits him hard in the face, twice, and her son is on the floor and there is blood on his face and his clothes and the rug, and the revolver is in Wesley's hand now and his hand isn't shaking and she doesn't know if his finger has the strength to pull the trigger or not, but the gun is leveled and steady and ready to put a bullet in her child.

She stands up and screams, Stop! Or means to scream, but it comes out a whisper, and she says it again and again, trying to make the word louder, but it is still a whisper: *stop stop stop stop stop.* She sees Wesley hear her, sees the subtle change in the way he holds himself. But he keeps the gun aimed at Dennis a half second longer before he drops his arm and turns around and goes outside. She expects the door to slam but it doesn't.

Later, after she has brought Dennis back from the emergency clinic, his nose packed and splinted, but before Wesley has returned from wherever he has gone, she will clean up the dishes. One fork is on the floor, a smear of sauce there on the rug beside the blood, but otherwise everything is so ordinary. She will know, scraping the food into the trash and scrubbing the plates and drying the glasses, that she will not do these things here again. That there will be no more meals together. No more family. No more grace.

She will remember the way her son's rage made her see his father in him for the first time. She will remember the way Wesley hesitated before lowering the revolver, the way she knew, in that moment, that what he kept from his face was fear, and that fear was more dangerous than anger.

And the next day, when Wesley says to her, A person shouldn't have to share his home with someone who wants him dead, she will not disagree.

Amen.

On Monday, September gave way to October. Big cardboard crates of pumpkins appeared outside the doors of Henderson's Feed and Farm, displacing the weathered old bachelors who usually stood there, one boot sole against the wall, spitting into the gravel. The diner across the street painted cartoonish bats and ghosts on its windows. And the banner Wes had been half waiting to see went up across Main Street, down by the old prison. Looked to be the same one they'd hung when he lived here, faded and frayed. It was tied fast to two streetlamps, knot upon knot, and half-moon slices had been cut into the material so when the wind barreled through the canyon it wouldn't tear the banner down. BLACK RIVER HARVEST FESTIVAL, it said, and below, in smaller letters, THIS SATURDAY.

"You going to stay for it?" Dennis had asked that morning. Wes pretended he'd forgotten. Pretended to think about it. Then he'd said yes, and let it go at that, because he still hadn't told Dennis about the parole hearing, and now he could put off telling him for another week.

He hadn't forgotten about Harvest, of course. Wes had first stepped onto the Harvest stage when he was six years old, a skinny kid with a ¼-size fiddle. Folks had been prepared to listen politely, applaud dutifully. And then he'd played "Devil's Dream," a showoff of a tune most of them had heard before, but never so fast and never so good. Harvest was where he'd first played for an audience, where he'd met Claire, where he and Lane and Farmer were the headliners seventeen years running. Time was, no one left Harvest until Wes played his fiddle.

When Claire told him she wanted to come back to Black River, he'd immediately calculated the time to Harvest. It hadn't seemed so many days. He'd imagined driving with her there in the truck, slowing to ease over the ruts when the asphalt gave way to oiled dirt a half mile outside town. He'd imagined parking at the end of a long ragged line of pickups, imagined taking Claire in his arms the way he had when he'd carried her, giggling, over the threshold of the house after their wedding. He imagined her wrists overlapping at the back of his neck, her head against his chest, the plain scent of her hair beneath his nose. He'd imagined carrying her to a seat midway back from the stage, on the side nearest the river, sitting there with her in the cool autumn sun and watching the musicians as they took their turns up on the stage, neither he nor Claire listening, both of them hearing the same long-gone music instead.

Harvest was held in a wide fallow field east of town. By late morning, when Wes arrived, parked cars and pickups lined both sides of the road and spilled into the dry lot opposite the field. It was the best day you could ask of October: sunny and cool, only a few clouds in the sky casting rounded shadows onto the mountain slopes. There was a hint of wildfire smoke in the air, a niggling sting at the back of the throat, and though it was from a distant blaze, it mingled uneasily with the scents of fried dough, beer, straw.

Wes walked alone along the shoulder of the road behind parents tightly clutching the hands of children, a group of teenagers laughing too loudly, a man he didn't recognize carrying a black guitar case. He let himself be funneled along with the rest of them through the entrance to the festival, marked with stakes and twine punctuated by triangular plastic flags. The field had been mowed, the stubble tamped down by dozens of boot soles. Along the periphery a couple of old pieces of farm machinery—a harrow, a rake wheel—sat rusted and folded up like the giant husks of dead insects. Down on the far end of the field was an oversized metal shed where the county kept three snowplows and a two-story load of coarse sand. Tucked way off beneath the mountains was the river. Hard to see unless you walked straight to it, but if you got up on the stage it stared you right in the face.

Wes wandered slowly through the crowd, pushed his way along the corridor formed by the rows of food booths. Folks packed tight, lined up to wait for booze or ice cream or elephant ears, or, if they were really brave, for Rocky Mountain oysters. Signs tacked to every available surface reminded everyone that the profits went to the Corrections Officers' Welfare Fund. Wes stood in line at one booth and thought about the unpaid bills stacked on the kitchen table in Spokane, the unopened statements that must be scattered on the floor below the mail slot, the notices still making their way through the postal system. He thought about the fact that Claire had reached her annual maximum benefit cap in May, that he hadn't paid the mortgage since July, that all four of his credit cards were maxed out. He thought about his depleted bank account and the crushed manila envelope in his duffel back at Dennis's, not quite a thousand dollars in cash inside. Then he thought about the welfare fund and how they'd picked up what the insurance wouldn't after the riot. When he got to the head of the line, he bought a beer he didn't want, paid with a fifty and didn't wait for the change.

On the far side of the food corridor the festival forked apart: crafts in one direction, games in another, the stage straight ahead. Wes found a spot to stand near the back of the crowd, behind the rows of straw bales that served as seating. It was a good stage for a small-town event like this. Not real big, but high, and bound overhead by an upturned squared-off horseshoe of metal latticework, speakers on either side, lights above. A few more bells and whistles than he remembered. There was another banner across the front of the stage, as tired as the one on Main Street, and a few pumpkins and cornstalks arranged near the speakers. A bluegrass band was playing now. Wes didn't recognize them, but they were young. A guitarist, a bass player, banjo and mandolin pickers. A fiddler.

He wasn't bad, the fiddler. Kept a good chop going, played a fast break. But he was getting by on the speed of his fingers. That was enough for most folks in any given audience: a quick melody, a fast bow, fingering that was so far beyond anything they could imagine doing themselves they thought that made it good. But the thing about a fiddle was that it was more like the human voice than any other instrument in the world. You could make it sing. You could sustain a note for as long as a breath, longer. You could draw that bow across two strings at once, or slide it from one string to the other in a single downbow, and in doing that you could sound a piercing cry and a low sob at once, joy and sorrow made one.

There were open seats up ahead, but Wes stayed where he was. The band rounded off one song, launched into another. "Salt Creek." Wes knew it, of course; it'd been one of his band's standbys. His fingers tried to tap out the notes against his thigh, but they crossed and tripped over each other, and he pulled them into a painful fist. Forced himself to be still and listen. A strange thing to stand here and listen to a man who was a good fiddler but nowhere near as good as Wes had been. Wasn't sure if it was a rare pleasure or an especially exquisite torture. He liked hearing this familiar music played well, with familiar scents in the air and familiar ground beneath his feet. There was something right in that. But it also just about killed him to be so close to a stage he'd stood on so many times in his life, a stage he'd commanded, and know he'd never stand on it again.

Lane had changed the name of the band at least once a year. Lane Gregory and the Lockdown Lads, or Lane Gregory and the Prison Posse, or something equally ridiculous. A fluid series of names for a fluid band. Lane, Arthur and Wes had played together for nineteen years. Others drifted in and out: there had been a couple mandolin players, a second guitar for a while, a standup bass for a few short weeks. They played an even balance of bluegrass and old-time, with a little straight-up country mixed in for good measure.

At Harvest they were always the final act, got an hour where the other bands had twenty minutes. They'd play their usual set: upbeat songs people knew, or that sounded close enough to ones they did; maybe a few of those old cowboy ballads Lane liked, the ones that showed off his voice but tested the audience's patience for pathos. And all those songs were good, but what they really did was give everyone time to wrap up whatever else they might be doing, to make their way over to the stage. Because Wes had played here every year since "Devil's Dream," and folks knew what was coming. Lane and Farmer would step back, and Wes would step forward. And that stage belonged to him alone.

He had a repertoire of tunes that numbered in the hundreds, all learned by ear, all held there in his head, ready to be brought forth by his fingers at a moment's notice. A nearly endless stable of notes and melodies at his command, and even that wasn't enough. He composed his own tunes sometimes, pieces that went beyond improvisation, beyond a hot lick or a fast break. He never set out to do it; the tunes came into being as he played alone, forming themselves from notes that joined together almost without his deciding to join them. One of those tunes, especially, Wes let himself be proud of. It was a slow piece, not what you'd think folks would want to hear at what was essentially a big party. Not quite a waltz. More an air.

Low notes first, building to a melody that rose into the highest register, then broke back down into the low notes again. Back and forth. Lingering on hope, never escaping melancholy. It was a piece that had evolved over the years, started as a simple thing with an A part and a B part, each repeated once. He'd built it into something more over time, found that he never played it precisely the same way twice. He added ornaments, took them away again. Experimented with double-stops, added new parts, shifted keys in the middle. To this day, he didn't know its final form, didn't know how it would sound if he could play it now—if he could have played it for Claire when she asked—and that, more than anything else, was why he would never forgive Williams.

Always there was a moment toward the end of the tune, a long single high note Wes could hold seamlessly for several bow strokes, the string pressing sharp against his fingertip, his wrist fluttering in the slightest of vibratos, when he knew that everyone at Harvest was listening to him. He'd look out across the field and see them watching, from the stage all the way to the glittering river. No talking. No laughing. No drinking. Hundreds of faces, all turned his way, all listening to the music he made, all knowing there was something true in that wistful note, that even in the midst of the festival there were things here, in this canyon, in these lives, that were always painful and sometimes beautiful.

The moment didn't last long. The note had to end—though sometimes Wes wondered if he might sustain it forever—and when it ended people drifted out of the collective pause. By the time Wes took his fiddle from beneath his chin and nodded his head in an awkward bow, all was back to the way it had been three minutes earlier.

And afterward, one day, there had been Claire, shy; Dennis, a dark-haired four-year-old clutching her hand; and Farmer, a sure smile on his lips and in his eyes as he introduced them. You play beautifully, Claire had said, and though Wes had heard the words from many others, many times, they'd never before brought a flush to his cheeks. That song, she said. The one you played alone. What's it called?

Hasn't got a name.

She hadn't even had to think about it. You should call it "Black River," she told him.

Wes applauded with everyone else as the bluegrass band took their bows and left the stage. There was a general exchange of people in the audience while cords and microphones were rearranged, as some folks drifted away and others came to find seats and settle in. A group of teenagers claimed the straw bales in front of Wes, and they folded their gangly limbs and leaned into each other as they sat. Eighteen years working security at a shopping mall had left Wes with an earned dislike of teenagers in packs, and he thought about moving, but then Farmer walked onto the stage, Scott trailing him. One of the girls on the straw bale giggled loudly and whispered something to the boy beside her. Up on the stage, Farmer settled onto a stool near the back, out of the way. He'd dressed up; his jeans had a crease down the front, and the pearl snaps on his shirt shone in the sun. Scott had made no such concession to the occasion. He wore skinny black jeans and a plain black T-shirt. Red sleeves reached from the base of his fingers to his elbows; they looked like socks with the feet cut off. Scott's eyebrow piercings glinted, and his dyed hair was in such disarray he might've just gotten out of bed, though Wes supposed he'd actually worked to make it look like that. He approached the microphone with his customary sulking shuffle. He didn't introduce himself, didn't speak at all, just looked back at Farmer once and sang his first note as Farmer played his first chord.

His voice was startling. It was the clearest of tenors, nothing like his shambling speaking voice, and he hit each note so roundly, with such ease, that it seemed his range might be limitless. Scott hadn't lied: he was a singer all right. The song he chose was just as surprising as his voice. "Mary Morgan." It was one of those old campfire ballads with a misleading tempo, so when the tragic twist came it was a surprise that seemed either improbable or inevitable, depending on one's mood and disposition. It told the tale of a rancher's daughter who falls in love with a young man who has joined a roving band of horse thieves. Her father forbids her to see the horse thief, but she steals away in the middle of the night to meet him. When she returns, long past midnight, the rancher hears her in the barn and, in the dim moonlight, mistakes her for the horse thief. He gets his rifle and fires, not realizing he has taken his own daughter's life.

Scott really sold it, made you think it'd happened here, and not so long ago. When he sang the chorus — *Wait for me beneath the willow, my Mary Morgan* — it might have been with the voice of the grief-stricken young horse thief. It was, Wes realized, the first time he'd seen the kid express emotion that went beyond sullenness and anger. His audience wasn't rapt, though. Wasn't even polite. The whispering had started soon as Scott stepped onto the stage, and it hadn't quit. Folks clearly knew who Scott was — and who his father was, or *where* he was, at least. In front of Wes, two of the teenage girls were sharing a pair of earphones, their heads touching; he could hear the thrum of the bass from where he stood. One of the girls had blond hair, blond as Claire's had been, and he wondered briefly if Scott knew her, if he thought she was pretty.

Onstage, Farmer played calmly, purposefully, keeping out of the way of Scott's voice. Scott grasped the microphone in both hands and kept his eyes cast down, never looking at his audience. Wes closed his own eyes and listened as Scott started the final chorus. *Wait for me* . . . His voice soared, and Wes felt it deep in his chest and recognized what had once been his, this thing for which *music* was such an inadequate word. This magic, this enchantment, this prayer. It went beyond talent, Wes decided. He believed in gifts, and this, what Scott had, this was a gift.

The applause was halfhearted, and Scott didn't wait to acknowledge it; he was off the stage before it died down, which was quickly enough. One of the boys on the straw bale laughed, a braying guffaw, and said, "God, what a fucking faggot."

Wes found Scott out behind the craft booths, next to the river. The boy was sitting on the ground against a large rock, an untouched candy apple in one hand. He spun the stick and stared intently at the red candy gloss, as though it might show him visions.

"Hey," Wes said, and Scott looked up.

"I didn't know you were here," he said.

"I used to fiddle here," Wes told him. "When I was younger."

"This whole thing's pretty lame." He picked a shard of nut off the sticky surface of the apple.

Almost made Wes angry, but if he'd had the reception Scott did, maybe he'd have felt the same. "Don't think I've ever heard a kid your age sing so good," Wes told him. He didn't offer praise lightly, and maybe the kid sensed that, because the pale skin on his neck flushed.

"I told you I could."

"I guess you did."

"Mr. Farmer helped me pick the song. I'd never heard of it."

"It's a good one. You did it justice."

"He said he used to play with you." Scott glanced once at Wes's hands, then away again.

"That's right."

"You know he was a prison guard?"

"Yeah." Wes eased himself to the ground beside Scott, held a hand to his forehead to shield his eyes from the sun, already low over the mountains. This time of year it just skimmed the sky. "Lots of folks around here are."

"I was kind of surprised when Dennis told me." Scott turned, but his eyes were shadowed. The mountainside behind him, across the water, was covered in ponderosa pine and western larch. The needles of the larches had gone fiery yellow, and it looked like half the trees on the slope had started to burn from within. "I mean, he seems like a pretty decent guy."

"He is. I known him a long time." Behind them, in one of the craft booths, a woman laughed loudly, a shrill false sound. *Tell him,* Wes thought. Wouldn't be so hard. *I was a CO, too.*

"Most of those people are real assholes, though." Scott dropped the candy apple on the grass. "You should hear the stuff my dad says goes on in there."

The scent of fried food was starting to make Wes queasy, like it used to at the mall. *Tell him.* "Scott," he said, "did you mean what you said in the truck the other day? About wanting to learn to play the fiddle?"

Scott turned to look at him, and the breeze lifted his hair at the crown of his head. Looked a little like bird feathers. Delicate. "I guess so."

"'Cause I was thinking about that, and if you're interested—serious about it, I mean—I could teach you."

"For real?"

"Yeah."

"Wow. I mean, that would be awesome."

Wes stood, and Scott quickly followed suit, brushing dried grass from the seat of his jeans. "Don't waste my time if you ain't gonna stick with it," Wes said.

"I don't quit stuff."

"All right. You work with Dennis on Saturdays, right? Can you hang around an hour after he's done with you?"

"Sure." An anguished expression abruptly crossed his face. "I don't have one, though. A fiddle."

Wes gazed past him, toward the dark water. Moved so fast, but didn't look it from here. "I got one you can use to start."

~

Wes's father had loved the fiddle. The violin. The sounds made by four strings and hollow wood. He played old-time music mostly, but he also knew Irish tunes, and Scottish, even a few Cajun and Gypsy. He knew the history of each tune, the odd stories and anecdotes that clung to folk music like burrs. He read books about music, slowly, the strip of leather he used as a bookmark making its way through each volume just a few pages at a time: theory texts, biographies of Paganini and Heifetz, histories of classical and folk music alike. On the third Saturday of each month, he took Wes's mother into Elk Fork to hear the symphony. He believed the Chaconne from Bach's Partita No. 2 in D Minor for unaccompanied violin was the world's only perfect work of art, and he listened to it every morning, a daily devotional, the way other men studied Bible verses or snapped out two dozen pushups.

He'd had talent, his father, but mostly he'd had a well-matched combination of passion and work ethic. Wes hadn't realized it until years after his father's death, but his father must have understood that his skills would never match his desires. He would never receive the praise of an audience of strangers. He would be shackled always to notes composed by others, and even then there would be strict limits; Bach's Chaconne would remain forever out of reach.

Wes always imagined this realization as an epiphany, and it is at this moment, in his constructed memory, that his father turns his attention to lutherie. He built the shed out beside the house, just beyond the first line of pines, and he furnished it slowly. Wes was ten, eleven. He remembered the room filling gradually: a workbench first, largely empty. Tools appearing one by one. Full-size color posters of revered Italian violins, with drawings and charts and measurements on the reverse. Paper-and-pencil sketches of scrolls, f-holes, corner blocks and purfling. Battered old violins from which his father stripped the varnish or pried the tops. And, eventually, pale, perfect blocks of white maple and spruce, narrow strips of ebony and pear. Curls of wood scattered like dry leaves across the floor.

The violin his father chose as his model was a Guarneri del Gesù, not as sweet as most Stradivaris, but more powerful. One instrument. He built it slowly, over the course of a year. The scroll was rough, and the corners were sharper, the f-holes canted more steeply than in most fiddles. The varnish was light, more yellow than red, a color many people wouldn't—didn't—like, but that showed off the fine grain of the wood beneath. Plain ebony pegs, an ebony tailpiece with a mother-of-pearl Parisian eye set into the center, four silver fine tuners.

Wes hadn't found it until three weeks after his father's funeral. He'd gone into the shed intending to pack up the tools, because his mother wouldn't or couldn't, and the fiddle had been hanging from a wire above his father's neat, bare workbench. It was already set up, and when Wes took it down from the wire he found the strings still bright and unblemished by rosin, though they were flat in different intervals (three days would pass before Wes could bring himself to turn the pegs his father had last touched). There was a label inside, visible through the left f-hole. The year—1966—and, where another luthier would have inscribed his name, Jeremiah Carver had written only *For my son*.

~

Wes ate at Farmer's that night. The older man had corralled him into it at Harvest. Wes's first instinct had been to decline, but the thought of another meal alone with Dennis, at that damned table, persuaded him.

Farmer emerged from one of the barns when Wes arrived at half past six. "You'll have to forgive me," he said, gesturing at his oil-stained shirt. "My irrigation pump quit again. Third time in two months. Been trying to get it going."

"Place has grown," Wes noted.

Farmer grinned. "Yeah. I've got a good stud and some nice mares. I breed a few colts every year and sell 'em. Keeps me busy."

"Well, it sure looks good."

Farmer took the compliment with his usual grace, then said, "I'll get the grill going soon as I change. You want a beer?"

"Sure."

Wes sat on the yellow farmhouse's small porch and looked out at all Farmer had built here. The horses had been a hobby when he was working at the prison, but Wes saw it had become far more than that since. A hell of a thing, especially considering Farmer was living on his pension from the prison. Did thirty-five years there. He had always been one of those COs who knew how to leave it at the gate. Back when they were both on the main cellblock, Wes would sometimes see Farmer at work and then see him at home the same day, and it was like talking to two different men. Farmer the CO was good at his job, serious and alert but able to walk the fine line between authority and rigidity. He kept his dignity no matter what the inmates threw at him — even when it was their own shit — and as he moved up the ranks, he earned and retained the respect of everyone who worked with him or under him. Farmer the horseman and husband, on the other hand, changed in the locker room in a town where most COs wore their uniforms home. He had a gentle manner and sense of humor, believed that God heard prayers, and, Wes suspected, never stopped thinking about the wife he'd accidentally killed on a lonely highway all those years ago.

The sun was sinking toward the tops of the mountains to the west, and Wes let his gaze follow it down to the land that used to be his. The house was barely visible, just slices of white through the pine. As he watched, a horse and rider appeared on the other side of the far pasture fence. A black horse with white forelegs, a bareheaded rider who sat straight in the saddle. The pair stopped near the end of the fence, and the rider rested his hands on the horn of the saddle, let the horse lower his head to graze. When he made the effort, Wes could hear the clink of some piece of metal on the tack. He wondered if Dennis could recognize him from that distance.

"All right," Farmer said, stepping back onto the porch and handing Wes a frosty bottle. "I got plenty more where these came from."

"Thanks." Wes glanced back across the pasture, but Dennis was gone.

"You're looking awfully pensive," Farmer ventured. "What's on your mind?"

"Nothing much."

"Try me."

He almost lied. Said *Music,* or *The time we got drunk after Harvest and Lane woke up on your roof,* or even *Claire,* because that, at least, was always partly true. He took a long pull on the bottle. "I was thinking about that night I came here looking for Dennis."

Farmer's jaw tightened, and Wes resisted the satisfaction he felt in his gut.

Three months after the riot. The first time Dennis ran off, the first of many. (Claire never knew, thought the first time he disappeared was two months later.) He was fourteen. Way past midnight, Wes had woken to the sound of the front door shutting, and he'd gotten outside in time to make out Dennis's skinny form shimmying under the hot wire around the broodmare pasture. Claire was still asleep, and Wes was careful not to wake her while he dressed. He'd driven down the narrow access lane between their place and Farmer's, only to find Farmer himself standing in the doorway of his barn when he got there.

"Evening, Wesley," he'd said, as though it were just past supper and not the wee hours of the morning. "Something I can help you with?"

Wes had walked straight up to him, hadn't missed the way Farmer stepped forward to meet him, leaned a little to match his movements. Wes got just inside the barn, and he was surprised by its warmth, by how sweet the hay made it smell. "Dennis ran off," Wes said evenly. "You ain't seen him, have you?"

"Nope. Something upset him?"

Wes shrugged. "He's a teenager."

"Don't always seem to think real straight at that age," Farmer agreed.

They'd stood there a few long moments more.

"I don't usually see you up this late, Arthur." Wes was suddenly aware of the feel of the barn aisle beneath his feet, the rocks embedded in the packed dirt pressing against the soles of his boots. "Got day watch tomorrow, don't you?"

"One of my mares is colicky," Farmer said. "Got to sit up with her."

That's when Wes had seen him. Just when he was ready to let his suspicions go, to assume his stepson was lying low out in the pasture, Dennis had let his curiosity get the better of him. Wes spotted his face peering out from the open doorway of one of the stalls, the barn lights casting a mocking halo on his glossy child's hair before he ducked back inside.

Farmer saw Wes see Dennis. Wes knew he had. Farmer's gaze had been set on Wes's face; he'd have seen his eyes dart away, seen the twitch at his jaw.

"Well," Wes said carefully, "you give me a call if you see him, all right?"

"Will do," Farmer agreed. Lied right to him, blue eyes innocent as could be. Like he already knew Wes wasn't gonna call him on it.

Lord only knew what Dennis had told him. Maybe nothing, maybe it'd all been assumptions on Farmer's part. Thought he was hitting Dennis, Wes supposed, treating him bad. Black River had its share of wife- and child-beaters, most of whom were repentant come morning. Not everyone could leave it at the gate, and some of those who took it home didn't know what to do with it when they got there. (Lane's wives left him for good reason.) Wes, though, had never lost control. Not ever. Not even in those first weeks back at work after the riot, when every other CO in the prison, Farmer included, would've looked the other way if Wes had decided to take out his frustrations on the inmates now and then. Folks almost expected it of him, as though he was beholden to some kind of equation that stated being hurt meant he was gonna turn right around and hurt someone else. But Wes, though he'd had plenty of anger, plenty of rage, had never laid a hand on anyone, Dennis included. Not till years later, till that last night with the gun. But there was a reason Wes didn't challenge Farmer that night in the barn, though it was the first time Wes recognized one of Farmer's lies, the first time he saw how easily they came to him. The anger that had been kindled in Wes with the riot hadn't begun to lessen with time the

way he had first thought it would. It lived in him like a chronic disease, like a cancer, multiplying, growing, coursing through every part
of him. Better, maybe, that Dennis was out of reach just then.

"That was a long time ago," Farmer said now. There was a caution
in his tone Wes wasn't used to. Sounded borrowed.

"You asked what I was thinking," Wes said. Took another swallow
of the beer. "Don't mean that's what we got to talk about."

So he and Farmer spoke about safe things while the meat grilled,
unimportant things. The new housing development, the new pastor,
the new stores. All the things that had changed that didn't matter. They
went inside the kitchen to eat, and Wes saw that this, at least, had stayed
the same; Farmer had kept his house just as it was when Madeline was
alive. There were lace valances over the windows, a yellow-checkered
cloth on the table, and a cross-stitched Bible verse—one of the gentle
ones—in a frame over the sink. Madeline had liked cats, Wes remembered, and Farmer kept one now, a small calico. It crouched primly
on a windowsill and watched them through copper-colored eyes. How
did Farmer do this, coexist with his wife's memory day after day? Wes
thought about his own house, back in Spokane. Doors locked, blinds
drawn, drafts stilled. It had been just two weeks, but he imagined the
house as if it had been left untouched for years. A veil of dust over everything, the color leached from the furnishings, stale air suited only to
ghosts.

A banjo case stood propped in the corner of the room, half hidden
behind Farmer's guitar. Wes nodded to it. "That Lane's Gibson?"

Farmer looked, like it might've appeared since he last glanced that
direction. "Yeah."

"You ever play it?"

He shook his head. "You know I can't get a decent roll going. The
fingerpicks trip me up." He sliced a strip of meat from his steak. A
sharp movement. "I keep thinking I ought to find some young up-and-
comer to give it to. Too good an instrument to be gathering dust in a
corner."

"But?"

"But it's twenty years on and I still ain't done it."

Wes wondered if Farmer, like himself, found he could no longer think of Lane without thinking of the way he'd died. Seemed an unfair thing: so many memories of good times, of music and county fairs and the worst dives and long applause, of practices in Wes's living room or Lane's garage or on Farmer's porch, of drinks and laughter shared, and all of it, all of it, superseded by imagined images of a crushed skull and glassy eyes.

The sudden silence lingered uneasily, and then Farmer cleared his throat. "I been meaning to talk to you about this hearing, Wesley."

"I'd rather you didn't." Wes concentrated on holding his fork. Damn thing like that took concentration now.

"I'm not saying you should go and I'm not saying you shouldn't, but there are some things you ought to give some thought to beforehand."

Wes picked up the knife with his right hand. It had a narrow molded plastic handle, and Wes couldn't force his fingers to close on it with any degree of workable pressure. "I guarantee you I spent plenty of time thinking about Bobby Williams already," he said. "We really gotta let him spoil dinner, too?"

"Ain't exactly my favorite topic of conversation either, but—"

"I don't want to hear the 'but,' Farmer. I got no interest in talking about this with you or anyone else." Wes heard his voice rising before he could check it, but Farmer didn't flinch.

"I'm not aiming to be rude, Wesley, I'm really not. I just want you to go into this with your eyes open."

The knife slipped from Wes's grip and clattered onto his plate. Farmer glanced down and saw Wes's untouched steak.

"Oh, Jesus," Farmer muttered. "I'm so sorry, Wesley. I didn't think."

"It's fine," Wes said quickly, loudly, over Farmer. "Fine. The arthritis is all. These hands, they're no good for anything anymore."

"I should've thought."

"No, it's fine," Wes said again. He tried to force a smile, but felt it twist into a grimace on his flushed face. "Can't do the simplest things sometimes."

"Here, let me." Farmer reached awkwardly across the table, averting his eyes, and Wes stared at the little calico while the other man cut his meat for him.

～

The threat of a baton above his head. Blood already in his hair.

"Take off your shirt."

The buttons at the cuffs first, then the buttons down the front. Ten altogether.

"Unlace your boots."

His broken ribs grated when he leaned over, but he held the pain behind his teeth. Unknotted the laces, slid them from their hooks and eyelets two at a time.

"Tie your ankles to the chair. Tight. Do it right."

The last easy things he ever did with his hands.

～

He had a morning routine of sorts now. Coffee at the house, then the short drive to the near end of town. He'd park the truck, buy a second cup of coffee at the kiosk in the Jameson's parking lot and walk the length of Main Street to the IGA, where he'd buy cigarettes or beer to replace those Dennis had shared with him, or if those things didn't need buying, a copy of the *Elk Fork Herald,* or if he didn't want to face the headlines, a single random item from the shelves, the price of entrance, justification for walking the aisles. A waste of time and money both, he knew that. But it was fair exchange for an hour in which he could pretend not to think about Dennis or Claire or Williams.

"Hey!"

Wes turned to see Scott marching across the parking lot toward him. The young woman in the espresso kiosk pushed his coffee across the counter along with his change, which Wes deposited in the jar with *Tips* scrawled across it. She didn't thank him.

"Hey!" Scott called again.

"What, you forget my name?"

"You told me you were a musician," Scott said, stopping short a little too close to Wes, as though he'd gotten so near without meaning to. "You said you could teach me to play the fiddle."

"I was, and I can." Wes took a sip of his coffee. It was a little burnt. "Ain't you supposed to be in school?"

"You lied to me."

"I did no such thing."

Scott's eyes were all pupil, like he was drugged on his anger. Lines had etched themselves into the skin of his forehead, all the starker for his youth. "You weren't a musician. You were a fucking CO."

Wes stepped right into the kid. "Quit staring at my shoes. If you're gonna swear at me, you'll look me in the eye while you do it."

Scott took a half step back, caught himself—he was quick, like Dennis had always been—and met Wes's eyes. One hand went to the earbuds dangling from his sweatshirt collar, and he twined the cords around his fingers until they doubled and twisted. "Maybe you played on the side or whatever, but you worked at that freaking prison just like every other asshole in this town."

"Listen good, Scott." In the street, a gust snapped the Harvest banner hard against its restraints. "Being a CO? That was to feed my wife and my stepson and keep a roof over their heads. Because that's what a good man does; he provides for his family." Wes lowered his voice, pitch and volume both. "Though I guess you might not know that."

"Shut up about my dad. You don't know shit about my dad."

"I know he's locked up, and I don't need to know more. Ain't your fault, but it is what it is."

The kid was getting ready to punch him, or bolt. Hard to say which. "You're still a liar."

"You grow up in this town, you go to work at the prison. That's how it works." Wes had forgotten to get one of those cardboard sleeves for the cup, and the coffee burned his fingers through the paper. "But God's honest truth, Scott: when I think about what I used to do when I was a younger man, music's what comes to mind."

Scott was shaking his head over and over, each movement sharp and automatic. "Nope," he said. "No. No way." He leaned into Wes, tried to get him up against the wall, but Wes didn't move and Scott backed off with a snarl. "You COs all think you own this shithole of a town, and you think you're like God or something, just because you have an ugly uniform and you put people in prison."

"People put themselves in prison," Wes said automatically, and Scott's face collapsed into a grotesque grimace.

"You liked it and you know it," he said.

Wes sighed, took another long sip of coffee. He held the liquid on his front teeth until the heat shocked the nerves and only then did he swallow, pressing his tongue against the lingering pain. "You ever been in there?" he asked finally, gesturing with his cup to the old prison across the street.

Scott looked, shoved his hands into the pockets of his coat. "No. We were supposed to go one time on a field trip, but I skipped." Found Wes's eyes again. "Nobody cared."

"Come on, then. I got something to show you." He started across the street. Didn't hear footsteps behind him until he was halfway across.

They'd turned the old prison into a museum a few years after Wes and Claire moved to Spokane. Pulled a few tourists off the interstate during the summer months with tacky billboards featuring a cartoon ball and chain. There were a few rooms of exhibits and educational materials, but the real draw was the opportunity to tour the old prison itself, to walk through the narrow, damp corridors and duck into one of the tiny, close cells, to touch stone and brick and imagine who else had done the same years ago. Wes had never been inside the museum, but Claire had, on one of her visits to Black River, and it was because of her he knew what he was looking for.

There was an older woman behind the desk in the lobby, someone who looked vaguely familiar to Wes, like she might have been the wife of someone he'd known a little, once, but he passed her with just a terse nod. He bypassed the entrance to the prison itself and instead turned right and walked briskly through the first exhibit rooms. Kept his eyes ahead, but in his peripheral vision Wes saw the glass-fronted displays of shanks confiscated from inmates—makeshift knives fashioned from toothbrushes and spoons and broken broom handles, or cobbled together with disposable razor blades and lengths of thread unraveled from clothing or bedding—and the neat panels on the walls that explained the history of the old prison and of law and order in Montana as though it was all a neat, purposeful progression to some sort of idealized present.

Scott almost ran into him when Wes got to the last room and stopped. Credit the kid a little for following him. "So what's the deal?"

Wes stepped to one of the panels, a smooth sheet of plastic mounted at an angle to the wall, like a drafting table. The title was neat and ordered and printed in black, black ink: THE 1992 PRISON DISTUR-BANCE. *Disturbance*. Always liked that. Like calling a war an *action* or an *operation;* everyone knew it was a war but understood that the politicians didn't want to call it one. 'Ninety-two had been a riot—and if you asked anyone in town about it, that's what they'd call it—but *disturbance* must've sounded better to someone with a desk and a brass nameplate.

Wes scanned the panel, the plastic cool beneath his fingertips, and tapped the line when he found it: *. . . two officers were killed and a third was held hostage for thirty-nine hours before . . .*

"I'm the third officer," he told Scott. "You want the gory details, I'm sure they're on the Internet somewhere."

Scott looked down at the panel, back up at Wes. "I didn't—"

"I'll be at the house Saturday if you still want those lessons. Put new strings on the fiddle for you." Wes left the kid there alone. He dropped a ten at the front desk for the woman to fold into her donation box, and then he pushed back out onto the street and into the cold.

When Wes got back to the house he heard hammering. Rhythmic, bright, almost tuneful. He'd intended to make an entrance. Stride in, back Dennis up against a wall, demand to know what the hell he was thinking, telling Scott he'd been a CO, knowing full well how the kid would react. But something about the hammering stopped him, and he stood there beside his truck, listening to the melody of metal on metal.

After a couple minutes he followed the sound to the workshop. He scarcely recognized it. It'd been transformed into something purely functional, industrial, with none of the charm or comfortable snugness of his father's shop. Maybe there was a wash of nostalgia over his memory of the place, but he wouldn't have guessed metal was so very different from wood. Dennis, back to the door, stood over his anvil, right leg thrust forward, left leg back. Wes could see him brace himself before each strike of the hammer. He worked quickly, but unhurriedly. Gray-white flakes of metal scattered across the concrete floor below the anvil, marrying with spirals of wet, trailing water droplets. Behind Dennis, the coal forge rumbled and glowed, the light ever changing, and Wes could feel its heat even from where he stood in the wide doorway.

Dennis wore safety glasses with earplugs at the ends. The hammering didn't seem loud to Wes, but hour after hour, day after day, perhaps it took its toll. He himself didn't hear as well out of his left ear as his right, his fiddle having stolen, over the years, a shade of the very sense it loved best. Abruptly, Dennis stopped hammering and dipped the horseshoe into the bucket at his feet; the water boiled and hissed. He spoke without turning. "Why are you still here, Wes?"

"Watching you is all."

Dennis stepped sideways, used his tongs to pull an orange-glowing length of straight metal from the forge. "In Black River. I meant why are you still in Black River."

"You want me to get a motel, all you got to do is say so."

"Jesus, Wes, I don't want you to get a motel. I want you to go home." He began hammering again, and spoke between strikes: a few words, *strike,* a few words, *strike.* "We took care of Mom's ashes, and that's good. You went to Harvest for old times' sake or whatever, and I guess that's good, too. But I don't understand why you haven't gone back to Spokane." Dennis's posture seemed suddenly fatigued, and each ring of his hammer sounded a bit louder and duller than the one before. He glanced up only once, a stolen look while he wiped sweat from his brow with the back of his wrist, quick enough to deny. He repositioned himself, shifted his feet and squared his shoulders; when the hammering started back up, it was again the familiar sharp ring.

Wes crossed to the workbench on the other side of the anvil, where he could see Dennis's face. Hotter still here, the heat just about scraping skin. He ought to tell Dennis about the hearing. But the more people he told, the more real it became. The harder it would be to back out.

"Tell me this," Dennis said at last. "What possessed you to offer Scott fiddle lessons?"

"He expressed an interest."

"Don't give me that shit, Wes."

The shoe was already half formed, curving gently around the horn of the anvil. Incredible, this something from nothing. This gift of shaping, creating. He wondered if Dennis appreciated it for what it was. "He's got talent."

"For the fiddle? Suddenly you're clairvoyant?"

"For music."

"There are boatloads of people in the world with musical talent, Wes. Why Scott?"

"You want to help him," Wes said. "So do I."

"Bullshit. You think he's grand larceny waiting to happen."

Wes picked up a rasp, ran the pad of his thumb over the rough surface, feeling the snag of skin. "I really don't see how it's your business, Dennis."

Dennis stopped hammering, thrust the half-shaped shoe back into the forge. He pulled off his glasses, tossed them onto the workbench. "It's my business, Wes, because I care about that kid. It's my business because I don't trust you to see him as a person, not a protégé. I don't trust you to see past what his father has done, and I don't trust you not to ruin him."

Jesus.

"Look, Wes." A deep breath. "I know you loved Mom. I know that. You were devoted to her and that didn't change when she got sick, and I'm grateful to you for that, I really am. You were . . . a good husband." Wes heard the grind of teeth, and Dennis's voice took on a hard edge. "But you've never been a good father."

What Wes wanted to do: Overturn the anvil stand. Sweep his hand across the workbench and send the tools clattering across the concrete floor. Yell until his lungs ached. What he did: Took a single step forward. Tested his voice before letting it slip his lips. "This ain't about you."

"You sure?"

They held each other's gaze, and Wes thought of the thousands of other times he'd stared into Dennis's eyes, years ago. The way Dennis never, ever backed down, not in the moment and not later. Time and space never settled his temper. It'd frightened Wes, the way Dennis could sustain anger. Made him feel helpless—and nothing kindled rage in Wes's soul like feeling helpless.

He missed the way this room used to smell back when he was a boy, when it was his father's shop. Like wood and oil and varnish. Churchly scents, almost. Now it smelled only of heat, as though the fire in the forge leached too much oxygen from the air, left it hard and brittle.

"I just saw Scott in town," Wes said at last.

Dennis dropped his eyes. "Ah, shit."

"Now maybe you don't believe it, but I been trying hard to be civil to that kid, because I know you're trying to help him."

"It wasn't—"

"And I'm having a real hard time understanding why you suddenly decided to rile him up when you know—"

"Wes," Dennis said, "I didn't tell him, all right?"

"Don't interrupt me, Dennis."

"Then listen, for fuck's sake."

Wes clenched his teeth hard. "Hell of a mouth on you."

"This isn't a church, Wes. It's my place of business. On my property. You came here."

Wes forced himself to breathe, the way Claire used to tell him to do when he was angry. Always been easier with her hands on his shoulders, her kiss atop his head. "Okay," he said tightly. "What is it you got to say?"

"I need to show you." Dennis shut the forge off, and the deep roar of the bellows vanished, left a tentative silence behind. The coal still glowed in its belly. Dennis crossed to the workbench, flipped through a stack of papers held down by an old rasp. He found a manila envelope, pulled it free. "Scott was asking about you and the band," he said. "I sent him to get this out of the house the other day. Didn't mean for him to go through it himself." He tossed the envelope across the table between them.

Wes pulled a thin pile of photographs from the envelope. The one on top had been taken at a barbecue in someone's backyard, and showed Lane, Farmer and Wes playing on the patio. It was an old picture, creased at one corner. Wes squinted at it, but couldn't remember exactly where or when it'd been taken. There were a half-dozen other pictures of the band, at dances, at Harvest, in the yard behind the church. There were other photos in the stack, too, a kaleidoscopic vision of the Carver family. A snapshot of an eight- or nine-year-old Dennis grinning from the back of one of Farmer's horses. A photo of Claire holding up a sweater on Christmas morning. One of Wes and Claire together, Claire's hand in his, Wes's smile only half materializing. And then, on the bottom, a picture no one in the family had taken. It was one of the identification photographs the DOC took of newly minted COs. Plain blue background, harsh light.

Wes wondered if Scott would have recognized him if not for the card in his hand with his name printed on it. Wes had been twenty-one, just, and wore a deadly serious expression. He remembered he'd been trying for confident, in that brief moment opposite the camera, but he'd known all too well that he had no experience and was about to start a job in which that was the only thing that really counted. His hair was cut short and parted severely, and his eyes looked backlit, the way a person's did when the sun shone straight into them.

"Why've you got this?"

"Found it in the house after you left," Dennis said, and something in the way he answered made Wes wonder if he was lying. The photograph was public record, though, released to the media during the riot; Dennis could've gotten it any number of places. And maybe it was something Claire had kept after all; she was good at that, in the way women could be, good at keeping memories in physical form.

Wes stared at his younger self. When that photograph was taken, he had not yet walked a tier, met his wife or known how much pain one person could cause another. "You shouldn't have left it where Scott could get at it," he said.

"Guess I know that now."

Wes stared past Dennis into the forge. The coal had cooled to livid red, but it still burned too bright to keep his eyes on it for long. "I haven't gone home yet because there's a hearing," he said quietly. "Williams has come eligible for parole."

Dennis crossed his arms over his chest. Opened his mouth once, closed it straightaway. Finally he said, "They'd let a guy go after doing what he did?"

"They let people go who killed people, Dennis. Ain't gonna change the laws on my account."

"What are you going to do if they let him out?"

The muscles alongside Wes's spine all tightened at once. He thought about it, about Williams standing outside the double line of fence. Outside the gate. They'd send him home, of course—home for Williams was way out east, toward the Dakota border; Wes had looked it up—but he'd have a couple days to get there, and it was possible—possible—that in those couple days Wes would occupy the same space as him.

What would he do.

"Hopefully it don't come to that," he said.

~

"I've probably saved your life," Williams said. Second day. After the burns and the cuts, before the breaks. "Out there"—a thumb jerked toward the locked door of the control room—"out there your skull is busted, your insides ruptured, your windpipe crushed. Out there they'd have already tore you apart ten times over." A grin Wes tried not to look at, too wide, all slick white flash. "When you think about it like that," Williams said, "I'm your goddamn savior."

———

Wes heard Dennis's truck roll in just after two on Saturday afternoon, but he didn't stand until he heard both truck doors slam. Dennis came into the house first and held the door for Scott, who stepped tentatively into the living room, though Wes knew the kid had been here before. He wore good work boots today, laces tied, and a dark pair of Wranglers, but from the waist up he was still clad in his favored black. He held his head a little strangely, canted to one side, and Wes saw a bruise at the corner of his left eye, fading but not gone.

"How'd work go?" Wes asked, when Scott made no move to speak.

"All right," Scott said. "Dennis got stomped on by this big-ass draft horse."

Wes glanced at him.

"I wear these ugly old shitkickers for a reason," Dennis said, stepping on the heel of one boot and pulling it off. "They got steel toes, metatarsal guards, the works."

"That your way of telling me you're fine?"

"That your way of asking?"

Wes sighed, turned to Scott. "So," he said, "you want to learn to play this thing?" He nodded to the hearth, where his fiddle waited in its velvet.

"Yeah," Scott said, and it was like Wes had released him; he went across the room and knelt to look at the instrument, put out a hand but pulled back before touching it.

Dennis met Wes's eyes. "You care if I stay?"

"It's your house."

Dennis nodded, disappeared down the hall. Wes took two chairs from the table and set them facing each other in the living room, a few feet apart. Knee-to-knee, as his father used to say. Maybe a little silly with just one fiddle, but it was the only way Wes knew to do this. He put Scott with his back to the door. Wes pulled the case to the side of his own chair, sat with the fiddle on his knee. "You never held one of these before?" he asked. "Never took violin lessons in grade school, nothing like that?"

"No."

"All right. You kind of balance it here on your collarbone," he said, bringing the fiddle home to rest beneath his jaw. He remembered what his father used to tell him: *halfway between head and heart.* Wes had always loved that phrase. The way it summed up all you needed to know to play the fiddle right. He could almost feel his father's hands on his body: a light touch on his right shoulder, his left elbow, adjusting his posture. His father's quiet voice. *Halfway between head and heart.* Wes couldn't bring himself to say it now. "You settle your jaw on the chinrest real light, okay? Don't clamp down on the thing." And he held his fiddle across the space, had to fight not to close his hand around the neck when Scott took hold of it.

He was awkward, more awkward still when Wes added the bow, but he got that same look on his face he'd had at Harvest, a determination so intense it was almost grimness, and Wes guessed he'd stick with it a while at least. Wes taught him how to draw the bow, how to keep his right wrist loose and his left wrist straight, explained how to practice his bow hold anytime, anywhere, with a pencil. He showed him a G major scale and made him play "Twinkle, Twinkle, Little Star," even though the kid made a face. "You got to start with something you know by heart," Wes told him. "I know you know this by heart." Scott fumbled for the notes, but after a few minutes he was sliding his fingers to more or less the right places without prompting. It was more than most people could do at first, and Wes told him so. Once he looked up and saw Dennis standing in the doorway, arms crossed. A few minutes later Wes looked again and he was gone.

"Can I ask you something?"

A break in the lesson. Almost over anyway. All the "Twinkle, Twinkle" either of them could take.

"Sure."

"Do your hands hurt?"

A sound from the kitchen. No, a stopping of sound.

"Yes."

"All the time?"

"Some days worse'n others."

"The . . . guy who did it."

Wes waited.

"Did he know you were a fiddler?"

"I think," Wes said, "he just knew it hurt."

"You see that black eye?" The first words out of Dennis's mouth after dropping Scott back home. His hand still on the front door.

Wes looked out the window. The horses and the mule were gathered at the gate, coats metallic over muscle in the fading light. Their tails swished out of rhythm, tangling together before parting again. "Yeah."

"Scott tell you how he got it?"

"Didn't ask."

"Didn't ask," Dennis repeated. He came into the room, his boot heels sounding solid on the wood. He had a heavy step for such a slim man. "Shouldn't surprise me, I guess. You never did care why I got into fights. Only that I did."

Wes thought about that for a minute and knew it to be true. He crossed his arms, tucked his fingers into the crooks of his elbows out of habit. "Kid's got a tongue. He wants me to know something, he'll tell me."

Dennis shook his head. "Not everyone considers stoicism the highest of all virtues, Wes."

"You're the one spent most of the day with him. Did he tell you?"

No answer. Instead: "How are you going to teach him?"

"You saw the lesson."

"How are you going to teach him when he's had enough of 'Twinkle, Twinkle, Little Star'?"

Wes thought about not answering, shutting the conversation down with a couple sharp words. He'd taught before. Never for a living, but once in a while folks would approach him after a performance, or they'd call the house and leave a message Claire would pointedly pass along, and then he'd find himself sitting in the living room on a Saturday afternoon with a beginning fiddler who usually had more enthusiasm than talent. (And, of course, there was Dennis.) Wes had always taught his students the way his father had taught him: by ear. He'd play a tune through, twice. Then he'd play the first few notes of the A part over and over until the student joined in on his own fiddle. When the student could play those notes in unison with him, Wes would move on to the next few bars, and the next, and then on to the B part. He kept time with his foot on the floor and played harmony when his students could reliably carry the melody. Sheet music never made an appearance, and to this day Wes could barely read notation. So what was he going to do when Scott was ready for something more than kids' songs? "I ain't sure," he said finally.

"I've got an idea," Dennis told him, and disappeared down the hall. Wes heard him rummaging in the bedroom closet, and he returned a minute later with a sturdy shoebox. He offered it to Wes.

There were cassette tapes inside, a few with cases, most without. The lettering on the labels was precise, sharply angled. Claire's handwriting. Wes turned a few of the tapes over. Dates only. "You kept these?"

Dennis shrugged.

They were mostly performances, Wes knew. Recordings made from a distance at Harvest, or in a school gym. Coughs and chatter intruding upon the notes, dozens of pairs of feet stamping dance steps over the music. A few of the tapes—the later dates—preserved afternoons in this house, one fiddle, his fiddle, moving from one tune to another with whatever purpose he'd had in mind that day. Wes had never listened to these. When he was younger he'd only been able to hear his errors, and later, after the riot, he didn't dare listen. He'd wanted to get rid of them—had one of his rare, real fights with Claire about it—but she'd flat-out refused.

"I know it's all at speed and a lot of it's with the band," Dennis said. "But maybe it'll at least help Scott get familiar with some of the tunes."

Wes nodded. Met Dennis's eyes and nodded again. "Thank you."

Dennis reached into the box, tapped one of the tapes with two fingers. "That one's got 'Angelina Baker,'" he said. Flipped another tape. "And this one has 'Cripple Creek' on the B side."

"You know these."

Dennis nodded. "I know them all."

He sat alone in the living room the next afternoon, the shoebox balanced on his knees. Fourteen cassettes, with twenty-three dates. This, all the extant proof of what he once was. How many more recordings might there have been, if not for the riot? Wes selected one of the cassettes at random and wrestled it into the tape deck in the stereo beside the television. Hissing silence first. Then his voice, as simultaneously familiar and strange as the sound of one's own voice always was. "That thing on?" And Dennis, seven or eight, voice still pitched high: "The little wheels are moving." His own self again. "You ready?" "Yeah!" "Okay, here we go."

And he lit into "Hop High Ladies," played it fast as he knew how. Here was his fiddle: the rich, round, woody sound of it. Part of him wanted to fast-forward until he found a slower piece, something with long, sustained notes, so he could savor the sound, welcome it, wallow in it. But he was transfixed by the tune playing now, by how *easy* it had been. Wes closed his eyes, and though he did not move—his arms stayed at his sides, his hands relaxed, fingers curled into their new skewed normal—he could feel himself playing. The weight of the fiddle in his left hand, the bite of it at his collarbone, the pressure of the strings against his fingertips, the smoothness of the ebony beneath. He could feel how it had been to play like this, too fast to think about the notes, each of them just miraculously *there,* exactly when and where they were needed, the tune unraveling almost of its own accord, seeming to bring him along almost as a simple courtesy, an afterthought.

There were other sounds on the tape, too, beneath the music. A mischievous little boy's giggle, a steady thumping. More distant, a single ring of metal on metal, the duller clank of glass or ceramic on a countertop. And then, when the playing stopped, his fiddle eased into silence, Claire's voice: sweet, gentle, a little huskier than he'd expected the first time he heard her speak. "Denny, must you always be such a whirling dervish? He's going to bring this house crashing down, Wesley. Something a little slower this time, please."

He stopped the tape player, pressed the rewind button. *A little slower this time, please.* God, these things that had been his, these voices, so close. Rewind, again. *This time, please.* Again. *Time, please. Please. Please.*

~~~

Monday he woke to snow. It was coming down hard, but wouldn't stick; Wes could tell by the way it didn't gather on the gravel, the way there seemed to be fewer flakes in the air the closer they got to the ground. A little early for the first snowfall of the season, but not remarkably so. Wes knew there were probably curses flying around Black River; most folks dreaded the coming of winter in a place where it could stay for five months at a stretch. Wes, though, had always liked winter. The way it sounded. The way the gray tint that winter brought to the world seemed almost audible, a certain hushed and muted quality over everything. Calm.

He saw Rio a moment later. Couldn't have said why the sight startled him so. Horses did lie down from time to time; he knew that. And Rio wasn't flat on his side; he was settled on his chest a few yards beyond the gate, legs gathered at his side, head up. The way normal horses rested. But the red horse and the mule were standing a few yards away, nose to tail, hunched a little against the cold, ears turned back just a bit. They didn't look unhappy, really, but they knew they were standing in a storm. Something about Rio was . . . off.

Wes pulled on his chore coat and boots and then crossed the yard, the snow stinging his cheeks. The black horse watched him come, his white-rimmed eye unsettlingly human. Wes stopped at the gate. The red horse and the mule sauntered over, eager to see if he'd brought food, but he waved them off, and they backed away with an annoyed toss of their heads. Wes crossed his arms over his chest, wished he'd put on a hat. He clucked at Rio the way he'd heard his father do when he wanted his hunting horses to move. Rio's ears pricked sharply forward, but he didn't get up.

The gate had a chain wrapped around it, a bull snap on the clasp. Wes tried to pull it open, but the spring was too strong, the wedge slickly dotted with melted snow, and he couldn't get a grip on it. Metal rattled against metal. He leaned down next to the fence, but heard the telltale metronome click of the electricity. "Goddamn," he said aloud. With his coat off, he could just squeeze between the metal pipes of the gate, but it was an uncomfortable fit, and he cracked the back of his skull against the metal. He clapped his hands as he walked toward Rio, clucked again. This time the horse got his forelegs out in front of him and tried to stand, but his hind legs didn't straighten, and he ended up sitting on his haunches like a dog. Wes saw the heavy muscles of his quarters tremble before Rio settled back onto his sternum. He shook his head and neck, sending a crystalline spray of ice into the air above his mane. Then he stared back at Wes, blinked once, twice. Wes understood. He used to think the whole "my knee knows when it's going to rain" thing was a crock, an old wives' tale. But the cold pained him now, sharpened the ache that was always with him, bolstered the stiffness in his joints. And Rio, whose arthritic joints were weight-bearing, must have been even more troubled when the temperature dropped. Wasn't that he didn't want to get up—he couldn't.

Another squeeze through the gate, a brief call to Dennis's cell. Dennis swore when Wes told him Rio was down, said he was coming right away. Back outside, Wes crossed to the shed beside the workshop. Inside, Wes found a green horse blanket with a silver duct-tape X across a tear on one side. He bundled the blanket into his arms and went back into the pasture. Orange baling twine knotted a dangling buckle to the fabric, and it jingled lightly with each step. Wes spread the blanket over Rio's body so his back and rump were covered, the straps and buckles loose on either side.

No Dennis yet. Wes knelt in the grass. Snow melted into his jeans, chilled his skin. He patted the horse on the neck, belatedly remembered his father telling him that most horses preferred to be stroked. Rio's hair was smooth beneath his palm, and softer than Wes expected.

He let his hand glide down Rio's neck, over and over, and once he slid it beneath the blanket, afraid the animal was as cold as he was. He was shocked by the heat that surrounded the horse's body. He glanced at Rio's face: the same sharp white-rimmed eye, ears flopped a little to the sides. If he was unsettled, Wes couldn't see it. He slipped his other hand beneath the blanket and rested his palms on Rio's shoulder, let the animal warmth soothe his own aches.

Dennis's truck came up the drive too fast, and he stalled it out next to the gate. Slid out the passenger side and left the door open, the dome light inside glowing yellow against the gray veil of the day. "Shit," Dennis said. He opened the clasp on the gate—easy, so easy—and slid a hand across his mouth as he trotted toward them. "Shit, Rio. Don't do this to me today." Rio whickered softly, and Wes stood. Dennis put his hands on his hips, paced hard, a step to the right, a step to the left, again. He stopped abruptly, pulled his cell phone from his pocket and stared at the screen. He took several steps backward and a wide step to the side—searching for a signal, Wes supposed—then dialed and listened. He didn't speak before snapping the phone shut. "Arthur's not picking up."

"Why do you need him?"

"Might be we can get Rio back up," Dennis said, and his voice had lost all its assertiveness. Sounded more like prayer than certainty.

"I'm right here, Dennis."

Wes had meant it to sound gentle, but Dennis looked at him sharply. He glanced back at Rio. "You put this blanket over him?"

"I worried he was cold."

"That was good," Dennis said. He went down on one knee next to Rio, rubbed a hand over one ear. Rio bumped Dennis's shoulder with his muzzle. Dennis spoke without standing back up. "It'll take ropes."

Wes glanced at his hands. The skin was red with cold, the pain starting to needle its way up his arms. "I can wrap 'em around my wrists."

"That's not safe."

"You want to get this horse up or not?"

Dennis worked quickly, and soon there was a halter on Rio's head and a pair of ropes looped under his barrel and behind his haunches. The red horse was still grazing, but the mule provided an audience. "All right, buddy," Dennis said quietly, and Wes wondered why he hadn't thought to speak to the horse during the long stretch of time he'd sat with him. "You ready?" Dennis asked, and Wes nodded.

He coiled the ends of his ropes around his arms, and felt an instant of reflexive panic when the cotton tightened around his wrists. Then Dennis was hauling on his ropes and on Rio's lead, and he was saying, "Let's go, let's go, let's go," and Wes didn't know if he was talking to the horse or to him, but he leaned on his own ropes and clucked again for good measure. And Rio tried for them, he did. First the forelegs stretched out, and then he heaved his body upward, but again he only made it to the dog-sit position, but Dennis didn't quit and so neither did Wes, and he saw Rio's muscles quivering and he heard Dennis groan and he felt the rope bite into his wrists. And then Rio was standing, legs splayed, wavering a bit, but up. Dennis dropped his ropes, and Wes let his fall, too. Rio took a hesitant, unsteady step forward, and Dennis was there to greet him, his hands on either side of the horse's face, and he leaned in until his forehead met his horse's, and he stayed there. The snow had almost quit now, but it dusted Dennis's hair and Rio's mane, and Wes didn't know if he should stay or go.

"Winter's hard on him," Dennis said, his head still touching Rio's. When Wes looked at him again, he saw his eyes were closed. "After last year I swore I wouldn't put him through another." His tone was strange, the usual hard edge gone, and Wes heard a Dennis he'd thought had disappeared years ago. A Dennis he'd long forgotten how to talk to. "I swore," he said again.

~

Wes hadn't thought he'd be so disappointed. He'd already moved the kitchen chairs, already taken his fiddle down from the mantel and held it waiting on his knee. He didn't turn in his chair, but at four the clock chimed and there was no sound of gravel beneath tires, no hesitant step on the porch. He waited, fingers tightening painfully on the neck of the fiddle, until the clock chimed its solitary notice of the half hour, and then he packed the fiddle into its case and carried it out to his truck. He drove to town and stopped at Jameson's; the first cashier he spoke to gave him directions.

Scott Bannon and his mother lived near the end of a dirt road that dead-ended up against the mountains, in a white trailer with rust stains streaking from beneath the window frames and a tacked-on porch that listed sharply to one side. A trailer like that would've been crowded next to a couple dozen clones in Spokane, but here it was settled on its own three-acre lot. Not much else on this side of town: a couple other trailers, a few run-down houses, a bar that catered to the most hopeless drunks, a lot where the logging trucks deposited their sap-bloodied cargo to wait for the freight trains. It was the side of town away from the river, on the far side of the interstate and the railroad tracks, the side that stayed dark longest when the sun rose, and was battered hardest during storms when the wind whipped through the canyon.

Wes parked his truck in the gravel drive behind a blue sedan with a green driver's side door. Up close, the trailer bore some small evidence of care: a few potted geraniums still hanging on in the autumn chill, a wooden *Welcome* sign beside the door. He hesitated on the front steps. Maybe he wasn't doing the kid any favors. Seemed like he had enough trouble fitting in; encouraging an interest in music that had peaked in popularity more than a hundred years ago hardly seemed likely to help. But he remembered the eagerness in Scott's eyes that first lesson, the way he'd grinned the first time he'd pulled a clear note with the bow. Wes opened the screen door, knocked on the aluminum behind it.

He knew her. Scott's mother. He recognized the black curls, the telltale cigarette wrinkles above her upper lip. Hell. The phlebotomist from the blood donation center.

"Mr. Carver," she greeted smoothly. "Good to see you again."

Wes nodded. "Yes, ma'am."

A small smile broke over her face, and she bit her lower lip. "Lord, don't call me that. It's Molly."

Another nod. He could picture that name now, on a plastic nametag pinned over the breast of her violet uniform. The sunflower sticker above it. He tapped his own chest belatedly, said, "Wes."

"Wes, then." She didn't offer her hand, and Wes was impressed; it usually took folks a few failed handshakes with him before they trained themselves out of the habit. She opened the door wider and ushered him inside. He stood on the small woven rug just inside the door. Hated this. It was all right for this woman, this Molly, to have seen what she had there in the hospital — the tears and the scars — but it was damn near unbearable to stand here and have to look her in the eye, knowing those things had been seen.

"I didn't realize," he muttered. "That you were Scott's momma, I mean."

"Sixteen years and counting," she said, with a smile that seemed equal parts genuine and put-on.

Wes followed her into the main room of the trailer, taking in the uneasy scents of someone else's home. Here was the turnabout, the chance to see her life, and Scott's. A couch upholstered with an ugly knobby fabric. A tube television set with a rabbit-ear antenna perched on top of it, one branch jutting into the center of the room. Two prints on the wall, replicas of vintage French travel posters (he knew nothing of this woman, but somehow the posters surprised him, and he wondered if they'd been here when she'd moved in). Magazines on the coffee table, *Rolling Stone* and *Spin* and *Good Housekeeping*. Claire used to read that, the *Good Housekeeping*. She liked the advice columns about people's family problems, used to tell him about them over dinner as though gossiping about neighbors, but near as Wes could tell, no one ever wrote in with the kinds of problems people in Black River had, the Carvers or the Bannons: *My teenage son nearly shot my husband in the face, and then my husband made me move two states away and leave my child behind. What do I do?* Or: *My husband is in prison and now I'm trying to raise our son among the people keeping his father locked up. Please help.*

"Sorry it's such a mess," Molly said. "I've never been much of a housekeeper. Good intentions and all that, but by the time I get home in the evening . . ."

"It's fine," Wes said, though when Claire had still worked, early in their marriage, she'd kept their home neat, too.

Molly smiled, and Wes smiled back, and though the couch was right there, neither of them sat.

"The reason I'm here is we had a fiddle lesson scheduled," Wes offered. "Scott didn't show up and I was concerned is all."

"He didn't call you," Molly said. It wasn't really a question, so Wes didn't say anything. He looked at the posters on the wall. Camels on one. An old-fashioned airplane on the other.

Scott chose that moment to appear in the doorway to the hall. "Hey."

"You told me you called Mr. Carver to reschedule your lesson," Molly said tightly, smile still in place.

Scott shrugged.

Molly turned back to Wes. "We go see his father on Wednesday afternoons," she said. "You know about his—about my husband?"

Wes nodded once.

"Every Wednesday," she said, and looked back to Scott. "You know that."

"It's not gonna kill him if I skip a week."

"He depends on us, Scott. It's difficult for him right now."

Wes felt his teeth clench, and Scott sneered. "Guess he should've thought of that before he held up a CashExpress, huh?"

"I ought to go," Wes said, and together Molly and Scott said, "No!"

"No," Molly repeated. "You're here. Scott's not dressed for a visit, and I'll be late if I don't leave now." She tried for another smile, but her eyes were weary with the effort. "They make you jump through a lot of hoops at the prison."

Wes tested the words before he loosed them. "I'm familiar with the process."

Something crossed Molly's face then, pieces sliding into place, maybe, memories of his rolled-up sleeves coming up against realities of how a man might come to have a name and six small circles scarred into his skin. Realities that might set him against her, his past against her present. Whatever she understood in that moment, she kept it to herself. "I really can't thank you enough for . . . well, for everything," she said quietly. "I've never seen anything catch Scott's fancy like this fiddle music."

He recognized the words for the peace offering they were. "Glad the fiddle's being played again," he said. "Been too long."

Her eyes went to his hands, a quick and involuntary movement. Wes pretended he hadn't seen, and when enough seconds had passed, put his hands in his pockets. "What do I owe you for the lessons?" Molly asked.

"Nothing."

"Nonsense. For your time, at least."

"Scott's a good student," Wes said, careful not to look at the boy. "Got a lot of talent. It ain't—it's no burden to teach him. You don't owe me nothing."

Molly seemed ready to argue, but she glanced at the clock and turned to Scott instead. "Friday," she said. "You better be dressed for visiting and ready to get in the car the second I get home."

"Whatever," Scott said, crossing to open the door for his mother. "Bye."

"I'll give your love to your dad," Molly told him, stepping out onto the porch.

"Bye," Scott repeated.

"You ever use me like that again, we're done," Wes said, when they'd sat on opposite sides of the couch in the trailer's living room. Scott glanced at him once, then reached for the fiddle case on the floor. Wes put his boot on top of the lid. "You hear what I said?"

Scott flopped back against the cushions, crossed his arms over his chest. "I hate going there," he said. "Every week he wants to know how school is going, and every week I tell him it doesn't matter, does it, 'cause he gave my college fund to his bookie. Then my mom starts crying and my dad yells at me for upsetting her, and then a guard"—he spat the word like an epithet—"tells us if we can't follow the rules we'll have privileges revoked. That sound like how you want to spend your afternoons?"

"What I asked you," Wes said deliberately, "was did you hear what I said?"

Scott scratched an eyebrow piercing, his eyes still on Wes's, and after a long few seconds, he said, "I heard you."

Wes took his boot off the case, nudged it toward Scott.

They warmed up with the G major scale, moved on to "Twinkle." Damned if the kid hadn't actually practiced that bow hold with a pencil like Wes had shown him. Wes gave him a handful of the cassette tapes—Scott looked at them like they were artifacts, and Wes had to ask if he had something to play them on—and then he taught him "Old Joe Clark." He'd hoped the kid might know it—a common tune—but he didn't, so Wes sang the notes, glad he'd picked something he remembered the lyrics for. Never had a memory for words like he did notes. He was uncomfortable, had never much liked his own singing voice. He could carry a tune all right, and he supposed his baritone was pleasant enough, but when he was in the band he'd been happy to leave that glory to Lane. Even Farmer occasionally sang lead, maybe one or two songs a set, but Wes lent his voice only to the three-part harmonies so many of the bluegrass songs required, leaning toward the microphone rather than stepping to it, keeping his fiddle and bow at the ready. Eager, always, to return home to his instrument.

"I'll start looking around for a fiddle for you," Wes said after the lesson, his own fiddle and bow back in the case, the brass clasps fastened. "Till then you can come by Dennis's and play on this one. I'm usually there. Happy to teach you anytime." He stood, but Scott stayed on the couch, and after a few seconds Wes sat back down, too.

"Can I ask you something? Else?"

Wes remembered where this question had led at the first lesson, grimaced inwardly. "Guess so."

Scott picked up the pile of cassettes Wes had given him. Moved the one on the bottom of the stack to the top, back again. Finally put them down on the coffee table. "You know how they used to hang people here?"

"Where's that, now?"

"Here. In Montana. Vigilantes and stuff."

"Oh. Sure." Wes felt like he'd missed the beginning of the conversation. "Lots of that going on back when they first made this place a territory."

"There was a display about it in the prison museum last week." Scott pressed his knuckles against each other in his lap. "And I was thinking it might have been better."

"What's that, exactly?"

"When they just up and killed you if you fu— Messed up."

"Some of those people didn't murder nobody or nothing," Wes said. "Some of them were just thieving."

"Still a crime."

"Well, I guess I don't think we got the right to decide when to take someone else's life," Wes said. "I think that's up to God." This was a respectable answer, he knew. Hadn't yet decided whether it was, in fact, what he believed.

"I don't believe in God," Scott said. He turned to face the window, and the bruise on his face seemed to disappear into the light.

Wes watched him carefully, trying to decide what it was about the kid today that left him so uneasy. He couldn't help but feel he was missing something important, not hearing it, not seeing it. The harder he looked, the more elusive it became. "You all right, Scott?" he ventured.

The kid didn't look at him. "They're letting my dad out next month," he said. "We're going to go back to Miles City."

"That a good thing?"

"Are you shitting me?" A quick sideways glance. "Sorry. But yeah, it's good." He brushed a hand through his hair; Wes could see the red roots. "I can't stay here anymore. I can't. God. You have no idea."

He fell silent. Wes glanced out the window. The mountains filled the pane, nothing but sharp pine and risen earth. Sometimes he just wanted them gone. Wanted to set his eyes on horizon. *I can't stay here anymore.*

"That eye healing up okay?"

"It's all right," Scott said. Something in his tone. Wariness, or anger. Too subtle to say which.

"I just wondered," Wes said. "Because it's lasted a good few days and I couldn't help notice you never said nothing about it." He thought to look at Scott's knuckles; they were smooth and unbroken.

The kid leaned over the arm of the couch and twisted the knob on a radio; he spoke as soon as the sound filled the room. "You remember that time you gave me a ride from Elk Fork?"

"Yeah."

"It wasn't the starter. That's what I told you, right? The starter?"

"Think so."

"What really happened was these guys at school poured bleach in my oil tank," Scott said. No inflection. "That totally wrecks the engine, you know that?"

Wes licked his lips. "I'd guess it would."

"Yeah," Scott said, still in that dead monotone. "I got about as far as Milltown and then my car started smoking like crazy and I pulled over and it wouldn't start up again. I mean, I thought it just up and died, but I had it towed to Elk Fork and the mechanic figured it out."

"You tell anyone about this?" Wes asked.

"Well, I had to tell my mom," Scott said. "She kind of wanted to know why my car was ruined all of a sudden, you know?" He went silent for a minute. "I didn't tell Dennis, though, because he'd freak."

"I meant the police," Wes said. "You tell the police?"

Scott shook his head.

"That's a crime, what those boys did. Ought to be reported."

The kid smirked a little, let his eyes go unkind for a moment. "I don't get how a guy like you can be so fucking naïve," he said. "It must take a lot of work."

You have no idea.

～

Wes knew he'd been standing in the IGA aisle too long. Someone would notice soon, if they hadn't already, and he'd have to try to explain, and he doubted he'd be able to get a single word out with his throat this tight. It was dish soap that'd tripped him up. Dennis was almost out, had asked Wes to pick some up next time he went to buy cigarettes. And here Wes stood, four shelves of jewel-bright bottles in front of him, and he couldn't remember which one Claire would buy. Thirty years she'd used the same kind, he knew that. Thirty years it'd sat beside the kitchen sink, thirty years he'd looked at it, and now he couldn't remember the brand. He'd thought it was the purple kind, the kind with *Lilac Fresh!* emblazoned across the front of the label, but it didn't smell right when he took the cap off. None of them smelled right. Each time something caught his eye — the picture of a lemon in the corner of one label, the tinted orange plastic of a bottle — he felt certain he'd remembered, but when he took the caps off, none smelled like his wife's kitchen.

He knew he'd lose things with time, that this was how a person kept from going mad with grief. Already immediacy had begun to fade from his memories of Claire; already he found that when he tried to focus on certain details, they slipped to one side or blurred into uncertainty. But this, the dish soap, this inconsequential thing, this was the first memory to vanish entirely, beyond the grasp of conscious recall. It didn't matter — Dennis wouldn't care; Claire had probably chosen the brand for frugality's sake, nothing more — but it shattered him.

"Wes? Wes Carver?"

Wes turned to see a man standing beside him in the aisle. He was maybe ten years younger than Wes, carried a basket filled with frozen pizzas and beef jerky. Wes swallowed hard, took a deep breath to clear his lungs of the disappointing fragrances. "I know you?"

"Clancy Johnson," he said. "I worked the overnight with you years back, when you were on Two South."

"Oh." Wes could see that he was a CO now — the way he stood with his feet a little farther apart than most people would, the suspicious glint behind the otherwise friendly gaze — but he couldn't claim he remembered the guy. He'd worked Two South just after the riot, and those days, getting through his shift, even on a quiet night, took about all he had.

"Good to see you again," Johnson said. He tugged on his sleeve. "I heard you're gonna speak at Williams's hearing."

"Looks like."

The other man slammed his palm against the shelf, and a single bottle of dish soap fell to the floor. Wes glanced at it in case it was the one he'd been searching for, but no, Claire hadn't liked strawberry. "Man," Johnson said, "can you believe this born-again bullshit?"

"Born-again."

"As if a cocksucker like Williams could ever find Jesus. Christ," he added, with no sense of irony.

"Not sure I heard about that," Wes said. He felt the dull tightness of grief in his gut morphing into something sharper, queasier.

"Oh, yeah. Williams's been claiming he's seen the light, turned into a good repentant Christian. Never reads nothing but the Good Book, prays with the chaplain, the whole nine yards. They've even got him leading some Bible study group twice a week."

An odd fact: the COs weren't supposed to know what the inmates had done to get locked up. Or at least they weren't told. Public record, of course—an officer could look it up if he cared to—but it wasn't really necessary. Half of them bragged; the rest an officer could guess, or heard about through gossip. Williams, he'd bragged. Late one night he'd broken into a farmhouse belonging to an elderly couple. Bound husband and wife with duct tape, then spent hours terrorizing them before stealing all the cash and jewelry in the house. The husband came out of it with what the police report Wes later tracked down called "numerous contusions and lacerations." The wife suffered a stroke that the coroner testified might not have killed her had she received immediate medical treatment. ("Had a real good time that night," Williams had whispered in Wes's ear.)

"I wouldn't worry about it," Johnson said now. "Only people dumb enough to fall for that reformed-sinner bull are inmates' girlfriends and—"

"Parole boards," Wes finished.

PART III

Burn

Claire has never seen Arthur Farmer in his uniform before. He is one of the few officers who change into street clothes before leaving the prison, so when she opens the door at two in the afternoon and sees him there on her porch in his crisp blue shirt and slacks, brass bits gleaming, she knows. Wesley.

An *incident,* Arthur calls it. Stumbles over the word. It is so obviously not his own, a parroting of something the administration has said, bureaucratic euphemism. When he finishes speaking, Claire steps toward him and he opens his arms to her and she raises her hand and slaps him hard across the face. She feels it all the way up in her shoulder. Arthur takes it — a blink, nothing else — and his calm makes her want to hit him again, but she crosses her arms over her chest and steps back when he reaches for her.

When? she asks.

Not quite an hour ago, he tells her. I came as soon as I could.

Not quite an hour. Is that fifty-nine minutes? Forty-five? Thirty-one? So much could have happened in not quite an hour. Wesley could already be dead. Jaw slack, eyes glassy. Or they could be hurting him. Landing blows on his body, slicing skin and what lay beneath. Worse. Claire forces herself to imagine every possibility, every potential pain and terror. She wants no more surprises. Wants nothing else to shock her the way this has. She must start to look crazed, because Arthur risks reaching for her again, and this time she lets him steer her to the couch.

Maddie's gone to pick up Dennis at school, he says. I'll stay with you until she gets here, and then I'm going back to the prison. I'll stay until I can bring him home to you.

Vague phrasing. *Bring him home.* Claire is sure it's intentional. Care on Arthur's part not to make a hollow promise.

At that moment, Wesley is already in the chair in the control room. Ankles bound with his own bootlaces, wrists fastened behind him with his own handcuffs. Williams is slouched on the floor opposite, back against the wall. He has found Wesley's cigarettes in the desk drawer and lets one dangle, unlit, from his lips.

Mac Dalloway comes by in the evening. Stands just inside the door and looks somewhere over Claire's head while he asks if there's anything he can do. He works the ground-floor tier, two levels below Wesley. One level below Lane. He is here because he feels guilty, because it could so easily have been him. Like Arthur, he is still in his uniform. It's as though the men are reluctant to leave the prison behind while their brothers remain inside, so they carry it with them on their backs. Before Mac leaves, he tells her about the candles. People are putting them in their windows, he says. All over Black River. Three. One for Bill, one for Lane. One for Wesley.

It's a nice idea, Madeline says when he has gone.

There are tea lights in the cupboard over the stove, Claire tells her.

Except there aren't. There are matches, the box still wrapped in cellophane; it crinkles when she folds her fingers over it. But no candles.

Maybe in the linen closet? Madeline asks.

No. Candlesticks, in the back, not real silver but chrome, flaking at the base. Claire throws them back inside and they clank against each other.

Now it isn't such a nice idea, these three candles in the window. Now it's a necessity. She is negligent for not having lit them before, even if she didn't know. She should have thought of the idea herself. Every minute that passes with her windowsill unburdened by flame is a minute that might somehow, through some ugly magic or mysticism, hurt her husband. Madeline comes up behind her and puts her hands on Claire's shoulders; Claire shrugs her off. Already she's sick of being comforted. Claire doesn't want comfort. She wants Wesley, and barring that, she wants hysteria. She wants to embrace it, succumb to it, fling herself into it headlong and let it take her.

How can there be no candles in this entire fucking house?

At that moment. Five hours in. Bobby Williams is putting out cigarettes on the soft underside of her husband's forearm. Six touches of ember to flesh.

She goes out for the candles herself. Madeline doesn't want to let her—Claire sees it in the way she lets her pressed lips turn down on one side, a gesture she's inherited from their mother—but Claire already has the keys to the old farm truck in her hand. Stay with Denny, she says. There is hay on the bench seat, pierced through the worn upholstery, and it presses uncomfortably against Claire's thighs as she drives.

She gets the candles at Jameson's. They have already put a box at each register, blocky white votives. The girl who sells them to her is young, still a teenager. Someone's daughter. Claire knows her but can't think of her name. The girl watches Claire with unabashed fascination as she puts the candles in a paper bag. It will be like this all the time if Wesley doesn't come home, Claire thinks. I will be The Widow.

It's okay, the girl says when Claire tries to hand her a dollar. I think Mr. Jameson would want me to give them to you.

Claire holds the money between them for a moment, across the counter. It's an old bill, soft and limp, a little damp between her fingers, and it flutters under their breaths. Thank you, she says finally, and puts the dollar back in her purse.

At the frontage road, she turns right instead of left. It is only just night, and both horizons glow. West for the sun, east for the reflected blaze of lights at the prison. The first a restful sort of light, an easing into dark, the second harsher, a fighting against it. And there, at the far end of Main Street, is the prison. It is ugly enough on its own, uglier still juxtaposed against the gently ordinary buildings of her adopted hometown. The parking lots are full, police cars and media vans spilling into the space below the great gray wall. Lights everywhere, the harsh sentinel lamps rising above the wall and its towers, and below, the sharp square lights of the news crews and the frenetic, spiraling reds and blues of the emergency vehicles. Claire spots Wesley's truck in the officers' parking lot: a green Chevy, bought last year from Arthur Farmer for five hundred dollars. If Wesley doesn't come home, someone—maybe Mac, probably Arthur—will drive that truck back to the house. Already Claire knows they won't park it properly, will let the tires edge off the gravel drive, forget the emergency brake.

Claire parks on the side of the frontage road, an empty field stretching between her and the rear wall of the grounds. She could get closer, head back up Main toward the prison gates, but then she will be amid people. They will know her, and then there will be cameras in her face and men pushing the cameras away and other men trying to comfort her. They are good people, these officers—her friends' husbands, her husband's friends—but they spend their days enforcing rules, suppressing emotions, intimidating and refusing to be intimidated. They won't know what to say, and will try to say it anyway.

She gets out of the truck, the candles rolling away from her, white wax gathering dirt and hay. There is broken glass in the grass at the side of the road, a single sagging strand of rusty barbed wire linking skewed fenceposts. She wades through the knee-deep grass, steps over this first feeble fence. Moths fly up and halo her face before disappearing into the night. Claire notices the cold for the first time this season. Her skin much cooler than the blood beneath.

He is there. In the main cellblock, near the top; his tier is the highest. That's all she knows. She has never been inside the prison. She doesn't know what color the walls are, how many cells on a tier, how wide the walkways. It's terrifying, these gaps in her knowledge. They make Wesley seem farther away, already beyond her reach. If she could create an accurate picture of him in her mind—where he is kept, how the light casts on his face—she might protect that picture, protect him.

How many yards away is he? She isn't good with distances. But not so many. Not so far. It would take mere minutes to walk to him, if only she could. But there are walls. Fences. Concertina wire. It is piled along the top of the perimeter wall, coil upon biting coil. She has always thought it an odd name, *concertina*. A beautiful word, musical, a word Wesley might like. *Wesley.*

She wants to scream his name.

He wouldn't hear her. Couldn't possibly. But she can feel her voice collecting in her chest, rising in her throat. A sound the shape of his name. *Wesley.* Her husband, her love, her trusted one, her idiot for staying here and working this miserable, dangerous job, and hasn't he done it all for her, her and her son, and if he dies, it will be all because of her, won't it, and he's right there, goddamn it, *right there,* and no one can get to him. And even if she screams his name until her voice abandons her, he won't hear.

Claire is on her knees in the field, fistfuls of dried stalks and blades in her white-knuckled hands. She closes her eyes and grinds her teeth together and waits until the need to scream has been forced back down to wherever it lives. Until she can part her lips and hear only breath.

While she is there in the grass, Williams carves his name into Wesley's skin. His shank is an appalling example of inmate resourcefulness, a sharpened shard of fiberglass from a mess hall tray, a strip torn from a pillowcase wrapped around one end for a handle. It is not quite as sharp as a real knife would be, and he has to press hard. The *O* gives him the most trouble. He goes over it more than once.

That night, after first Dennis and then Madeline drop into sleep, Claire stays up and watches the three flames dance in the window, each reflection nearly as brilliant as its living twin. The one in the center, she has decided, is Wesley's. It starts to smoke sometime after midnight, gasps, disgorging short bursts of swirling ethereal black. She should blow it out. Trim the wick and relight it. She should. (She doesn't.) After another hour or so, long after the startling scent of ash has deadened into familiarity, the flame settles again, stretching steadily back toward the ceiling.

Williams sleeps for a few hours. Wesley does not.

How to fill the minutes. The hours. She sits on the couch. Lays a hand on the telephone. Notices the way the sunlight moves across the living room, an elongating patch of bright. She lets her sister sit beside her and tell her comforting things. She tries praying, silently, but she doesn't know how, and she doesn't want something Wesley believes in to feel so much like a lie, so she stops.

Arthur calls every hour on the hour. There is nothing for him to say. (At ten-sixteen a.m., just over twenty-one hours into the riot, the inmates climb onto the catwalk and send Bill Harris's body through the cellblock window. He is dead already, but the fall breaks his neck. Afterward people will say this is when they should have gone in—Claire will disagree; they should have gone in before Williams had a chance to torture her husband—but the warden decides negotiation is the word of the day. Arthur tells her none of this when he calls.)

Madeline boils macaroni and dresses it with mayonnaise for lunch. This was Claire's favorite meal when she was a child; she is both touched that Madeline remembers such an inconsequential detail from so long ago and angry that her sister thinks such a small thing could possibly matter now. She eats only because Dennis refuses his own meal until she has finished hers. Twenty-four hours of riot. Twenty-four hours at least since Wesley has eaten. He must be hungry. In some part of herself, Claire realizes this is a trivial concern, the least of her fears, but it's a comprehensible worry. Nothing like blood. Nothing like death.

At half past four, Sara Gregory calls and tells her about Bill. (These first rumors say he was beaten to death—it's strange the way the details build; by the end of the next day Claire will hear that his spleen ruptured, that he bled to death without a single drop leaving his body—but the autopsy will reveal a heart attack. Scared to death. The reality, when it trickles out in bits and pieces over the coming weeks, is this: Bill was in the ground-floor guard station, safely behind iron. The riot began when the inmates doused him with gasoline from the auto shop, lit a mop on fire and threatened to push it through the bars unless he gave them the keys. He did, and died anyway. Claire cannot blame him for giving in, but for the rest of her life, a black whisper in her heart will insist he got what he deserved.)

They say he's been dead since yesterday, Claire. Since the start.

Claire hears the unspoken words, and though she doesn't like Sara, not even now — maybe especially not now — it's a relief to offer even false comfort to someone else. Lane and Wesley are fine, she says. Her voice is so steady it surprises her.

But there's no way to know that.

They're fine.

When she hangs up, Claire carefully winds the spiral coil of the phone cord. She takes her hair out of its braid and twists it up into a bun. Then she thinks about Bill, and she thinks about Wesley, and she goes to the bathroom and vomits up the macaroni.

His fingers are last. Williams breaks them slowly, over the course of the day and night. Right hand first. This is one of the only details Claire will learn directly from Wesley, one of the only things he tells her. But he doesn't say, My right hand. He says, My bowing hand.

She has finally fallen asleep, and the phone wakes her. Four-seventeen a.m. Arthur on the other end.

He's alive, Claire. She will be so grateful to him, when she thinks of this later, for speaking those words first.

Where is he?

We just went in. We've got the cellblock back. I was the first one to him.

Is he all right?

They're taking him to St. Pat's in Elk Fork. Get Maddie to drive you. I'll come as soon as I can.

What am I going to see?

Silence.

Arthur, don't you think about what to tell me. Just say it.

They tied him up. Gave him more than bruises. It was . . . methodical.

Silence again.

I'm sorry, Claire.

What about Lane?

I can't say.

Can't?

The deputy warden is driving out to see Sara right now.

Oh. Oh, God.

The litany: Dehydration. Concussion. A four-inch laceration above his right ear. A bruise building below his left eye, transitioning from swollen red to dark mottle. Blood crusting black on his lower lip, a broken tooth behind the split flesh. Two fractured ribs, a heel-shaped bruise shading the skin above. Abrasions around his wrists and ankles. Six cigarette burns. Five carved letters. Nine broken fingers. (Claire thinks of it another way: A broken pinkie. A broken ring finger. A broken middle finger. A broken index finger. A broken thumb. Another broken pinkie. Another broken ring finger. Another broken middle finger. Another broken index finger. And she could parse it further still, because she learns that most of those fingers have more than one shattered bone. Condylar fractures, the doctors tell her, split into the joints. Williams didn't just snap. He twisted.)

Wesley refuses most of the medicine the nurses offer. The pain's not intolerable, he says, and who will argue with him? He knows intolerable. Claire sees it wearing him down, though, sees the way he doesn't quite look at her, his gaze a few degrees off. He has been in the hospital three days; they are talking about letting him go home soon. He is restless here, and while Claire doubts her husband would be an ideal patient under any circumstances, she thinks it is especially difficult for him now. He goes very still whenever the doctors or nurses are in the room, holds his breath when they touch him.

I wish you'd let them give you something more for the pain, she says. They are walking down the hallway outside Wesley's room. He takes short steps, but they come steadily, one after another.

I don't like the way it makes me feel.

How's that?

Like I ain't entirely here.

Maybe that's not such a bad thing right now, Wesley.

His eyes shift to hers. Let's go back, he says.

She helps him turn; he can't hide the wince. His ribs this time, she thinks.

The nurses don't like her being here so often. They cluck at her about visiting hours, try to guilt her into leaving by telling her Wesley needs his rest. But they don't know her husband. He is wearing sweats and a bathrobe she had to buy for him two days ago at Jameson's, because he doesn't own such casual clothing. His hands are useless; he can't feed himself, can't bathe himself, can't dress himself. He will not accept help from anyone else. Will not rest in front of anyone else. The nurses don't know what it costs him just to be here.

It's gonna be all right, Claire.

I know.

I love you.

It's not something he says often. I love you, too, she says.

I love you, he repeats. They are back at his room; Claire pulls the door closed behind them. That's all that matters, Wesley says. I love you, and you're here, and we're together.

She stays quiet. Puts her hand on his arm, above his elbow. She wants to take his hands in hers, but they are too swaddled in gauze and tape.

The rest of it ain't important. I know that.

Wesley . . .

There's a chance I might play again, he says. Can't look at her when he speaks. She tries to guide him to the bed, but he won't allow himself to be moved. Even if the doctors don't think so, he says, there's a chance.

Shattered was the word they used. Claire has seen the x-rays. *Shat-*

tered doesn't begin to describe what Bobby Williams did to Wesley's fingers. They had to go in and take out bone fragments. They're still talking about amputation.

Baby, she says. She wants, suddenly, to shut him up. To put her hands over his mouth, hold his jaw closed.

It was just a hobby, he says.

And she sees the tears building in his eyes, and knows something inside him will break if they fall. Claire has never seen her husband cry, and she doesn't want to. She rises on her toes to kiss him, and as she does she takes his face in her hands, and she wipes the tears from his eyes before he can know they are there.

After he comes home, Claire waits for the nightmares. She is prepared to comfort him, ready with soft words and a light touch. A small, shameful part of her actually looks forward to it. She is so eager to help, and Wesley so reluctant to let her. In the dark, just back from the dreamworld, maybe he'll allow it. But either the nightmares don't come or Wesley bears them with stillness and silence. (She suspects the latter, because when she wakes she often finds his eyes already open, and she can smell the sweat damp in his hair.) Instead, Dennis is the one with plagued dreams. He is fourteen, but starts to call for her in the middle of the night the way he did as a young child. His voice must wake Wesley, too, but he lies unmoving beside her, so Claire rises and finds her slippers and robe and crosses the squeaking hardwood hall to Dennis's bedroom, and she sits on the edge of his bed and brushes his hair back over his forehead and tells him over and over that everything is okay until he believes her and lets sleep take him again.

Claire comes to know about the riot—the times, the details, what her husband endured while she waited—because she reads the reports. Wesley almost never speaks about his hours as a hostage, and when he does, it is only a few words, which appear between them as if by accident. Always the sense that Wesley wishes he could take them back. Always the certainty that he conceals more than he reveals. So Claire drives to Elk Fork one day while he is at work, sits at a metal table in an over-air-conditioned room in the courthouse and turns the pages of the file.

She thinks of the way the little Wesley has told her has seemed wrenched from his lips against his will, and she tries to imagine her husband voicing the words on these pages, admitting to all this pain and fear. Such detail, line after line. So vivid. She is wearing a good dress, and has put on makeup, something she rarely does. She remembers it only when she touches a page and leaves a smear of red lipstick on the pristine paper, realizes she has had her hand to her mouth as she read.

The warden resigns. The situation, it is acknowledged, was handled badly. A plaque is set into a boulder just outside the gate, Bill's and Lane's names engraved on it. They plant some flowers nearby, but they are annuals, and no one replaces them after the first winter.

Almost a year beyond the riot, Claire will come home from Jameson's and find Wesley bent over the bathroom sink, blood twining over his wrist and off his fingers. A jackknife with slicked blade gripped awkwardly in his other hand. She stares at his blood, impossibly red against the white porcelain, and thinks, *It's not the way I would have expected him to do it.* She has always worried about his revolver, certain that if he ever took this route, he would leave as little to chance as possible. She has never worried about the knife. (All this in a moment. A moment in which she would have expected to scream, drop her bags, faint. Exhibit some symptom of shock. Instead, the shock comes a heartbeat later, when she realizes she is shattered but unsurprised.)

Then Wesley looks up, and she realizes this isn't suicide. The blood wells from higher on his arm, above the wrist. Beads red over his scars. He opens his hand, lets the knife clatter and settle on the countertop. He straightens but doesn't say a word, offers no explanation, as though he already knows nothing he can say will satisfy. As though he doesn't need to justify this. His green eyes are steady on hers, unapologetic.

She will learn to ignore these new scars just as she ignores his old ones. And she will even understand why he did it, will imagine the hurt of carrying his devil's name on his skin, will remember that her husband is a man starving for control. But though she tries—she tries—she will never forgive Wesley for those seconds between the sight of blood and the meeting of their eyes.

"The hell is this born-again bullshit?" Wes demanded.

Farmer stood in the center of his round pen, pivoting on one heel to follow the horse trotting around the rail. He'd glanced over when Wes pulled his truck up next to the barn, but didn't quit working the horse. Glanced up again when Wes crossed the yard to the hitching rack just outside the pen, but again, didn't quit working.

"Farmer. What's this shit I'm hearing about Williams?"

No answer. Three days Wes had been trying to catch Farmer to talk, and now that he had, the other man just kept fooling with that damned horse. It was a buckskin, with a yellow coat and a black mane and tail, a matching stripe down the center of its back. Young, Wes guessed. Still kind of skinny the way colts sometimes were, like no amount of feed could keep up with the speed at which they were growing. There was a battered old saddle on its back, a rope halter on its head. Every time it passed the place where Wes stood, the talcum-fine dirt in the pen got kicked up and found its way to Wes's lungs.

He waited until the horse was on the far end of the pen, raised his voice. "Were you ever plannin' on fucking telling me?"

"I tried that time you came to dinner," Farmer said, "but you weren't having none of it." He slapped the coiled rope in his left hand against his thigh, and the colt broke into a high-headed lope. "I'd have told you before the hearing if no one else did, but frankly, Wesley, I figured I'd let you hear it from someone else if I could."

"Yeah? Why's that?"

"'Cause I knew you'd be pissed as all get-out. Fact that you're swearing up a storm tells me I wasn't wrong." He slowed his pivot a little, said "Easy" in that same low voice Wes had heard Dennis use before, and the buckskin fell back into a hurried trot.

"Well, someone tells me that Bobby Williams of all people has gone and—Farmer, would you leave the goddamned horse alone for two minutes and talk to me?"

Farmer turned toward Wes and quit moving. Abruptly, the horse slowed to a walk and then came to an uneasy halt, legs awry as though frozen midstep. "Good boy," Farmer said absently. He tugged on the brim of his hat, crossed slowly to where Wes stood, but stayed on his side of the pipe fence. He looked very much the cowboy today: jeans, the hems brown with dust, stacked over work boots with curled kilties; a chore coat with cuffs that looked chewed on; his well-worn bone hat. A new uniform. He raised one foot to the first rung of the fence, pushed it forward until the boot heel hit, crossed his arms over one of the other rungs. Then he looked at Wes in that way he had that let a man know he had Farmer's full and unwavering attention.

Why the hell did Wes want to talk to Farmer about this, anyway? So they'd been friends once, married to sisters. So they'd played in the same band and worked the same shit job. That was all a long time gone, and there was plenty Wes didn't like about the man, shared history or no. He was too good at everything. Too ready to involve himself, to provide balm for other people's troubles. Altogether too eager and too earnest. But perhaps that was itself the reason—because while Wes and Farmer had sat in the same pews and listened to the same sermons all those years, Wes was pretty sure Farmer heard something in them he didn't, something that let Farmer believe it all without the doubts Wes had to battle through.

He waited Wes out now, not rushing him. The horse walked across the soft dirt, neck and tail swinging with each step. It stopped behind Farmer, stretched its neck to sniff at the back of Farmer's head, nostrils flaring.

"Nice colt," Wes said.

Farmer held out a hand without turning, and the horse took one more step forward, accepting the reward of a gentle touch. "You didn't come to talk about the colt."

Wes mirrored Farmer's posture, leaned forward over the hitching rack, crossed his own arms at the wrists and let his hands hang loose. Yes. That felt right. Casual. "How long ago this supposedly happen?" he asked. "Williams . . . seeing the light?"

"Been awhile, Wesley." Farmer moved his boot, and the pipe rang. "I heard about it before I took my pension. Probably ten years ago. A little more, maybe."

"It's all cooked up to impress the parole board."

"Most likely."

There had been plenty of inmates like that. Always with a Bible on their bunk, a frayed ribbon marking the page. Painstakingly copied verses of scripture and maybe a cheap print of a bland, blue-eyed Jesus on the wall of their cell where other inmates put up girlie pictures. Lining up for the call to chapel even before the COs announced it. For most of them, Wes knew, it was a calculated decision, designed to look good on paper when it mattered. For a few, religion seemed like a hobby, the way weightlifting or watching the soaps were hobbies for other inmates. And maybe — maybe — it was more for some. For some.

Wes leaned sideways, spit. Felt his molars find each other and grind hard. "Farmer, you don't think he could have really changed." He looked up. "Do you?"

Farmer's eyes searched his, and Wes wondered what he was looking for. If he found it. "I don't know, Wesley." Farmer slid back the gate's bolt and slipped out, closing the welded pipe against the colt. The horse took one step backward, then turned and crossed the pen, muzzle bent to the dirt. Farmer joined Wes at the hitching rack. He moved slowly, as though he were living in a world in which everything happened at a slightly lesser speed than it did for everyone else. "Do I think a man can come to religion and be the better for it? Yes, I do." He glanced back at the mountains suddenly, at the sun hovering above. "But do I think Robert Williams can be that man? That I just don't know." Wes tried to catch Farmer's eye, but now the other man seemed to be deliberately avoiding it, fixing his gaze just a little over Wes's shoulder. "What Williams did to you was evil, Wesley. I know that. I don't know as I could forgive it, if it'd been done to me. I mean, I seen some of what he did to you," he said, his voice dropping low, "and I seen some of how much it's hurt you since. But no one was there when Williams did what he did but him and you, Wesley. Way I figure it, that means you know him best. Better than anyone else on God's earth. There ain't no one can say whether he might've changed but you."

Wes liked church. The ritual of it, the way going every week without fail made him feel like he was doing something decent, something unequivocally right. Odd, he supposed, that he should cling so hard to a habit that had done his own father so little good.

This week the reading was from the Gospel of Mark, the sermon all about the rewards of faith. Wes expected frustration during services—his mind ran a constant stream of objections against his efforts at faith—but the anger was new. There was something pathetically trite in being angry at God, and for such a clichéd reason: *How could He do this to me?* Wes had avoided that kind of anger after the riot, after his hands went crooked and stiff. But losing Claire . . . Williams up for parole . . . these things were too much. *The rewards of faith.*

Wes lingered in the sanctuary at the end of the service, managed to be one of the last to reach the lobby. The pastor was there. Greetings, some brief small talk. Wes calculated, let just enough emotion show in his voice and face. Garnered an invitation to talk in the office.

Wes had been there once before. Alone, a kid of fifteen. He'd sat silently as the pastor at the time offered his enlightened view of the spiritual fate of suicides, providing unasked-for reassurances that Wes's father was in a heaven that even then Wes couldn't really believe in. The office had changed little: small, a sharply angled ceiling, brown and white wallpaper with visible seams. He didn't remember the chairs, but they were old, the seat leather shiny and sunken, the brass buttons on the arms tarnished. An odor in the air like coffee exhaled from damp mouths.

"I'm very sorry for the loss of your wife," the pastor said, and Wes waited for the platitude, the biblical wisdom, but it didn't come. His estimation of the man rose a notch.

"She was . . . ," Wes said, meaning to say something like *special,* but more accurate, less trite, and could think of no right word and so left the sentence hanging, unfinished. The pastor seemed not to notice. He was even younger than Wes had thought; he'd been fooled by the receding hairline. Wes wondered how a man so young could be certain enough of God to go into the ministry, and he wondered if he would still be a pastor a couple decades from now. "I ain't really here to talk about her," Wes said finally.

The pastor sipped at his coffee. Wes had declined when the other man offered it, and the pastor hadn't tried to cajole him into it, but hadn't put his own mug away, either. "I heard about the parole hearing," he said.

"You got a history with this?" Wes asked. "Family in corrections, anything like that?"

The pastor shook his head. "A sister in social work," he said. "Closest I come."

"Ever done prison ministry?"

"I've never been called to do so."

"You think it does any good?"

The pastor didn't answer. Wes watched him, but broke off eye contact after a few seconds. Not like him. "I get the sense," the pastor said, "you want to ask something else."

There was a crack in the leather over the arm of the chair. Wes's fingertips found it, worried it. "You've heard about the hearing," he said. "So you know about the riot."

"I know you were held hostage," the pastor said. "I know you were tortured."

Wes's fingers tightened on the arm of the chair, and he found he couldn't relax them at will, like they were spasmed. He despised the word. *Torture.* The label made it worse. (Was this what Claire had felt when she heard the word *rape*?) He thought of torture as something that happened to political prisoners, to mobsters in movies, to people who knew things other people wanted to know. What Williams had done to him had been cruel, yeah. Brutal, even. But torture? Aggravated assault, maybe. That's what they'd called it in the paperwork. "The inmate who did it says he found God."

Another long silence. The smell of exhaled coffee was getting to him. The size of the room. The fact that he was saying these things aloud and hoping for a reply that would help it all make sense.

"You believe he's being dishonest."

"He's an inmate." Wes met the pastor's eyes. "Saying he's dishonest is redundant."

No judgment. "Tell me this, then," the pastor said, steepling his hands in front of his face. It was an odd gesture, somehow too old for him. "If it were true—and just go along with the 'if' for a minute, say this guy's suddenly become the world's best Christian—would it change the way you want this hearing to turn out?"

Wes heard Williams's laugh in his memory, bursts of hot air against his ear. "No."

"Why not?"

He felt the flare of temper, reined it in before the pastor could see it. "Because a person doesn't deserve to walk around free after doing what he did."

"So it's a matter of justice."

"Guess so."

"Then is there any reason you can't hope the man has welcomed Christ into his heart and still hope he's denied parole?"

"He doesn't deserve it."

"People usually don't deserve forgiveness," the pastor said, his voice frustratingly gentle. It was a lulling sort of voice, the kind that made a man want to listen. "But forgiveness doesn't forestall justice."

"That so."

"I realize that the prospect of forgiveness can seem unfair. Like you're being asked to take on yet another burden when you've already endured so much. But there's something freeing, I think, in the realization that forgiveness is a choice God has given you the power to make, independent of anything this man has done, or will do. And you must understand that there cannot be true justice—and now I'm talking about justice for you, justice in the big scheme of things, not legal justice—without forgiveness."

Wes leaned forward in his chair, waited until the pastor mirrored him. "Look," he said. "I never told anyone this before. I kept it from my wife. Not 'cause she wasn't strong enough to hear it, but because she shouldn't have to hear it. That whole time during the riot, Bobby Williams never once looked at me. He looked *through* me. Like I wasn't nothing to him, not even a person. You know how you sometimes hear about a kid who kills the neighborhood dog for fun? Just to see how long it will take, and what noises it will make while it dies? Williams was that kid, and I was a dog he found. He's soulless. Or—what do they call it now?—a sociopath. But there's something not right about that man, and it wasn't right when he was born, and it ain't gonna be right till the day he dies." He sat back, forced deep breaths into his lungs, forced his hands to relax. "Tell me, Reverend, you think someone without a soul can find God?"

The pastor sighed. So much compassion there on his face. So much it made Wes sick. "I believe," he said, "that all men, even wicked ones, have souls. And I believe in the power of Christ's love to lift up all—"

"I didn't mean forgiveness," Wes interrupted. Couldn't listen to all that.

"I'm sorry?"

"When I said he doesn't deserve it, I didn't mean Williams doesn't deserve forgiveness." Wes closed his eyes. The pastor waited. "I mean God. He doesn't deserve God." He opened his eyes again. The pastor was still watching him, and nothing obvious had changed on his features, but Wes saw something different in his eyes. Suspicion, maybe. Or merely sorrow. "A man like that doesn't deserve to believe," Wes said, "when I spent my whole life trying and still can't do it."

The red horse and the mule were missing when he returned to the house. A couple halters dangling from the hitching rack, Dennis's truck parked beside the workshop. Wes squinted toward the slopes, but he saw no glint of sun on silver, no movement through the trees. Rio stood alone in the pasture, looking, so far as Wes could tell, none the worse for wear after his struggle during the snowstorm. He watched Wes from across the yard, and though Wes liked the black horse, he didn't like this. The way he watched.

Wes opened the passenger door of his truck, twisted his key in the lock on the glove compartment. His revolver was satisfyingly heavy in his hand. It was a .38 Smith and Wesson Special with a six-inch barrel, the kind COs had used way back when officers still carried sidearms. His father's before him. When he was younger, Wes had been a pretty fair shot with a rifle; he was competent with the revolver, nothing more. It made him nervous in a way the rifle never had. Claire hadn't liked it, even before that night with Dennis. Urged him more than once to get rid of it.

He was careful now. The gun wasn't loaded, and he kept his finger outside the trigger guard. Sighted only at the pile of firewood beside the workshop, and felt guilty even so. Wes shot with his left hand now. Williams hadn't snapped his left thumb the way he had his right, and Wes had a marginally better grip with that hand. Enough years gone by that it no longer felt entirely awkward. He went to the range once or twice a year, fired off a few rounds and paid the price in pain later.

Wes knew as well as anyone that a weapon could be used against its owner. There was a reason today's COs checked their firearms at the gate. Dangerous enough to carry what they did. (His handcuffs. Lane's baton.) But all this talk of Williams. All these memories being stirred up. Wes would be lying if he said the weight of that revolver in his hand didn't make him feel better.

He took it inside the house. Laid an old dishtowel on the kitchen table. Found Dennis's gun-cleaning kit where he'd always kept his own, on top of the safe in the living room. Sat at the table and set to work. The revolver didn't really need the attention; Wes always cleaned it after he'd fired it. Claire helped him most times, sat silently at the table and completed the fine, precise work he couldn't manage. She pursed her lips while she did it, held her head cocked a bit too far to one side.

She'd never voiced her displeasure at those moments, but she hadn't needed to. He knew.

Slow work for his hands. Hard work. Wes wasn't even halfway done, still feeding a cleaning patch through the barrel, when Dennis and Scott came through the door. Dennis glanced at the revolver, the supplies arrayed across the table, but all he said was "Church good?"

"Fine," Wes said. Scott stood beside Dennis. He stared a little, but not much. A Montana kid, his father's son. Hardly the first gun he'd seen. "You going straight home, Scott?"

The kid shrugged. "Mom's working."

"You're welcome to the fiddle, if you want to play."

Scott nodded, went to the mantel. Dennis disappeared down the hall, and a moment later Wes heard water running. He traded the cleaning rod for a nylon brush, set to polishing up the rear cylinder opening. The ache already starting to drive in his hands. Scott had the fiddle out now, was warming up with "Cripple Creek." He was struggling a bit with the string crossings, but Wes held his tongue. Kid needed to work some of it out on his own.

Dennis returned to the living room, took a chair. He sat silently for a moment, watching Wes. Finally he asked, "Is that it?"

"The very same," Wes said. Same gun Dennis had aimed at him. Same gun he'd aimed at Dennis. (He'd wondered, from time to time, why Dennis had used the revolver that night. Wes thought he could have forgiven a punch, maybe even a steak knife impulsively taken up in a fist. But not the revolver.)

"Let me help you?"

Wes's first instinct was to refuse. But the ache in his hands was a mere harbinger of what was in store later, so Wes laid the gun on the towel and let Dennis slide it across the table toward himself.

Scott was on to "Angelina Baker" now, making a disastrous attempt at playing with drones. Wes waited until he quit in the midst of the B part, a frustrated skittering of the bow over the strings. "Try arching your fingers up a bit more," he said. He touched his left fingers to his right palm to show the angle. "Land more on the tips, not the pads. Won't catch the second string so much that way."

Scott put the fiddle back up on his collarbone, tried to follow Wes's advice, with moderate success. But Wes had made him self-conscious, and he soon left "Angelina Baker" behind for simple scales.

"Good ride?" Wes asked.

Dennis rolled the revolver's cylinder against his palm, squinted down each chamber. "Yeah," he said. "Chilly, though. Wind's starting to get winter-sharp up in those hills."

"Think it'll be a bad one this year?" Almost a month he'd been here, and still the weather seemed the only safe topic.

"We're overdue." Dennis fed the cleaning rod down the first of the chambers. "Pretty light winters the last couple years."

Scott eased off the scales. A few seconds' silence before he drew the bow again. Somehow, Wes knew what he was playing before the first note had finished ringing. Heard it in the pull of the hair, the way Scott tried to ease off the string toward the end. It took Dennis a few moments more, but by the third note he'd put the revolver down, met Wes's eyes. He found his voice before Wes did. "Scott . . ."

That song. His song. Uneven, the timing a little off, the intonation imperfect, all too tentative, but oh, his song.

"Don't play that." It came out a whisper, and Wes said it again, louder. "Don't. Don't play that."

Scott stopped, but kept the fiddle in place, the bow on the string. He didn't look angry, or indignant, only mildly confused. "What's wrong?"

He must have waited too long to answer, because Dennis jumped in. "Nothing, Scott. It's just, that song's got some meaning to our family."

"Where did you hear that?" Wes asked.

Scott brought the fiddle down from his collarbone, settled it on his knee. "It was on one of those tapes you gave me," he said. "I thought it was pretty."

"I wrote that," Wes said, and he heard his own voice like it was someone else's. Heard the words come gently, like the annunciation of a discovery.

"Really?"

Wes opened his mouth to answer, found no words. It surprised him. His fiddle had been mere wood and varnish, steel and silk, for years now. Decades.

Dennis watched Wes warily and Scott stared like a chastised child. "I'm sorry," he said. "I didn't mean to make you upset."

"It's all right," Wes said. He moved to the chair opposite Scott. He held his hands out for the fiddle, and Scott immediately handed it over. Such a fragile thing. So small for its sound. Wes moved his hands over its body: the head, the neck, the shoulders, the waist, belly and back. He knew this fiddle like he knew his own body, like he'd known Claire's. That intimate. That much a part of him. "It's called 'Black River,'" Wes said, "and someday I'll teach it to you. But you ain't ready to play it yet." *And I ain't ready to hear it.*

"Okay," Scott whispered. "I'm sorry."

"You don't got to apologize," Wes said. "I'm just stating a fact."

He handed the fiddle back, and then he taught Scott two new tunes. One was an old Scottish air, the other a hymn, and both had been on his mind when he'd first started putting together the melody that would become "Black River." Scott seemed satisfied with the new tunes, and Wes hummed them for him, over and over, till the kid had the melodies in his own head.

Afterward, while Scott packed up the fiddle, Dennis handed Wes his revolver. "All polished up," he said. Wes nodded his thanks. "I could pick something up for dinner after I drop Scott off," Dennis offered. "You got a preference?"

"I'll take him home," Wes said. "I could stand to get out of the house again."

Dennis shrugged. "Fine by me."

Wes tugged his coat on and put the revolver in the pocket. Liked the heft of it there. "Bring that fiddle with you," he told Scott. "I got something to show you."

Outside, Wes got in the truck and returned the revolver to the glove compartment, double-checked the lock before he let Scott into the cab. The kid sat with the fiddle case between his knees, the bottom of it resting on the tops of his boots rather than the floor.

"Things go okay when you saw your father on Friday?" Wes asked, as he steered the truck down the long drive. He weighed the fading sunlight, flicked the headlights on.

"If by 'okay' you mean we had our usual fight and my mom cried her usual tears, then yeah. It went okay."

"Sorry to hear that."

"Sure."

"Don't take that tone," Wes said. He pulled onto the frontage road. Passed Farmer coming the other way, raised his hand off the steering wheel in greeting. "I think you got your reasons for feeling like you do."

"Yeah, it sucks." Scott thought for a minute. "But at least after next month I'll be back in a town where not everyone hates my guts."

Wes supposed that was as close to philosophical as the kid could manage. Not bad for a teenager, really. Main Street was quiet, the sidewalks all rolled up. Good to see that Sundays were still like that some places. The bars would be busy later, of course—the rotating shift schedule at the prison meant every night was someone's Friday night— but the streets were empty, most of the shops dark, the signs on the doors flipped to *Sorry, We're Closed.*

The windows of the trailer Scott shared with his mother were dark. "When's your momma get home?" Wes asked. He pulled up behind a silver hatchback parked in the driveway, killed the ignition.

"By six, probably."

Wes nodded toward the hatchback. "Yours?"

"Yeah. My mom got it from a guy she works with. Said it was real cheap, but I know we can't really afford it."

"School going okay, then?"

Scott sighed. Wes counted it a favor that he didn't do worse. "Mr. Carver, I know you're trying to look out for me or whatever. But the stuff that sucks is gonna suck, and you can't do anything about it."

Wes thought about arguing the point, but the kid was right, wasn't he, so Wes just said, "All right," and nodded to the fiddle, still resting beneath Scott's hands. "You take that with you."

Scott glanced down, took his hands off the fiddle case. "It's yours."

"You need something to play," Wes said. "You're talented, no doubt about it. But you've still got to practice, and a few minutes here and there when you're at the house ain't gonna do it."

"I can't."

"I don't know if this is gonna make sense to you or not," Wes said after a minute, "but that fiddle's got a particular voice I don't hear from it all the time. It sounded a certain way when I played it . . . before . . . and it doesn't ever seem to sound that way when other folks try it. Not bad, understand? But not the way I remember it." Scott was watching him closely, but Wes couldn't tell what the kid thought of what he was saying. He looked away, squinted through the pocked windshield. Those damned mountains blocking out everything else. "When you started to play . . . my tune . . ." Wes closed his eyes, couldn't keep the notes from his mind, couldn't stop them from prickling in his fingertips. "I heard its voice today," he said finally. "I heard it when you played." He looked back at Scott, and he felt so weary. No energy left to hide what he felt. No effort to guard his features.

Scott looked back for a long moment—a brightness in his eyes Wes had seen only in flashes before, a dark and thoughtful sort of intelligence—and then he put his hands back on top of the fiddle case, one over the other. "I'll take very good care of it," he said.

Wes nodded, felt an ease over his shoulders. "I know you will."

～

He was having nightmares again. Didn't much remember them after he woke, but Wes knew he'd spent his slumbering hours back in that control room with Williams. What else could jolt him awake this way, pulse running away with itself, T-shirt clinging to his back and chest? By midweek, he was the sort of tired that made itself known in muscle and bone. He doubled up on coffee in the mornings and rode the caffeine as long as he could. Truth was, he didn't entirely mind the exhaustion. Made everything seem just a little less real. A little less immediate. Didn't change the fact that the hearing was less than two weeks away. Didn't change the fact that Wes had no idea what he would say, how he'd face down Williams. But it did make it harder to think about those things.

Wednesday morning was his appointment at the donation clinic, and he didn't want to go. The chair was too like the one in the dreams he didn't remember, too like the one in his memory. But Wes got in the truck and drove, because this was something he was good at. Keeping his word. Following through. Doing what needed to be done. He felt a bit better when he got to Elk Fork and the mountains backed off. The light was different here than in the canyon. Found its way to earth more easily. Wes thought, not for the first time, that maybe he should've moved the family here when he was still working at the prison, found a little house on one of the oak-lined streets, something with a wide porch for summer evenings, and flowerbeds for Claire. Would've meant a fair commute, of course—that much harder come winter, especially in those predawn hours before day watch, or the post-dusk ones after evening watch—but he could've managed. Maybe such a simple decision—live here, not there—would've changed something.

Wes sat in the truck in the hospital parking lot for a long time. He'd arrived ten minutes early, and he sat in the cab for fifteen. Thought about not going inside. Might've done it—started the engine, driven away—had it not been Molly waiting for him. Molly, who he'd looked in the eye, who had invited him into her home. No. A comb through his hair, a tug on his collar. Then he was outside, across the parking lot, through the doors that drew themselves wide for him. He took the stairs to the second floor. (He couldn't remember what floor he'd stayed on those days after the riot. Third? Fifth?) In the donation center, he had to wait despite his tardiness, and he ignored the chairs, paced the perimeter of the reception area. He slowed when he passed the door. Still time to walk out. Probably wouldn't be the first time someone had done it.

Molly smiled broadly when she came into the waiting room. "Good morning, Mr. Carver."

"Wes," he corrected, doing his best to match her expression.

"Wes," she agreed. Pink scrubs today. Nametag still had that glittery sticker on it. Molly led him back to one of the donation chairs and drew the curtain around the cubicle without his having to ask. "Sun still shining out there?"

"Yeah." He perched uneasily on the edge of the chair, didn't yield to its curves and angles. "Plenty bright."

"Good," she said. "I get so edgy this time of year knowing winter's on its way, and when it comes I won't see the sun for ages. That little flurry the other day gave me a scare." She stepped toward him, and Wes felt his breath catch in his lungs. Only the blood pressure cuff. He let her position it on his arm, tried not to notice it tightening. Wes half hoped this might be one of those days they told him, *Thanks, but not today. Come back some other time.* "Perfect," Molly announced, pulling the cuff off.

He forced another smile.

"Can I give you a hand with those buttons?"

His very words from that first visit, back at him. "I got it today, if you give me a minute."

Molly turned her attention to her tray of instruments. Courteous as ever. "Wes," Molly said, and her tone was different this time, not unfriendly, but not overlaid with that professional cheer. "I can't say how much I appreciate your giving Scott your fiddle to use, but—"

"I don't want to hear the 'but,'" Wes said. The button on his right cuff came free. Two round scars showing in the sudden gap. "He can't get all the practice he needs during lessons." The left button always so much harder. No grip at all with his right hand. "My father built that fiddle," he said. "I ain't gonna try to convince you it don't mean a lot to me. It does. But it deserves to be played. And Scott deserves to play it."

Molly glanced back at him like she might argue, but something she saw in his face changed her mind. He checked himself immediately, tried to soften his eyes, relax his jaw. "He's been playing one song I really like," she said after a moment, and hummed the first few phrases, tentative and quiet. The notes came out lower than Wes would've guessed from her speaking voice.

"'Weaving Way,'" Wes said. He gave up on his fingers, brought his cuff to his mouth and tugged the button free with his teeth. Molly came to his side, drawing the cart close. She took his right wrist in her hand, and Wes couldn't stop himself pulling back for a second. She didn't seem to notice, just turned his wrist until his arm was positioned the way she liked. Wes hadn't realized till this moment how much he'd been counting on Molly to see through his veil of false composure to the unease beneath. How much he'd been counting on her to suggest— maybe even insist—that he go on home today, try again another time. But now she was swabbing his elbow with the alcohol, and he let the slightest flinch show itself, and still she said nothing. *You done this a hundred times,* Wes told himself. *You can do it again.*

"I got a call this morning." Molly was beside him now, tourniquet in one hand, needle in the other, but she stood very still and cast her eyes down. "There was a fight at the prison," she said. "I don't know exactly what happened. But Connor—my husband—was involved. A guard was hurt." She glanced at his face, quick, down at his bared arm, at the floor. "Minor injuries, they said." Footsteps on the linoleum beyond the curtain. Molly lowered her voice. "He's in segregation now," she said. "There's no chance they'll release him next month."

"You're not leaving, then," Wes said, barely aware of the words as they left his lips. He couldn't concentrate on this, could think only of how easily violence sprang into being in that place, how quickly an ordinary situation could turn bad. How it had come to him in a single moment when the riot began, a sudden awareness that what he had first thought to be a minor scuffle—nearly routine—was something else entirely, something it was too late to extricate himself from, something that was about to engulf him totally.

"No," Molly said. The word like a sigh. "We're going to have to stay. And I know how hard that's going to be on Scott. So I'm glad—so glad—that he can spend time with you, and with Dennis. With men who are . . . better . . . than his father."

It cost Molly something deep to say that. Wes knew that in some part of himself, knew he ought to offer her gratitude or reassurance or condolences, but he hesitated, and now she was asking him if he was ready and he lied and said yes, and there was a needle in his arm, seeking his vein. And he knew he'd granted permission, knew that in a moment the needle would be in place and the small pain would end, and it would be fine, it would all be fine. But something else inside him knew only that he did not want to be sitting here, did not want his skin exposed this way, did not want to feel any more pain than he already did, and that something was stronger, that visceral response sharper than the rational one, and then he was standing, the needle on the floor, the tourniquet limp beside it, and Wes was stammering what he meant to be an apology, but all that came out was "I can't." He looked at Molly, saw confusion cede to compassion in her eyes—he didn't *need* her pity—and he pushed his sleeves down, saw the right one bloom red where it touched the single drop of blood sliding toward his wrist, and then he was past the curtain and out the door.

He woke again that night. He lay on the narrow bed, listening to Dennis's light snore across the hall, to the absence of Claire's gentle breaths beside him. Sometimes she had woken with him when he'd had a nightmare, but more often she didn't. He'd found that comforting, somehow. Proof that what troubled him was in the past. That it was safe again.

No more sleep tonight. Wes rose slowly, easing out of bed so the creaking springs wouldn't disturb Dennis. He pulled on his jeans and padded barefoot down the hall. He fumbled blindly on the kitchen table for Dennis's cigarettes and lighter, then let himself out onto the porch. Cold outside, too cold for just a T-shirt, but Wes sat down on the steps anyway. There was smoke in the air again, not from wildfire but from fireplaces and woodstoves. It would gather and linger in the canyon over the next weeks and months, the scent growing sharper and heavier until the air became chill enough to sear the nostrils. Until all a person could smell was the cold itself.

Autumn had been Claire's favorite season. His, too, once. He'd never quite got over the schoolboy way of thinking of fall as the start of a new year. For a long time that was a good thing, the thought of an entire year stretched out before him, waiting to be lived. When Wes's life was easy, it meant the promise of more good things to come. When it wasn't, it meant hope that the new seasons would be better than the last. But now, without Claire, he couldn't muster the optimism.

He hadn't thought of her today, at the clinic. Not once, not even there. Spent the better part of the past two years in one hospital or another, at her side, and today he'd been so full of memory and fear, so full of goddamned Bobby Williams, that he hadn't thought of her until he was in his truck, halfway back to Black River. Wes just wanted this over, wanted Williams out of his life. He wanted to get back to grieving, because hard as it was to bear, there was something pure in his grief for Claire. What he felt in those days after her death so filled him, so commanded every moment, he knew it was just a hairsbreadth from love itself. Like the same note played an octave apart, at the same time, ringing and resonating together.

Wes watched his breath appear faintly before him with each exhalation. He squinted into the dark but couldn't see the horses. He could hear them, though, beyond the circle of light cast by the security lamp mounted on the side of the workshop. A shifting of weight over frosting grass, a clink of steel shoe against hoof sole, a long, trembling sigh.

He tapped the cigarette pack against his thigh, set one between his lips and managed the lighter in only a few tries. A greater plume of breath into the air now. He had to decide what to say at the hearing. He had to have a plan. Otherwise he might end up in that room with Williams and freeze up. Stammer. Bolt the way he did at the clinic today. Worse. But what to say . . . The parole board would have the files, the records. They'd know what Williams had done in that farmhouse out on the eastern plains, and they'd know what he'd done in that control room during the riot. Those things alone wouldn't stop them from letting him out. There had to be more, something he could say, something he could make them see.

The security lamp lent a greenish cast to his skin. Wes held his right hand out before him, turned it palm-up. He liked the way the light made the skin seem not quite his own, the scars a little less real. The one in the middle of his forearm, third from his palm, that had come first. He remembered the smoke blown in his face, the laughter in his ear, the first touch of burning ash to flesh. But he wasn't sure he remembered the pain. Not well enough to put it into words that might let someone else think they could understand it.

Williams had found Wes's cigarettes in the desk drawer almost immediately, tossed his own aside in favor of the more expensive brand. Wes remembered watching from the corner of his eye, afraid to look directly at Williams. Seemed like looking a wild animal in the eye, better avoided. He hadn't hurt much yet. The crack over his head, the boot to his ribs, a fist to his face when he hadn't immediately responded to the sole question Williams had asked so far. (Why had he finally answered "Wesley" rather than "Wes"? Why the name Claire used?) Williams had a reckless way of moving, entirely without caution, and he smoked the cigarette with a certain brashness. He wore Wes's uniform shirt over his own T-shirt, and it was too big for him, the cuffs falling over his knuckles, close to the cigarette's lit tip. He seemed to be paying attention mostly to what was going on outside the control room—to the shouts and occasional screams, the ringing of metal on metal, the sickly scent of something burning—and Wes was glad. He was relieved that electric attention wasn't on him, hopeful he might be simply warehoused here, bound and uncomfortable but otherwise more or less unharmed.

"You must think I'm awful rude," Williams had said suddenly. Hadn't looked at Wes when he spoke, and Wes seized that, pretended—childishly, pointlessly—that he didn't realize Williams was talking to him. Williams had walked slowly around the small room, to what would come to be his customary place behind Wes. Knelt behind the chair, leaned around to speak into Wes's ear. "I smoke this in front of you and don't share." Blew a lungful of smoke across Wes's face. The cigarette appeared in front of him, still one or two drags left before the filter, tip smoldering gently. "Finish it off?" Williams pushed it toward his face, and Wes had tilted his head away, eyes on the far wall, lips pressed shut. Not yet knowing what was coming, exactly, not with certainty, but it was there, pushing at the edges of his consciousness, refusing to be kept at bay. He couldn't look, couldn't respond, because his eyes would betray his fear, and even his voice, ever trustworthy, might not protect him.

That laugh. That laugh he had never forgotten, low and languid. "Better put it out, then."

Wes held his cigarette out in front of him now. It glowed hard in the dark, brighter for the absence of strong light nearby. He remembered the heat just before the cigarette had touched his skin. The moment before the pain. He remembered the scent of it, the smaller, closer acrid burn twinning with the stench outside the control room. He remembered the sound, the breathy hiss and crackle. But he didn't remember the pain itself. Not in his waking hours, anyway. There was a haziness cast over the memory of the worst pains, the details surrounding them sharp enough that the missing core went almost unnoticed. Maybe that was some gift of God, a gentle hand shielding the eyes of his memory from the harshest moments. But he *needed* those moments. Needed the worst of it, bright and present.

Claire didn't believe in an afterlife. Didn't believe she would be somewhere out there in the blackness, above in the stars, watching over him.

Wes pressed the tip of the cigarette to the unmarked flesh above his right elbow. Oh, yes. Yes. Now he remembered. The searing he'd tried to jerk away from even before feeling the brunt of the pain, the way Williams had followed his movements so smoothly, the strain of muscle against steel, the way the burning built and heightened and still Williams didn't lift the cigarette from his skin. Now he remembered the bracing, the way it had taken every physical effort, all the strength and discipline he could muster, just to stay silent. God, that such a small scrap of fire could cause such pain!

"Jesus, Wes!" A hand on his wrist, the cigarette no longer pressed to flesh, the glowing embers tumbling to the ground. Dennis was barefoot, too, and remembered it just as he went to grind the butt out, kicked gravel over it instead and buried the orange flame. "What the fuck are you doing?"

Now he remembered. Now he might put this into words. Now he had found the clarity he had sought. The man who had done this to him had done it not once, but six times. And when he tired of that, he'd tried a different sort of pain, and then another. Over and over and over. Laughing and laughing and laughing. The man who had done this to him was not deserving of parole. He was not deserving of forgiveness, or God's grace. He had not become someone else. The man who had done this to him could not have become anyone else.

"What the fuck, Wes?" Dennis's voice too loud in the night air. "What's wrong with you?"

"I couldn't remember what it felt like."

Dennis knelt in front of him, looked into his eyes a long time. He'd sounded angry, but Wes saw now that he was scared. Sorry for that. Hadn't meant anyone else to know. Dennis took Wes's hand in his, turned it so the greenish light hit the new wound. Bare arms. T-shirt. Wes realized it at once, tried to stand, to pull his hand back, but Dennis held his wrist, then both his wrists. "Jesus," he whispered.

"Give me back my hands," Wes growled. Enough himself to make it sound like the order it was, to drive enough authority into the words to command obedience. Dennis dropped his own hands to his sides, took a step back, gravel grinding beneath his feet. Wes stood, crossed his arms over his chest. Scraped his knuckles against the fresh burn, but hid the grimace.

"I had no idea," Dennis said.

"You know what he did," Wes said. "I know you do."

"Yeah, but I've never seen . . ."

"You were a kid," Wes said. "I didn't want you to have to see that stuff."

Dennis turned a slow circle, hands over his face. When he came around to face Wes again, he lowered his hands and dropped to a crouch in front of the porch. The gravel must've been sharp beneath his feet, but he didn't show it. "Don't hurt yourself anymore, Wes." He looked up. "Okay? Please."

Wes glanced down, finally nodded, so slightly. Dennis sighed, and Wes reluctantly sat again. Starting to feel the cold now. After a minute Dennis came to sit next to him. Easier that way. Didn't have to look right at each other. They stared together into the dark, listening to the horses, to the occasional crescendoing rumble of a tractor-trailer on the interstate.

"I don't understand," Dennis said after a while.

"I ain't gonna be able to explain it so you do."

He ought to go run some cold water over his arm. The pain was still bright, the way it stayed with burns. But Williams hadn't exactly given him ointment and Band-Aids, and he'd healed okay back then.

"Maybe you shouldn't go to this hearing." It was as hesitant a tone as Wes had ever heard Dennis take. He knew he was treading into territory that was none of his business.

"Got to. No one else is gonna be there. I don't go, you can bet Williams walks."

"So let him walk!" There was the arrogance Wes was used to. Something under it, though, something almost desperate. Wes glanced sideways, expecting to see Dennis's eyes on his scars, but his stepson was looking at him, waiting to meet his gaze. "Maybe they'll parole him and maybe they won't, Wes, but so what if they do? Let the bastard go back to East Jesus wherever. Let him live his miserable little life and die, and don't give him another thought."

"You don't understand."

"I understand enough," Dennis insisted. He touched Wes's wrist, thought better of it and pulled his hand away, the touch of his fingers so brief it was almost imagined. "I remember Mom taking me to visit you in the hospital, right after. You gave me the strangest look. Like you'd never expected to lay eyes on me again."

Across the yard, Rio stepped gingerly into the barest wash of light that reached the pasture, sidled up to the hot wire and raised his head over it. Drawn by the sound of voices, Wes supposed. His white eye glinted across the distance.

It'd be easier if night never lifted. If all Wes had to do was sit on this porch and watch the darkness while the world slept. He'd have liked that, liked to ignore the business of life, the troubles that demanded attention, action, during daylight hours. Here, now, the burn of cold on his bare arms had almost equaled the round point of pain above his elbow. Here, now, he could speak almost freely with the stepson he seemed unable to coexist with at any other time. Here, now, he could pretend that there was only this porch, this yard, these animals, the invisible river and road, the world the limit of his senses. No prison. No parole.

Long minutes of quiet. Dennis shifted beside him, and Wes heard the click of his teeth as he opened his mouth, shut it again. At last his stepson risked another touch, awkward, his hand hesitating, hovering just above Wes's shoulder, so close Wes could feel the warmth of Dennis's palm even before it finally settled.

—

He slept afterward, and woke late. It was darker than he expected in the bedroom, and a glance through the slats of the blinds confirmed that the sun had already passed its peak and crossed to the western half of the sky. Whole morning wasted. Wes couldn't bring himself to be sorry about it. First time he'd rested like that in days. Before dressing he passed his thumb over the fresh burn above his elbow. Still sharp. Soon it'd fade to a lesser hurt, reduced to something milder than the bone ache he lived with every day. Gone entirely, given enough time. He wondered if that'd happen before the hearing.

Wes skipped the coffee—didn't seem right to drink it when it was already afternoon—and settled for dry toast and the pulpy dregs of a carton of orange juice. He ate in the kitchen and listened to the metallic tapping he'd come to recognize as hammer and anvil. It was early for Dennis to be home, and Wes guessed he'd canceled appointments, found excuses to linger near the house.

He went out to the porch, leaned over the railing. Dennis had parked his truck near the hitching rack; the canopy was up, the small gas forge blowing. The anvil stood on its stand a couple feet away, the hammer resting—for the moment—beside it. Rio was tied to the hitching rack, ears flicked backward, posture stiff, and Dennis was bent almost double near one of his hind hooves. It wasn't the way Wes had seen him work on horses before, the animal's leg propped over his own. Instead, Rio's hoof rested with the toe grazing the ground, and Dennis worked his knife from there. As Wes watched, Dennis stifled a grunt and slid down to one knee. Rio shifted, putting his weight back onto the hoof Dennis was trying to work on. Dennis stayed on the ground but straightened, pressed his palm to the small of his back.

"One more time," he said a few seconds later, cupping his hand beneath Rio's fetlock. The horse pivoted his hoof back onto the toe, and Dennis hunched over again, his knife switched out for a rasp. Got only a few seconds' work in before Rio put his foot back down.

"That don't look very comfortable," Wes called.

Dennis stood, tried not to show how much it strained him. "Yeah, well," he said, "working like this is a little harder on me and a lot easier on him." He crossed to the anvil but didn't pick up the hammer.

Wes stepped off the porch, walked cautiously across the gravel. Dennis was watching him, but Wes went to the horse instead, stopped on the other side of the hitching rack and brushed the back of his hand down the side of Rio's neck. "How long it take you to do his shoes?"

Dennis shrugged. "Couple hours, give or take."

"And that red horse," Wes said. "How long it take you to do him?"

"Hour." The word came out sideways, like it hoped not to be noticed.

"Less?" Wes asked.

Dennis looked away. "Sometimes."

Wes patted Rio one more time. Dennis was firmer with him, Wes knew, his pats more like slaps, but Wes couldn't help but feel there was something fragile about this black horse, something that made him want to touch him only gingerly. "You're patient with him."

"Ain't his fault he hurts."

Wes turned to look at Dennis. "How long till he hurts enough it don't matter how patient you are?"

Dennis's mouth tightened. So hard, Wes thought, to see his mother in him. In almost every way he looked nothing like her. Different hair, different skin, different eyes. The lines of his body hard and angular where Claire's had been soft. But the slight wariness Wes saw in him now, the fine veil of caution over his features . . . that he shared with his mother. "Not long," he said finally. "But not now."

It didn't look like anyone was home when Wes pulled up to the trailer Scott shared with his mother—blinds drawn, no light showing in the gaps—but Scott's hatchback was parked out front, and Wes had cruised Main Street from end to end twice, scanning the crowds of kids just out from school, with no sighting of Scott's familiar slouch. (And he needed to find the kid—any thoughts of Scott's hurt on finding out about his father's revoked release had, like Claire's memory, succumbed to his panic at the donation clinic yesterday, just one more thing he'd had no time to notice among thoughts of the hearing and the riot and Williams.) The frost had lingered here in the deep shade of the mountains, and the patchy lawn outside the trailer sank stiffly beneath Wes's feet. He rapped twice on the door, waited. Heard footsteps approach. He looked right at the peephole, but said nothing. Wasn't gonna beg the kid to open up.

Scott opened the door but left the screen shut. He hadn't made his hair stick up the way it usually did, and it fell in a soft spray across his forehead. He looked hard at Wes, but didn't seem able to muster the energy needed for the glare Wes guessed he was trying for. "What do you want?"

"You skip school today?"

Scott snorted. "Are you a truant officer now or something? Would that be a step up from prison guard, or a step down?"

"I was looking for you in town is all. Didn't see you." Wes took a step toward the screen door, and Scott closed his hand over the inside handle.

"Yeah, well," he said. "That's 'cause I was here. Being delinquent."

Wes sighed. "Let's start over, all right? I didn't come to fight."

"What the hell did you come for?"

"I want to teach you that song. The one you like. The one I wrote."

It shut the kid up, anyway. He blinked a couple times, took his hand off the door handle. "You said I wasn't ready."

"You're not. I ain't gonna teach you the whole thing yet. And you gotta promise not to try to play more than I teach you, got that?" He waited for Scott to offer the barest hint of a nod. "All right, then. Go get that fiddle."

"Don't you want to come in?"

Wes shook his head. "Bring it out here."

Scott looked like he thought Wes was nuts, but he disappeared down the hall. Wes stepped back onto the crisp grass. Breathed deeply of the sharpening air, scanned the overlapping swells of the mountains. Maybe he *was* nuts. Maybe what he could offer Scott wasn't enough, maybe it was pathetic next to the darker elements of the kid's life. But the music had always been there for him. It had always called him back to himself. Every afternoon, walking out that gate feeling like everything good in him had been drained away, or wound up tight inside, too deep to reach. During the darkest days of his own adolescence, after his father's suicide. Music had been his saving grace: that fiddle, perfect and polished, waiting in the workshop, waiting on the mantel. Could be the fiddle and its music held that sort of power only for Wes. But maybe he could share a little of it.

Scott kicked the screen door open and came into the yard, fiddle in one hand, bow in the other. There were two lawn chairs set up around the side of the trailer, and Wes nodded to them. "Ready to do this?"

Scott started toward the chairs, stopped. He turned halfway, so Wes saw his profile. "Did you already hear about my dad?"

Wes put his hands in his pockets, took one small step toward Scott, almost sideways, the way he might approach a skittish animal. "Your momma told me."

"You know they might add like a whole year to his sentence?"

"I'm sorry," Wes said, and it was half a lie. He wasn't sorry Connor Bannon's release was being revoked, not if he'd hurt an officer. But Wes knew it'd be hard on Scott, and he was sorry for that. The boy already rode pretty close to desperation.

"I can't stay here another year. I cannot." Scott looked away, at the mountains that loomed high over his home, and Wes tried to remember what it was to feel that a single year was so very long. "I told my mom I wanted to leave anyway. Go back to Miles City."

"Yeah?"

"She says I can't go on my own. That I'm too young."

"I know it ain't what you want to hear, but she's probably not wrong."

"Dennis was on his own when he was my age," Scott said, and it sounded like an accusation.

"Dennis got a good chunk of my pension in the mail every month," Wes said. "He didn't have to pay rent on no apartment, either. And it was still hard on him. Dropped out of school in the end."

Wes expected Scott to argue, but he didn't. "I told my mom that if I can't go back alone, we should go together. She doesn't like it here, either."

"And?"

"She won't do it." Scott was clenching the neck of the fiddle so hard Wes wanted to reach out and take it from him, but he forced himself still. "She thinks my dad needs us here." Scott laughed bitterly, and the sound was choked off as if he were crying, though what Wes could see of his face was dry. "He *needs* us. What bull. He doesn't care. If he cared, he wouldn't have gotten in a fight a month before his fucking release. If he cared, he'd think about what it might be like for me to spend every single day with kids who think they can shit all over me because their dads guard my dad." He spun on his heel, stared right at Wes — there was that glare — and swung the bow toward him like a weapon. "Hell, if he actually gave a rat's ass about me, he wouldn't have gotten arrested in the first place, would he? *Would he?*"

Wes felt reflexive anger trying to rise, but he forced it down, kept his hands in his pockets, his gaze level. Carved the edges off his voice so it was steady and low. "What do you want me to say, Scott? You want me to tell you life always works the way it ought to? That hard things never happen to folks who don't deserve them? That fathers always look after their sons the way they should?" He honed his voice, let it come a bit sharper. "I will, if you want. I can lie with the best of 'em. But you'd know it ain't true. And I can't fix that stuff. Wish I could, but I can't. What I can do is teach you the tune that fiddle knows best. It ain't much, I know that, but it's all I got."

Scott stayed quiet for a minute, but his white-knuckled grip on the fiddle loosened a little. A train whistle sounded through the canyon, fading even as it reached Wes's ears. A name for that sound. High lonesome. "I want to learn it," Scott said finally.

Wes nodded. "Good."

"We can go inside," Scott said, jerking his thumb toward the trailer. "My mom won't care."

"You ever tried playing that out here?" Wes asked, lifting his chin toward the fiddle.

"No."

Wes turned a slow circle on one heel, gave himself a panorama of the risen earth, the abbreviated sky. "I kinda hate these mountains," he said. "Make me claustrophobic, I guess. Feels like there ain't no way out." He stopped, facing Scott, saw that the kid felt it, too. "But that fiddle don't sound half so good outside this canyon."

"Because of the acoustics or whatever?" Scott sounded doubtful.

"Could be," Wes said. "Could be something else. All I know is I've played all over Montana, indoors and out, and it sings best here." He stopped, suddenly embarrassed. Sometimes his yearning for his lost music came out this way, without his intending to share it. Mostly it used to happen only in front of Claire, who always understood and never judged. But Scott didn't seem to share his embarrassment, appeared to take his words at face value.

"Okay," he said, "but I'm freezing my ass off. If we're gonna play out here, I have to go get a sweatshirt."

Wes took the fiddle and bow from him, and Scott disappeared around the front of the trailer. Wes walked to the lawn chairs, settled himself into one. It sank and creaked beneath his weight. He held the fiddle upright on his knee, the way he used to during breaks in practice, let the bow lie across his thighs. It was so tempting to put it beneath his chin, to bring bow to string. It was tuned now; he could draw open-string notes from it, maybe even one or two stopped notes before his fingers gave up. Might be able to coax the first couple notes of "Black River" out of it. Might be able to pretend for a few seconds he could still do what he'd always loved best. But Wes kept the fiddle where it was, waited for the eager readiness to dissipate from his hands and body.

The kid must've been trying on half his wardrobe. How long could it take to pick one black sweatshirt from half a dozen others? Wes tried not to feel the fiddle beneath his fingers. He listened to the train rumble past. He could see it through the trees lining the road: dulled blocks of color flashing by steadily, one after another. Wes found his foot tapping to the rhythm of metal grinding over metal. Lots of songs about trains.

Scott came half jogging back from the trailer. "Sorry," he said, tugging the sweatshirt over his head. "I guess my mom washed it, and I couldn't find it." He held out his hands, and Wes wasn't sure whether he was glad or sorry to hand the fiddle over.

"You know this tune pretty good?"

"Pretty good, yeah." A little color in his cheeks. Been listening to it a lot, then. Wes felt a hint of that same prideful pleasure he used to feel when people below a stage called for the tune by name.

"All right," he said. "Today I just want to go through the first melody line, okay? Just like this." He sang the first part of the tune softly, wordlessly, the first gentle rise and fall of notes. "Key of G. Start on open D."

Scott was eager—and he wasn't fibbing; he knew every note—but he attacked "Black River" the way he did the old-time dance tunes Wes had been teaching him, all rhythm and no elasticity. It was a beginner's way of playing—a talented beginner, yes, but still a novice—and Wes wondered if this had been a mistake, if it was simply too soon. The fiddle sang dutifully, and it rang nicely in the open air, but Wes knew it was capable of so much more than *nice*.

"Gently," he told Scott. "You want to draw the note like you're spinning it out of thin air." He rose from his chair and knelt beside Scott's. Carefully he rested his right hand on the back of Scott's, helped him guide the bow across the strings. And there they were. The first of his notes. He felt them resonate through horsehair and wood, as surely as if his hand had been the one touching the bow.

"Whoa," Scott said.

Reluctantly, Wes let go, sat back in his own chair. "Again."

Slowly it came to him. Slowly the sound Wes remembered returned, the fiddle's true voice filling the canyon, building and rising with the mountains, inhabiting the air. Sometimes Scott got frustrated—"Don't you get that most folks playing as long as you are still mucking their way through 'Oh! Susanna'?" Wes asked him at one point—but more often he got it right, or close to right. Didn't sound quite the way it did in Wes's head, of course. "Black River" had been, and always would be, Wes's tune first and foremost, his almost masterpiece, the song he heard in his head every day of his life, the notes he felt waiting in his fingertips every hour of the day. But Scott was going to have his own way of playing it, and it would be worthy. They played together for al-most two hours—two hours for a single melody line, not even a quar-ter of the whole tune—and Wes thought about stopping only when he realized the winter-white sun had already sunk below the high hori-zon of the mountains. He let Scott play it through once more, and he watched his face and saw the way the music transformed this boy, saw that he had been right in coming here with nothing more than a song, that it was enough for Scott as it had been enough for him. Saw that he had done something good.

~~~

Enough indulgence. Enough of letting Bobby Williams drive him from sleep. Enough surrendering to the queasy memory of fear. Morn-ing came and Wes was up with Dennis, the sun still closer to the east end of the canyon than the west. He drank his coffee, added a glass of orange juice to spike his blood sugar and got into his truck. It was just late enough he missed most of the commuters heading toward Elk Fork, and he had the interstate mostly to himself. Near Milltown a slew of police cars and ambulances flew past in the eastbound lanes, lights spiraling but sirens silent. Montana had its share of bad wrecks— the roadsides all littered with tiny white crosses—and Wes guessed they were headed to another. Even so, he drove as fast as he thought he could get away with—he missed the days when the official posted speed limit was simply "reasonable and prudent"—and cranked the radio louder than he usually liked it. Anything to keep up his resolve all the way to town.

Lord, it made him angry. The riot was twenty years gone. It had lasted just thirty-nine hours. Thirty-nine of the worst hours of his life, yeah, but still less than two full days. Didn't seem right that a few hours, however miserable, should still have such an effect on him so many years later. Plenty of folks had endured worse; he knew that. In some ways—not many, but some—he'd even been lucky. He'd heard rumors at the academy of what inmates sometimes did to COs during riots. Williams, twisted as he was, at least hadn't been interested in that. And all a man had to do was read the paper—any paper, any day—to realize that there was no shortage of people doing terrible things to other people. You picked up. You moved on. Wasn't quite that simple, maybe, but there was nothing stopping Wes from going to the hospital and asking for Molly and sitting quietly for a couple hours so he could do some good for another person.

Except when he got to the donation center, the receptionist told him Molly wasn't there. "She came in this morning," she said, "but she went home sick. You just missed her."

Wes set his palms flat on her desk. It was moments like this that made him a little glad he had so much trouble believing in God; he didn't like to think a higher power would toy with him this way. "She won't be back?"

The receptionist took a second look at him. Something came down behind her eyes, but he couldn't tell if it was guardedness or pity. "I don't think so, sir." She glanced behind her, toward the donation area. "Emma could help you, though?" It came out a question, and the receptionist seemed relieved when, after several seconds, Wes nodded.

Emma was younger than Molly, and a little skittish. Wes didn't mind. Made him feel like he ought to take care of her, and that made it easier not to think about himself. She helped him with his buttons, and Wes rolled his sleeves himself, careful to keep the fresh burn on his right arm hidden. His scars startled Emma, and she hid it badly. Her voice jumped an octave, and her smile broadened into a rictus. Twice she dropped needles on the floor, and when she had the lines in place and asked if he'd like a magazine, Wes took pity on her and said yes, he sure would. She brought him half a dozen, *Field & Stream* and *Popular*

Mechanics and *People.* He spent the next two hours dutifully flipping through them, reading about deer rifles and glossy cars and celebrities he'd never heard of, half afraid that Emma, in her nervous enthusiasm, might quiz him later.

Wasn't easy. Oh, he wanted to bolt. But he didn't, and when Emma came back for the final time and pulled the needles and taped cotton over each elbow, he was glad he'd stayed. It wasn't any sort of victory over Williams, not really, but it felt a little like one. The trial of it must've shown on his face, though, because Emma decided he looked too pale, and despite her jumpiness and his protests, she insisted that he stay another ten minutes and eat a pair of off-brand cookies.

He left the hospital feeling almost good. Maybe after school let out, he'd track down Scott again and try to teach him the next part of "Black River." Might be a little too soon, a little too challenging for his skill level at this point, but the kid had surprised him before.

He was almost to Milltown when the ambulance passed him in the opposite lanes. No lights, no siren. No reason to notice. Just that he'd come from the hospital. Just that he'd seen another ambulance going the other way this morning.

It was gonna be a pretty evening later. Cold, but in that clear, crisp autumn way that seemed like a last gift before winter hit. Maybe he should swing by the IGA before going back to the house, grill up some burgers for him and Dennis tonight.

The police cars came from behind, when he was a few miles from Black River. The first hit its siren to alert him, an abbreviated whoop, and he slowed and pulled half into the breakdown lane. The next came a few minutes later, the third another minute after that. He'd been going almost eighty; they were going faster. Wes felt familiar tension settling back over his shoulders, tried to shrug it off. No reason to worry about a few cop cars. Wrecks all the time on the roads here. Hunting season. Folks starting up their woodstoves after the summer off. All kinds of calamity in the world; it wasn't all coming for him. But each time one of the police cars passed and Wes slowed, he held his weaker speed when he pulled back into the travel lane.

Slower.

BLACK RIVER ▪ 165

Slower.
Slower.

~~~

He didn't drive through town. Didn't continue through the canyon to see what it might show him. When he got back to the house, the wind was blowing from the east, and it brought with it the high wail of a single siren, fractured against the mountain slopes. Dennis was sitting on the porch steps, and Wes wished he didn't have to go to him. He was still in his horseshoeing clothes: the heavy boots, the plaid flannel shirt with its tattered, turned-up cuffs. He leaned forward, elbows on his knees, hands clasped between them, and he looked like he was both waiting and not waiting. If Wes hadn't known better, he'd have thought Dennis was praying.

Dennis didn't look up when he approached, though Wes walked slow, the way Farmer had on that first day back in Black River. His stepson's face was still, so still. Eyes downcast but seeing something other than gravel and dirt. Wes wanted to leave. He feared this knowledge he didn't yet have. Maybe if sharing its burden could help Dennis, if it could soften the hard, weighty mask of misery that had taken hold of his features, Wes would have been more eager to ask. Since Claire's death, though, he often felt dangerously fragile, just a hairsbreadth from losing control.

The siren died abruptly, the echo lingering a few seconds more before succumbing to silence. "What is it?" His voice was too loud, compensating for his dread. "Is it the prison again?"

Dennis looked up sharply, like a hawk that had spotted prey. "The prison," he repeated. He stood, a slow unfolding of his body. Walked toward Wes, stopped, moved a few steps left, a few steps right. "It's not always about the fucking prison, Wes. Not every goddamned thing that happens in this town is about the fucking prison." Both hands to his forehead, pushing back through his hair. "Or maybe it is. Maybe it is. I don't know."

Wes felt his protective instincts evaporate. The pacing, the hard glint in the eyes, these things belonged to the Dennis he had known years ago, the Dennis he didn't trust and didn't like. "What's happened?" he asked.

Dennis tapped a cigarette from a nearly empty pack and cupped his hands to light it. He held the smoke in his lungs for a long time, exhaled in Wes's direction; the wind carried it away before Wes caught the scent. "Tell me something," Dennis said, turning his hand so he could see the tip of the cigarette. "When Williams burned you, did you scream?"

"What did you say to me?" Wes's voice low, the dangerous kind of low Dennis ought to have recognized.

His stepson moved close to him, too close, his face just inches from Wes's. "Did you scream," he repeated, "when Williams burned you?"

He'd clenched his jaw so tightly he'd cracked a molar. He'd pulled so fiercely against the handcuffs the metal sawed through his skin. He'd damn near passed out, his exhalations were so hard and his inhalations so shallow. But the control room was open to the tiers, and all the inmates would have heard, and Williams would have heard, and Wes knew his own voice was the last thing—the only thing—he still controlled, so the one thing he did not do was scream.

He shook his head, just slightly.

"No?" Dennis raised an eyebrow, though the eye beneath stayed cold. "Five cigarettes and you didn't scream?"

"Six," Wes said softly.

"Six," Dennis repeated, nodding to himself. "Right." He gestured toward Wes's left arm. A casual movement, one he had no right to. Shouldn't even know what was under that sleeve. "And what about when he cut you?"

It had been a different pain, easier to take in its way. Hurt more in the minutes and hours after than during, though the makeshift blade was dull enough it did plenty of damage on its way through flesh. The knife had frightened him more than the cigarettes. Williams sliced deep, and as he'd worked his way down Wes's arm toward the wrist, all Wes had been able to think was how close his arteries and veins ran to the surface. The blood slicked his arm—some dripped off the knob of his wrist, the rest curved beneath the cuff and into the cradle of his palm before slipping between his fingers and onto the floor, with a sound that was subtly not like water. He'd been too afraid of that blade to move. Too afraid to scream.

"No," he said.

Dennis's eyes were starting to take on that wild, desperate edge Wes remembered from when he was a kid. From that night at the dinner table. "So you stayed quiet through all that," he said. "Can't say I'm surprised, Wes. Guess I expected nothing less." He nodded to Wes's hands. "What about the fingers?"

Williams had given him time to dread. Wrapped Wes's right pinkie in his fist, coiled and uncoiled his own fingers around it like a man getting a better grip on a golf club or a baseball bat. Bent Wes's finger back slowly until Wes felt the warning pains shoot all the way to his elbow. So he expected—but was not prepared for—what came next: the sudden wrenching, the pop and crack of bone and cartilage and tendon, the explosion of pain. He hadn't been able to hold it behind his teeth that time, so he channeled it into words, into the longest string of profanity he'd ever let pass his lips, all of it directed at Williams, who had hardly seemed to hear. It took him hours to break the rest of Wes's fingers; he'd snap one or two at a time, take hold of another but then let it go, whole, twist another he'd already ruined hours before. Wes's eyes crusted with unspilled tears, and later, when they came too fast to hold in, they streaked his face. When Williams broke his thumb, the pain so seized Wes he leaned over and retched onto the floor. He lost what little control he still had during those hours, witnessed the unwavering command he'd always held over his voice abandon him. He gasped. He swore. He begged. And yes, after Williams started in on his left hand—the hand that had always danced so easily up and down the neck of his fiddle—he screamed.

"Well?" Dennis asked, the word almost an accusation.

Wes reached out and grabbed Dennis's wrist in his left hand, closed his right around his stepson's index finger and forced it back far enough to hurt. He saw the brief flash of pain and surprise rise behind Dennis's mask before the other man forced them off his face. It didn't shame him. "You'd have screamed, too," he whispered.

Dennis snatched his hand away from Wes—he did it easily, Wes's hands no match for Dennis's strength—and shook out his fingers once. "I've got no doubt of that," he said. "Hell, I'd have been hollering before the bastard ever touched me." He took a step back, and suddenly Wes felt he could breathe again. Let out a shuddering lungful of air. He could still feel the ghost of Dennis's finger in his fist, the landscape of calluses and half-healed nicks against his own skin. "I know better than to question your strength, Wes. Whatever's between us, I ain't ever been stupid enough to think I could stand up to half of what you've been through. But not all of us are you." He was pacing again, a few steps one way, a few steps the other. Arms crossed over his chest, eyes back on the ground. "Not all of us can hold it all in the way you can, Wes. We just can't. And you've never understood that. Never seen how hard it is for the rest of us, how we can only dream of that kind of self-control . . ." He was crying, Wes realized. Wet tracks through the dust on his face, a cracking voice losing the battle to conceal the sobs waiting to break through.

"Dennis," Wes said, as gently as he could, "tell me what happened."

His stepson stopped pacing. Looked up bleakly. "Scott took a gun to school."

Wes felt his gut contract, but he kept his features still. Better, maybe, if he hadn't, if he instead showed Dennis what he felt, but he didn't know how. Didn't know how to let that stuff show, and didn't know how to rein it in once he had. He swallowed, licked his lips. Held his voice steady. "Did he use it?"

Dennis shook his head. Sniffed hard and cleared his throat. "He pulled it out in one of his classes," he said. "Threatened a couple kids with it. A teacher. I don't know what happened exactly. They're still piecing it together."

Wes wished Dennis would sit, so he could sit, too. Felt a little lightheaded. "Where is he now?"

Dennis looked at him. No expression.

"Scott," Wes prompted. "Is he still at the school?"

"He left," Dennis said. "I guess he only stayed five, ten minutes after he pulled the gun. They were looking for him everywhere. The sheriff found me out at Jim Filmore's place. Thought Scott might be with me, or maybe came back here." He looked around the property, as though Scott might be waiting by the workshop or leaning against the hood of the truck.

Wes didn't prompt Dennis again. He waited and listened to the wind blow through the heights of the pines. So quiet. Wished it could stay this quiet always.

"I heard the whistle," Dennis said at last. "Don't think I've ever heard it so long or loud."

"No," Wes said. "No. I don't want to hear it."

"It was the crossing on that forestry road out past the new prison." Dennis's words reduced to a monotone now, the way people's voices got when they weren't sure they could say what needed to be said. "No one thought to look there. That road doesn't go anywhere."

Wes went down on one knee, put a hand to his face. Curled it into a fist, once, twice, three times.

"Those freight trains don't run on a schedule," Dennis said, as though making conversation. "They'd have looked out there eventually. On a different day they might have found him in time."

The tears surprised Wes. He hadn't cried for his father. Hadn't even cried for Claire. Come close, yeah, real close, but he'd always held it in. Only the physical pain Williams had inflicted upon him during the riot had made him spill tears, and that was reflex, nothing more. But now there were two glistening dark spots on the gravel beside his boot, and when he passed his hand over his face his fingers came away wet.

"I think it would have been instant," Dennis said. The words delicate on his tongue, like they might be easily damaged or torn. "Don't you? I don't think he felt anything."

Wes stood slowly. It was as though the pain and stiffness he always felt in his hands had spread throughout his body. Dennis was watching him, his arms still crossed, his shoulders hunched as though he were chilled. Those deep-set eyes Wes had never been able to trust were watching him, pleading. "Come on," Wes said, and put his hand on Dennis's back, between his shoulder blades. He guided him to the porch, and they sat together on the steps.

"I don't think he felt anything, do you?" Dennis asked again. He sounded like the child Wes barely remembered, the boy he had been back when Wes was a different man. "I think it was easy," Dennis said. "Don't you think so, Wes? That it was easy?"

Wes so wanted to take his hand back, but he moved it around Dennis's back to his far shoulder, and his stepson accepted the touch, leaned his whole body into Wes's, the way he had when he was very young, too young, probably, to remember. "Yes," Wes said. "I think it was easy."

～

After the riot, a makeshift memorial for Lane and Bill had sprung up outside the prison. Flowers and candles, letters and cards, photographs, the odd cross or whiskey bottle. Wes had never gone close enough to see any of it in detail, though it'd stayed there for months, long after he'd taken his first shaky walk back through the gate, the sutures from his second surgery still pulling at the skin of his right hand.

There was no memorial beside the railroad crossing on the forestry road. No flowers, no notes. It was the right place, though. A wide twist of metal in the tall grass beside the gravel track bed. A yellow tatter of police tape knotted to the pole of a crossing sign. Too many tire tracks in the mud. Wes parked at the edge of the road, half on the dirt, half in the long dying grass. He stepped out and flipped his collar up against the wind, jammed his hands into his pockets. He'd left Dennis at the kitchen table, a cooling cup of coffee at one elbow, the newspaper — still rolled — at his other. Half the headline visible: *Black River Student Threatens.*

The train had come from the east. Wes stood on a tie, squinted down the track. It didn't disappear behind the curve of the mountains for a good quarter mile. Scott would've seen it coming. Had to sit there in that little run-down car and see that light bearing down and hear the whistle and desperate braking. He'd have had time to embrace, or regret. Wes turned back to the west, walked toward his truck. The spaces between the railroad ties glittered with hundreds of tiny pebbles of safety glass, strewn over the gravel like diamonds. Wes had a sudden vision of those bits of glass, bright against Scott's dyed black hair. Hard not to think of the mechanics of it all. The collision, the force, the folding of careless metal around fragile flesh. Through flesh.

He got back in his truck and turned the heat up high, but didn't put it into gear. He'd had to come out here this morning. Not so much to see the place, though Wes believed there was something that forever marked a place where someone had died. He'd felt it up on the trestle where his father had met his own train all those years ago, and he'd felt it walking past the spot on Two South where Lane had been killed, and he knew he would always, always feel it in the house in Spokane, if he went back there. And he felt it, as he'd known he would, here at this lonely railroad crossing. But that wasn't why he'd come. He was starting to know something he didn't want to know, had been starting to know it ever since Dennis first told him about Scott. He'd kept it at bay all through yesterday afternoon and all night, but he wasn't going to be able to fight it off much longer, and he knew he'd better not come to know it for certain while he was with Dennis.

Wes took his hands from his pockets, held them in front of the dash vent. He thought about the last fiddle lesson. The way the instrument had started to sing again, the way "Black River" began to take shape in the canyon for which it had been named. That long trip for the sweatshirt.

He reached across the cab and lifted the latch of the glove compartment. It fell open easily. He took in the contents in an instant, looked again before letting knowledge root itself in his heart. Maps. A flashlight. Napkins left over from a fast-food restaurant. Registration papers, owner's manual, tire gauge.

No gun.

Dennis was gone when Wes got back to the house—his heavy horseshoeing boots and chore coat missing from the front closet—and he was still gone when the sheriff's deputy pulled up outside the house a few hours later. The dark green pickup coasted to a stop beside Wes's own truck; the weak afternoon sun reflected hard off the dark rack of lights atop the cab, and Wes squinted when he stepped onto the porch. The deputy was close to retirement age, his thick mustache and the short hair showing beneath his broad hat gone white. He walked stiffly toward the house, carrying a rumpled paper bag with a rolled-down top. He looked somehow uneasy in his uniform, though he must have worn it most of his life. "Mr. Carver," he said, and it didn't sound like a question.

Wes nodded.

The deputy reached the porch, extended a hand. "Deputy Randall Morrow," he said. "With the Elk Fork County Sheriff." The handshake was mercifully brief.

"I guess you're here about Scott."

Morrow shifted his weight onto his heels, put his hands on his heavy belt. The bag rested against his holster. "I understand you were close to him," he said. "I'm sorry."

"He stole the revolver."

Morrow looked relieved not to be the one to bring it up, but he frowned a little and said, "You should've called when you learned it was missing."

"Just realized this morning," Wes said. "Figured you boys would put it together in short order."

"Where did you keep it?"

"Glove compartment," Wes said. "Locked. Ain't exactly a gun safe, I know, but I never guessed he'd bust into it." That was true, Wes realized. He hadn't thought twice about letting Scott see where he kept the revolver.

"You really ought to keep your weapons better secured," Morrow said. His voice lacked conviction.

"Guess I know that now," Wes said evenly. He took a step back onto the porch stairs, so he was a couple inches higher than Morrow. Cheap trick. The deputy could've followed if he'd wanted to, but he stayed on the gravel.

After a minute, Morrow pulled the revolver out of the bag, handed it to Wes butt-first. "That yours?"

Wes took the grip in his hand, turned it so the barrel shone in the light. He thought of this gun in Scott's hand, aimed at other people, other children. He wondered how the weight of it—the weapon, what it could do—had felt to him. Whether he had liked it. He wondered, too, whether Scott had taken the time to put the revolver inside the trailer before coming back to sit beside Wes and take up his fiddle for that final lesson. Maybe he'd instead kept it tucked into the oversized pocket of his sweatshirt; maybe it had been there the whole time, that whole afternoon, waiting there while Wes deluded himself into thinking he was making a difference in Scott's life. Had it been that close, this secret?

"Mr. Carver."

"It's mine." Wes snapped the cylinder out. Empty, of course. "He didn't get the ammunition from me," he said. "I keep it separate, and it's all there. Counted it this morning."

"There was no ammunition," Morrow said. "Not so far as we can tell. The weapon was unloaded when it was recovered. We haven't found any cartridges at the school or at the site of the collision. It's possible, I suppose, that he dumped them somewhere between the two locations, but it hardly seems likely."

Wes passed his thumb across the rear of the cylinder, the voids of the chambers. Dennis had loaded the revolver when he'd taken it before their dinner table confrontation so many years ago. Wes had tapped the bullets into his palm after leaving the house that night; they'd rattled against one another in his trembling hand.

"One of the students we interviewed said it looked to him like the chambers were empty during the incident at the school," Morrow continued. He crumpled the paper bag into a tiny ball, clenched it in his fist. "But the sus—Bannon—was threatening him with the weapon at the time, and the student wasn't willing to bet his life on it." Morrow looked up at Wes, something reproachful in his eyes. "Those kids are awfully shook up."

"Don't you try to lay blame on me for this," Wes said.

"I wasn't—"

"I done what I could to help that boy. I know folks want everything to be someone's fault, but you ain't gonna make it mine." Wes turned the revolver around in his hand, extended the grip to Morrow. "I had my doubts about Scott Bannon from the day I met him. I thought for a while that maybe I'd been wrong, but I guess I wasn't. He stole that gun. Busted a lock to get to it. Go look if you want."

Morrow didn't take the revolver. "I came to give that back to you," he said. "What I ought to do is put it into evidence, make you come down and file some paperwork. Maybe you'd get it back someday and maybe you wouldn't. Maybe you'd get a citation. But the way things turned out . . . Bannon didn't hurt anyone but himself. I've worked this county all my life, Mr. Carver. I know who you are, and I know you've had more than your share of trouble in life. Didn't think you needed more. That's all." He turned around, started back toward his truck with the same awkward, ambling gait with which he'd come.

Wes watched him go, felt the burden of the revolver in his hand. He wanted to give it back, wanted to fling it into the river and never see it again. But he couldn't even bring himself to put it down on the porch railing. He loosened and tightened his fingers on the grip, felt metal and wood more firmly against his skin. "Morrow," he called.

The other man slowed, turned like he'd been expecting Wes to stop him.

"I ain't justifying what Scott did," he said. "Not by a long shot. Not ever. But those 'shook-up kids' ain't exactly all sweetness and light, either. Ain't as black and white as it seems."

Morrow nodded. "Never is."

At dinnertime, Wes set two places at the table and heated a can of stew. He kept Dennis's half warm on the stove for a long while, finally emptied it into a plastic container and put it in the refrigerator. There were a handful of business cards on the door of the refrigerator—a veterinarian, a feed merchant, a dentist—a lone, washed-out photograph of a much younger Dennis riding a much younger Rio, and three comic strips cut from a newspaper. Wes lifted the corner of one to look at the underside; it was from the Spokane paper. Claire must have snipped them out and mailed them.

Just before midnight, Wes heard Dennis's truck pull up. A few minutes passed between the sound of the cab door slamming and Dennis's tread on the porch steps. Checking on the horses, or finishing a cigarette. Dennis climbed the steps slowly. When he came inside, he glanced at Wes but didn't speak. He braced one hand on the doorframe while he untied his boots, eased them off his feet. A stiffness to his movements — whether the extra weariness of this day or the regular burden of hard work, Wes couldn't say. Hadn't paid enough attention before. Dennis shrugged off his coat and hooked it over the back of the chair nearest the door. He sat, pulled a second chair away from the table and lifted his feet onto it. "Used to be I could shoe a dozen horses a day, regular," he said. "Did eight today and I'm damn near crippled."

"There's stew in the fridge," Wes said, "if you want it."

"I'm not hungry." He was picking at a scab on his wrist, stopped abruptly. "Maybe later."

Silence fell. Wes listened to the clock in the hall count the seconds. Same clock they'd had years ago, but he didn't remember it being so loud.

"I stopped in to see Molly on my way home," Dennis said finally.

"How is she?"

Dennis smiled, that hard, unamused smile he never aimed at anyone in particular. If there was one expression of Dennis's that Wes had always hated, one expression he wished he never had to see again, that was it. "Well, she's not so good, is she?"

"I meant under the circumstances."

"I don't know, Wes. How do you answer a question like that? I mean, is there a good way to be when your kid's just killed himself?" He passed a hand over his face, letting his fingers drag against the skin. "I guess she's hanging in there."

"Does she have someone taking care of her?" Claire had told him there'd been so many people wanting to help Sara after the riot they'd had to make a schedule. Hard to imagine there was any such clamor to look after Molly Bannon.

"One of the nurses from the hospital was there," Dennis said. "Told me she was staying the night."

"That's good."

Dennis took his feet off the chair, leaned forward over the table, fingertips drumming absently on the wood. "The funeral's Saturday. It's going to be at some church in Elk Fork. Methodist, I think. Molly asked if you and I would each say a few words."

Wes sighed. He'd hoped not to have to get into this tonight. "I'm not gonna go, Dennis."

Dennis looked up, slow. "How's that?"

"I ain't going to the funeral."

A long moment in which Wes couldn't read Dennis's expression one way or another, and then that damned smirk again.

"Let's just leave it," Wes said. "Let's not get into a big argument right now. Can we do that?"

Dennis shook his head, one corner of his lips still turned up. "I am such an idiot," he said. "A naïve fucking fool."

"Dennis—"

"Here I was just starting to think that maybe I hadn't given you enough credit all these years. I thought—despite a lifetime's worth of evidence to the contrary—that maybe you were more compassionate than I realized. That maybe—and this is a fucking laugh—you'd actually changed." He spread his arms wide. "But it turns out you're the exact same rigid, sanctimonious bastard I remember."

Wes crossed his arms over his chest, leaned back in his chair. Tried to remind himself that his stepson was hurting. "I don't think that's fair."

"Fair?" Dennis stood, started pacing across the living room. It was too small to satisfy: a few steps one way, a few steps back. "Fair would be going to the funeral of a kid you pretended to care about."

"Don't you tell me how I felt about Scott."

Dennis stopped in front of Wes, set both hands on the table, leaned in close. Wes smelled horses on him. Realized he'd always associated this scent with him, the coarse wildness of it. "I know exactly how you felt about him. You felt about him the same way you felt about me. You never trusted him, you were always waiting for him to fuck up, you cared about him in a half-assed way only so long as he was trying his damnedest to please you, and now that he's disappointed you, you're abandoning him."

Wes sat silent as long as he could. Kept his hands curled loose on the tabletop. Tried counting his breaths the way Claire was always telling him to do. Even so, he couldn't keep his voice from rising with each word when he finally spoke. "First off, this ain't about you. Did I abandon you? Yeah, Dennis, I guess I did. I know I hurt you, and I know I hurt your momma, and I'm sorry for both those things. If I had it to do over again, I'd try it another way. But I was doing the best I could. I was in pain, too. I guess I can't expect you to understand that, but I sure wish you could."

Dennis leaned against the doorway leading to the kitchen. Looked like a gatekeeper of some kind. Weighing his story. His soul.

"Second, this ain't got nothing to do with being disappointed. Not now, and not back then. You didn't disappoint me; you threatened my life with a loaded firearm. And Scott didn't disappoint me; he terrorized a bunch of schoolkids. He gave himself power over people it wasn't none of his business to have. And that goes way beyond disappointment."

Dennis eyed him critically. He was a little too calm, and that made Wes nervous. Dennis was a live wire, and that could be unpleasant, but Wes was used to that. This calculating, considering Dennis was an unknown. He sighed, pushed himself away from the doorframe. "You need to get the fuck over the riot, Wes." He turned away and walked into the kitchen. Wes followed after a moment, found him leaning into the cupboard over the sink, stretching his arm into its farthest reaches. He pulled down a bottle hazed with dust, no label, amber liquid churning inside. Rooted around again and brought down two small, squarish glasses. He poured heavily into one, held the other toward Wes.

Wes shook his head. "I didn't take you for that sort of drinker."

Dennis downed the contents of his glass in two swallows, poured again. Sloshed a little of the liquid over the rim of the glass; it spattered into a constellation on the counter. "Only on days good as this one."

He lifted his eyes to Wes's; they were sharp and level. "First time I met Scott wasn't at that career day thing I told you about; it was outside Jameson's. He was out there smoking a cigarette and some other kids had cornered him, were saying all this shit about how his father took it up the ass, was the biggest bitch in High Side, that these things ran in families. I came *this close* to punching one of those boys, Wes. A grown man and I'd have hit some punk teenager. Only thing stopped me was Scott grabbed my sleeve." He shook his head. "Maybe I should've done it anyway. Maybe I'd be in jail and he'd be alive."

"Dennis . . ."

"I loved that kid, I really did. I don't know if you loved him, Wes, but I know you cared. So he fucked up! He already paid with his goddamned *life*. You're really gonna let some misguided sense of justice and righteousness and victimhood keep you from paying your respects?"

Wes held Dennis's gaze. "I wouldn't put it that way myself. But yeah," he said, "I am."

Silence. That fucking clock.

Dennis balanced his glass between thumb and forefinger, set the heels of both hands on the edge of the counter on either side of his body. He looked at the floor for a while, cleared his throat once. Glanced up twice before he spoke. "Wes," he said, and his voice carried more gravel than usual, "I'm going to say this real calm. I'm not yelling, I'm not swearing, I'm not storming around. That's because I want you to hear what I'm saying." He sighed deeply, seemed to draw himself straighter as he steeled himself for the words. He looked straight into Wes's eyes, and he said, "I need you out of my house. Tonight. Pack your stuff, get in your truck and get the hell out. I don't care where you go. I don't want to know. And I don't want to see you again."

Wes stared at the floor. Maybe there was still a way to salvage this. Maybe there were still words that could fix it. Actions. But how far back would be far enough? How much did he need to undo? The last few minutes? The last few days? Weeks? Years? Might there be a way to reverse all the worst things in his life, all the wrong decisions, all the misfortunes? Were there opportunities he'd missed, chances to

BLACK RIVER • 179

save Scott, Dennis, Claire, Lane, his mother, his father, himself? Surely there was a way. Why wasn't there a way?

"Dennis, can't we—"

He hurled the glass so quickly Wes hardly saw it coming. It shattered against the brick beside his head, and Wes felt bits of glass rain into his hair, felt a single drop of liquid—liquor, he thought, not blood—slide down the back of his neck. When he raised his head again, he saw that Dennis looked more shocked than Wes felt. His hands trembled slightly, and he crossed his arms and pressed them hard against his chest. He cleared his throat, but when he spoke his voice was husky, and steadier than Wes would have guessed it would be. "You can see," he said, "I need you gone."

PART IV

Divide

Claire returns to Black River in the spring, half a year after she and Wesley left. She goes on a Sunday, and before she leaves, Wesley lifts the hood of the truck and checks and rechecks the oil and the brake fluid and the wiper solution, until she says, You're going to be late for church if you don't quit.

He replaces the oil dipstick one last time, then lets the hood down, pressing on it with the heels of his hands to make sure the latch has caught. You drive real careful, now, he tells her.

I will.

And give me a call when you get there.

I will, Wesley.

And you tell Dennis I said . . . He steps away from the truck, from her. Half turns in the driveway and looks toward the horizon, so she sees his profile. Sees the way he lets his head drop a little before he speaks again. You just tell him I said whatever you think he ought to hear.

It is a good day to travel, sunny until she hits the first pass, and even the clouds over the mountains withhold their rain. Claire finds she has to concentrate on driving more than she used to—these days she gets behind the wheel only to go to the market, or when Wesley's hands trouble him more than usual—but it relaxes her anyway, especially once she has left the city and the largest towns behind.

Halfway up Lookout Pass, the radio surrenders to static. Claire lets it hiss for a few minutes, then reaches into her purse and pushes the cassette she finds there into the player in the dash. She left most of the tapes at the house in Black River—though she's not sure Dennis will want them, wonders if he hasn't already thrown them away—but she kept this one for herself. It is one of the first they recorded, no more special than any of the rest: just an afternoon, a token of what she once had in abundance. The warm-up scales, then "Fire on the Mountain" and "Jerusalem Ridge," "Horses in the Canebrake" for Dennis (she can hear her son laugh in the middle), "Abide with Me" for her, and, as ever, "Black River" for himself. The tape has started to warble a bit; each time she plays it, Claire worries it will spill from the dashboard in a tangle of soundless ribbon. Still she presses Play.

She pilots the truck up the steep curves of the pass, welcomes the embrace of the mountains and listens to the way things used to be.

Her son is outside when she arrives, leaning on the pasture gate. It was off its hinges when she lived here, but now it hangs straight and there is a black horse on the other side. The horse is leggy—young, Claire thinks—and skittish; he spins and trots to the center of the pasture as she steers past the fenceline. Dennis watches him go before he turns toward her. He is seventeen but seems older, his expression inscrutable in a way that is new to her. He is wearing the red shirt she has always liked on him, but she cannot remember ever telling him it is her favorite. As he walks toward the truck, his steps betray a shade of reluctance, and Claire thinks he's trying on the idea of being angry with her. She has prepared herself for this—maybe even longs for it—but when she gets out of the truck he is there to meet her. Hugs, a shy smile, a few clumsy words spoken atop each other. He loves her still.

Dennis does not offer to cook dinner, and Claire is glad. She has yearned to be back in this most familiar kitchen, and even the broken left front burner on the stove sparks a feeling of nostalgic fondness. Dennis has shopped in anticipation of her coming (the vegetables in the refrigerator are dotted with the artificial dew of the grocery shelves), but the pantry still reveals what seems to Claire a painful sparseness, a dedication to only the barest essentials. She is pleased, at least, to make Dennis a strong meal tonight. (And yet, she cannot help but wonder what Wesley will eat when last night's leftovers run out.)

Dennis does most of the talking at the table — Claire eats slowly but finishes while he still has half his meal on his plate — and he tells her about the unusually gentle winter, and a wolf he glimpsed last month down by the river, and most of all about the black horse in the pasture outside. His name is Rio, Dennis tells her, he is four years old, and someday he is going to be his horse. Claire thinks this is probably a wish, the sort of dream that is both necessary and destined to remain unfulfilled (it is not callous to think so, is it?), but her son surprises her.

He's twenty-five percent mine right now, he says, around a bite of potatoes.

How's that?

Uncle Arthur's letting me pay a little bit at a time. Right now I've got him paid up a quarter of the way, but he's still mostly Uncle Arthur's. Dennis grins then, and Claire's heart swells with the sight. I told him I thought that ought to do it, since Rio's a Quarter Horse and he's a quarter paid for and all. He thought that was pretty funny. Said it was a nice try but I still owe him the rest.

I'm glad you have something you love, Claire says. Immediately she wishes she had phrased it differently, or not spoken at all. The words linger uncomfortably.

Dennis cocks his head, gives her a peculiar look that seems to Claire to waver between a plain yearning for solace and a resolve to comfort her. I still miss you, her son says.

~

The summer after Claire moved to Black River — the summer after she met Wesley — they went camping together. He had three days off from the prison, and they left the five-year-old Dennis with Madeline and Arthur and then drove north into the Seeley-Swan Valley. They were almost to the campsite, following a winding logging road high into the mountains, when a deer bounded into the road and out again, and Wesley yelled, Watch it, as though the deer might listen. He braked hard and the truck skidded on dirt and stopped at an angle. He squinted into the woods and said, Ah, would you look at that. It took Claire a moment to find the deer—a small doe—but then she did, there in a stand of trees, and she saw what Wesley had seen. There was a hole in the side of the doe's face, wide and ragged and red, and a glimpse of glistening bone through the torn flesh. Wesley shook his head. They take a shot at her out of season and can't even do her the service of killing her, he said. And then, to her: Stay here.

What surprised Claire was his speed. He was out of the truck and had the rifle at his shoulder in a moment. He fired and the deer fell and the echo came back from the far mountains and Claire still hadn't released the breath she held on first sighting the animal. Wesley staggered down the hill, the rifle held out at his side. He walked to where the doe lay still and looked down at her and came back to the truck. I'll call it in when we get back to town, he said.

Later, at the campsite, when the gold and green of the fields and the blue and silver of the lakes had yielded to darkness, after Wesley had built a fire that lit the edges of his features and sent sparks rising into the air, she said, That deer today.

He looked at her.

Was it hard for you? To kill it?

It was the right thing.

Claire waited, but he seemed to think he had answered the question.

～

She goes back to Black River for two weeks every year. It seems paltry to her, two weeks out of fifty-two, especially when she lives just four hours away. (Always there is a moment, at the end of the trip, right before she leaves, when she thinks she will not get in the truck.) But soon Dennis is no longer a child by any measure, and Arthur is always there for him. Dennis calls twice a week, on Wednesdays and Sundays, and Claire sends him envelopes now and then: coupons she has clipped from the Sunday paper, recipes simple enough for him to try, photographs she has taken during walks in the park in which Wesley always seems to be just leaving the frame.

Still Claire has not found the words Wesley has asked her to offer Dennis on his behalf. Sometimes she tries, on a quiet evening during a visit. Dennis begins to fidget as soon as she mentions Wesley's name, will walk away if she doesn't change the subject. She follows him once, outside into the chill night, and he turns on her, his words sharp and much too loud (she will remember the hard bark even after she has forgotten the words themselves), and then he staggers backward, fists clenched, and orders her not to follow. He does not come back to the house that night, and she does not sleep.

In Spokane, Wesley works. He is a security guard at the mall, a job Claire thinks is beneath his dignity, but when she once gently mentions disability benefits, the look he gives her is so desperate she changes the subject at once. So he works, and just as in Black River, he comes home and showers and changes before he talks to her, and then he talks of anything but his job. There are lines at the edges of his eyes she has not noticed before, and sometimes she has to say something two or three times before he hears her. He sinks into his easy chair with a new caution, as though he does not believe he will be allowed to stay there long. Arthur Farmer makes a point of calling now and then, and Wesley makes a point of not being available when he does.

She can talk about Dennis if she wants to. Wesley will listen. At first she mentions her son only rarely, tentatively, when he is so much on her mind she thinks she will shatter if she cannot speak his name. But Wesley does not storm out, does not scorn her. (She wonders sometimes if he even hears her, he is so silent, but if she stops talking, Wesley will very quietly tell her, Go on now.) She tells him about her worries when Dennis quits school, about her pride when he starts his horseshoeing business, about the way he is almost another man entirely when he is with the horses. She talks, and Wesley listens, and he never says anything but, Go on now, and that is both enough and not enough.

There is a point, some years after the journey between Spokane and Black River has become familiar, that Claire begins to notice the exits. It happens in the middle of the drive, usually just shy of the climb toward the pass. She lets her eyes drift from the centerline and sees all the places she could get off the interstate, all the signs she could follow. All the roads she could take that would lead neither to her son nor to her husband.

But of course she doesn't take them. Doesn't want to do that, doesn't want to see where they go. Not really.

~~~

And Claire's blood and bone marrow turn against her. She accepts the medications, and all they bring with them. Once, twice, three times health seems within her grasp before it is again overtaken by disease. A match is found; she endures the transplant. She comes home; she hopes; Wesley prays. Now it is three days since she learned that those detested cells are back again, unvanquished.

When Dennis calls in the evening, Claire cannot talk to him. She has been in bed all day, though what she feels is not exactly illness, not exactly physical. She looks healthier, in fact, than she has in some months, like someone whose trials are close behind her, yes, but behind her nonetheless. But now she knows better, and when Wesley brings her the phone, a hand cupped over the mouthpiece, Claire shakes her head. It must surprise him—she has never missed the chance to speak to Dennis—but he just presses his lips slightly tighter before he nods and goes back down the hall. Claire closes her eyes and tries to drift back into the refuge of half sleep.

Tired is all, Dennis, Wesley says from the other room.

This ain't worth fretting over.

Don't you go thinking that way.

Claire hears him repeating the things her doctor said to them on

Thursday, but they sound different coming from Wesley's mouth. Where the doctor said, It's your choice, Claire, though you should know the outcomes at this stage are guarded at best, Wesley says, There's plenty of folks come out okay from situations like this, and your momma's stronger than most.

The doctor said, There is a cocktail that has shown some very limited success in post-transplant relapse cases, and Wesley says, There's a new treatment sounds real promising.

The doctor said, I'm sorry I don't have better news for you. Wesley says, You just rest easy, boy.

His voice is closer, and when Claire opens her eyes she sees Wesley in the hall. He leans against the bathroom doorjamb, eyes cast downward. He puts a hand to his face, swipes it beneath his eye, and Claire sees the dashed glimmer of a tear wiped before it can fall. The sight of it shocks her, and his voice as he continues to speak to her son is so calm, so steady, she can almost believe she imagined it.

I ain't worried, Dennis, he says.

(At the clinic, when they got the labs back, Wesley had gasped, a defeated, deflated sound, almost gentle. It was so soft and small Claire thought only she had heard it, so sudden she wasn't sure Wesley even knew he'd voiced it.)

And if I ain't worried, he says, you shouldn't be, either.

Claire listens as Wesley offers Dennis gift after gift. *She's strong. Just a bump in the road. I got no doubts.* She closes her eyes, and though she knows he is not saying these things for himself, is not saying them for her, just for tonight she lets herself be persuaded.

—

Does she know that this trip to Black River will be her last? She has started the chemotherapy again (again!), and though she and Wesley are dredging their last reserves of hope, she knows they are close to empty, and so does he. When she is ready to leave, he glances first at the kerchief in her hair (odd that she thinks of it that way, *in her hair,* when she wears it only to cover what's gone), then at her.

Maybe this ain't a good idea, he says. You going so far just now.

It's only for a few days, Wesley.

I know it, but I hate to think . . .

Afterward Claire will wonder why she does not fill the silence that follows Wesley's words. Maybe fatigue is to blame; she is so often tired now. Maybe fear, or even anger, buried so far down she doesn't recognize it. Maybe she suspects, deep in her bones, that any reunion, any tenuous bond between the two men she loves that is brokered only on her behalf will not sustain. Because Claire knows, in that moment in the driveway, that if she asks Wesley to come with her, to drive her to Black River and stay there with her while she visits Dennis, he will say yes. If she asks, he will go.

But she does not ask. He does not offer. There is a long silence between them, so weighted Claire is later certain Wesley comes as close to offering as she does to asking. Then a car drives past, and Claire blinks, and Wesley looks just slightly away from her. And she says, I'll call you when I get there.

Dennis is more like Wesley than he would like to admit. He, too, knows how ill she is, and Claire thinks he, too, would deny it if asked. He might even believe the denial, but she can see the truth in the way he keeps his voice softer than she knows it to really be, the way he checks his sharper edges and treats her with the gentleness he usually reserves for animals.

They do not discuss it. They talk at lunch and in the evenings, about the news and town gossip and television programs they have both seen. They go to Arthur Farmer's house for dinner one night, and he serves meatloaf Claire recognizes as her sister's recipe, and he calls her sweetheart, the way he did when she was young. Claire goes with Dennis to his horseshoeing appointments, and she sits in the truck with the door open and the heater on and she watches her son work. It is not the life she would have chosen for him—no diploma, outdoors in all weather, work that will break his body in the end—but she can see that what he does with these horses is a reprieve. Here he is focused, he is skillful, he is calm and sure. Here he is all the things he is not in the rest of his life.

I want to go riding, she says on her last day. She can see Dennis working to formulate an objection, so she quickly adds, I was born and raised in Montana, and I've lived my whole life in the West, and I've never been on a horse.

He is silent a moment more and then says, Okay.

He gives her Rio. She stands beside the hitching rack while Dennis goes back to the pasture to get the other horse, and she lets her fingers glide down the long bones of Rio's face and through his mane and up the edge of his ear, along the gentle curve to the tip, where the short hairs stand soft and delicate.

He doesn't usually like people to touch his ears, Dennis says from behind her. Claire takes her hand away, but Dennis says, All I said was he doesn't usually like it. Seems like he's good just now.

A horse's back is higher than Claire expected, and she wraps both hands tightly around the saddle horn. She knows it's a mere few feet of added height, but the house looks different from here, the trees, the pasture, the mountains. She can see the dark glimmer of the river. Dennis mounts the other horse and Rio follows him as he starts off across the pasture at a walk. Claire feels that the slightest breeze might cause her to tumble to the ground, but Rio walks steadily and Claire lets herself settle into the rhythm of his steps. (She will never tell Wesley about this; he would worry even after the fact.) Dennis takes her around the big pasture twice, then leads her through the aspens at the far end, beside the riverbank. They stop at the water's edge, the horses' front hooves just wetted.

So, do you feel like a cowgirl now? Dennis asks.

Ready for the rodeo, Claire tells him, and she is rewarded with the smile she had hoped for. She leans her head back to look up the sharp angle of the slope on the other side of the river. Do you ever ride up in the hills?

Dennis nods.

Next time we'll go up there, Claire says.

Next time, Dennis agrees, but the words grate a little leaving his throat.

Claire looks at him, and he looks at the water. She had hoped that being with the horses would keep that smoldering anger at bay, but Dennis seems unable to keep from feeding it, fanning it. She considers not saying what she means to say, but she should do it now. She must. You know I wish you and Wesley could be family again, she says.

Dennis turns to her so sharply his horse tosses its head and stamps a foot in the water, sending drops into the air. They land back in the river as widening circles that the current steals away almost before Claire can fix her eyes on them.

I won't ask you to go to him, she continues. I know you can't do that, not now and maybe not ever. But Denny, if he comes to you, will you let him?

Dennis doesn't seem to move, but his horse sidesteps one way, then the other, then turns a tight circle at the water's edge. And then he guides the horse past her and his features are set like stone and he does not look at her, but she hears the words as he passes, as faint as if they had been borne on the breeze from some distant place.

I will try.

~

On her way back to Spokane, she pulls off the road at the top of the pass, nudging the pickup into line beside the long-haul truckers cooling their rigs' engines. She gets out of the cab and walks to the edge of the road, steps just beyond the heavy guardrail. Here she can see for miles both ahead and behind. Always Claire has been aware that whether she is with her husband or her son, she is not with the other. She has tried to think of both places as her homes: Washington and Montana, Spokane and Black River, her husband's house and her son's. But instead of feeling that she has two homes, too often she has felt she has none.

Only here do both seem close. Only here are they not unequivocally divided by this landscape that magnifies and emphasizes distance. There, beyond those peaks, is her son, who does not know how to reconcile and may not want to. There, beyond those others, is her husband, who does not know how either, but (Claire has always believed and still believes) does know that it is right. Dennis, there, and Wesley, there. Both hers.

Claire stays on top of the pass for a long time, looking first one way and then the other, trying to keep both places, both men, in sight at once. To keep them together. It is not quite possible. But Claire knows that even this land — the cradle of canyon, these seemingly immovable mountains, this etched horizon — has not always been this way, and will not always be this way. What she looks upon now is a moment in history, and it will pass. Claire will not be here to see it, and she cannot say how things will be different, but she is certain: given enough time, even this will change.

There was just one motel in Black River, the sort mostly found on lonely highways in lonely towns that had been long since bypassed by interstates. This one had hung in there thanks to the prison; when Wes pulled into the gravel lot after midnight, he saw that the other vehicles all bore license plates stamped with county codes from the eastern part of the state. Folks wanting to visit inmates couldn't always make the trip in one day. The experienced ones flocked to the anonymity of the Motel 6 in Elk Fork; the rest came here and holed up in their rooms till it was time to go home again. The place was called the Sapphire Lodge, though there was nothing especially lodge-like about it, unless you counted the lone buck mounted over the registration desk, who'd had the misfortune to be stuffed by a taxidermist who seemed to believe animals ought to look surprised to find themselves dead. Wes talked the bleary-eyed owner into a discount; even so, it left him with a thinner stack of bills in his envelope than he'd have liked.

His room was clean and bland, little different from the half-dozen motel rooms he'd stayed in during Claire's transplant in Seattle. Unlike those, though, this one stood apart, its own small building separated by eight or nine feet from the units on either side. Quieter. He found himself wishing he were sharing walls. He'd have welcomed the mild irritation of others' voices, the murmurs that rose and fell but never coalesced into distinct words and sentences, the rattles and knocks of movements that weren't his own. In Seattle, he'd found that those things served as a promise that the larger world still existed, that there was something waiting beyond the fear and grief that had so totally absorbed him then, that he might someday get back to that safer and easier place.

He could think now, in this oppressive quiet, of all the things he should have said to Dennis, all the things he couldn't put voice to. That this was the second time in his life he'd been stunned by a suicide he should've seen coming. That he was angry at Scott, yes, that he couldn't explain the horror of knowing Scott had terrorized those people, absolutely, but more than that, he couldn't bear the thought of going to Scott's funeral and seeing his lips shut, his hands idle, forever. It'd be a closed casket—the train, the train, the train—but Wes would know. He'd see it anyway. Still hands. Silent lips.

He felt a familiar rending starting in his chest, small now, slight, as though his heart were tearing slowly, fiber by fiber. God, he missed her. Wes hadn't always been good about sharing his burdens with Claire. Held back too much. He wished he had all those opportunities back now, all those times he'd known she was yearning to help. Claire wouldn't have been able to make this new loss better, but she'd have known how to help him bear it.

He turned to his Bible instead and flipped through the pages, a book or two at a time. Couldn't find what he was looking for—didn't even know what that was—and he wondered what Williams looked for in these same pages. What he found. In the end, Wes read aloud from Psalms, and Ecclesiastes, and the Gospel of John. Then he read the story of the Fall, because that seemed important somehow, and about Lot's wife turning to salt, because no matter how the preachers tried to explain that one, it'd never seemed just to Wes. And finally he read the first verses of the forty-third chapter of Isaiah, over and over, because he had always understood that these were supposed to be comforting words. *When thou passest through the waters, I will be with thee; and through the rivers, they shall not overflow thee . . .* But though the words were familiar on his lips and gentle on his ears, they taunted him with the promise of a peace and solace beyond his faithless grasp, and they brought no comfort.

The week passed slowly. Wes kept the Do Not Disturb hangtag on the outside doorknob, and he left the curtains drawn. They didn't close all the way, and during the day he sat on the bed and watched the slim shard of sunlight slowly cross the carpet. He tried not to think of Scott, or Dennis, or Williams, or Claire. He tried not to think about suicides and hearings and mortgage payments he couldn't pay and how much his hands ached. He tried not to think.

Each day he went to the IGA, late, fifteen minutes before closing — the place empty, the teenage clerk glaring at him as he walked up and down the aisles — and then he went back to the dark motel and ate cold chicken or macaroni salad. There was a No Smoking placard on the bedside table where the ashtray would've been a few years back; Wes tapped his ash into a drinking glass from the bathroom. He sat and smoked, and he watched the light from the streetlamps. It was yellower than the sunlight, but duller, and it did not move.

Saturday morning Wes rose early. He showered and shaved painstakingly, then dressed in his best shirt, his suit, his oxfords, his tie. Took him more than an hour, but he'd given himself time. When he was ready, he sat in the chair beside the television and waited until the red numbers on the bedside clock showed him that he'd have to leave now, and then that he'd have to speed, and finally that it was too late to make Scott's service no matter how fast he drove.

The knock came several hours later. It was light, a woman's knock, and Wes knew he was paid up and had left the Do Not Disturb sign on the knob, so he wasn't entirely surprised when he opened the door and found Molly Bannon outside. She wore a navy-blue dress and no coat, though Wes had to brace against the cold. Her hair was loose and the wind snapped it into and then away from her face. She was pale, but her eyes were clear, the skin below them smooth and tight, and Wes wondered if maybe she was too deep into grief to cry yet. She held his fiddle case in one hand. "Dennis told me you would probably be here."

"Come in," Wes said, and he brought the door wide. The sun was already below the mountains, and it had snowed without his noticing. The white dusting came halfway down the slopes, an encroaching threat above the town.

Molly shook her head. "I just came to give you this." She nodded to the fiddle case, but made no move to hand it to him. "Scott left a note on it." Wes saw it now, a square of white paper attached to the lid with a piece of tape. When Molly didn't say anything else, Wes leaned down and took the note off the case. The tape lifted the top black layer of the chipboard with it, leaving a pale brown patch behind. He looked down at the paper. A single line in the middle of the sheet. Cursive. He hadn't known they still taught cursive. *Please give this back to Mr. Carver. It is his.* Wes flipped the paper over. Blank.

"It's the only note he left." Molly's voice was strong, strangely normal, but she was looking somewhere over Wes's shoulder, not really at him. "The only thing that . . . shows he meant to do what he did."

Did she know the gun was his? Wes wondered if this was some kind of test, if he was supposed to say it first. But maybe she didn't know. Maybe all she'd been told was "stolen handgun." He held the note out to Molly, but she looked at it like she didn't know what it was, and the wind tried to cheat it from his hand, so after a minute he took it back and put it in his pocket. "You sure you don't want to come in? There's a coffeepot. Probably ain't any good, but I could make you a cup."

"I just came to give you this," she said again, and this time she moved the fiddle case toward him. Their fingers touched when he took it from her.

Wes adjusted his grip on the handle, glanced down. "I meant for him to keep it."

"I know," Molly said, and met his eyes. "I'm not sure he'd figured that out yet, but I did."

Another sustained gust — arctic air, bearing winter down — and Wes felt gooseflesh rise on his arms beneath his clothes. He set the fiddle case at his feet, took off his suit coat. "If you won't come in, put that on at least."

She took the coat and held it by its collar for a long moment before draping it over her shoulders. Looked him up and down, and seemed to notice his clothes for the first time. "He tried once before," she told him after a minute. "A month after we moved here. I found him sitting in the shower with his wrists cut. It wasn't a 'cry for help,' either. He cut the long way. Deep." She drew one index finger up the inside of her opposite wrist. "If I hadn't come home early . . ." Wes thought about the long sleeves, the knitted arm warmers, the ubiquitous hooded sweatshirts. The things he of all people ought to have noticed. "I should have taken him home to Miles City then," Molly said. "I never should have brought him here in the first place. I wanted him to be close to his dad was all."

"You were just trying to do right."

"Maybe I wasn't. Maybe I came here because I was afraid to be alone with my son. Maybe I came here because I was trying too fucking hard to prove that I still loved my husband." Wes didn't have anything to say to that. He knew what this was. This was Molly saying things she couldn't say to anyone who mattered, Molly saying things to him because she was never going to see him again, because she already knew his secrets. "I should have taken him home before," she said, "but I'm taking him home now. I don't want him buried here."

"You gonna stay with him?" Wes asked. "In Miles City?"

Molly looked down at her shoes. Pretty shoes, open toes, wrong for this weather. Finally she nodded, slow, like she was making the decision right this minute. "Connor doesn't know yet. They didn't let him come to the funeral." She looked directly at Wes again. "What do you think of that?"

"It's a hard thing," he said.

"He's been crazy since they told him about Scott," Molly said softly.

Wes remembered walking inmates down to the warden's office. Sometimes they knew, if they had someone who'd been sick awhile, or old, but mostly they didn't. Wes remembered standing there, retreating behind his stone face, while the warden told the inmate he was *so sorry to inform* . . . And then the walk back to the cellblock. Always took longer, the walk back.

"I'm sorry," Wes said.

Sorry they didn't let your husband come to your son's funeral.

Sorry I didn't go, either.

Sorry it was my revolver.

Sorry I can do nothing for you but say sorry, sorry, sorry.

Molly took Wes's coat off her shoulders, folded it once the way Claire would have before holding it between them. Wes wanted so much to leave her with something. To offer something she could take with her. But the fiddle would bring no comfort, and Wes had nothing else. He took his coat back and understood that any chance he'd had to give was gone.

He dozed, and when he woke it was dark. Wes changed out of his funeral clothes and put his jeans and flannel shirt and boots back on. He was out of food and cigarettes. Twenty minutes till the IGA closed.

When he went outside, Wes found Arthur Farmer's truck parked in front of his room. Farmer was huddled inside the cab, hat tipped a little over his face. The engine was idling, a white plume of exhaust rising from below the tailgate, and Wes could hear the higher registers of a song playing on the radio. Farmer stepped out of the truck when he saw him. Wes tried to read his expression, but Farmer knew at least as much as he did about controlling one's features. Wes flipped his collar up against the wind—it'd died down a touch since Molly was here, but gone colder to make up for it—and pushed his hands deep into his pockets. "How long you been out here?" he asked.

"Hour or so."

"You didn't knock."

"You wouldn't have answered if I did," Farmer said, and it was just a statement, not an accusation.

Wes leaned against the side of the truck. He, Farmer and Lane had driven all over the state in a truck like this one, all night most of the time, chain-smoking and stopping on the side of the road to take a piss and twisting the radio dial trying to find something other than hellfire-and-brimstone preaching. They'd gone west to east and west again, from county fair to rodeo to honky-tonk to dive bar, hardly ever getting paid enough to cover their gas. Wes glanced into the bed now, half expecting to see instrument cases. Bags of horse feed, a couple battered buckets, a single frayed rope.

"So how was it?" he asked.

Farmer had let his eyes drift, but he brought them around. "What?"

"The service."

"It was hard," Farmer said, "but good. The preacher had a nice way with words, and the choir sang some. I didn't know Scott all that well, but I think he'd have liked that. The music."

Wes nodded a few too many times. "Many folks there?"

"Not many."

"Any kids?"

"None that I saw."

Wes looked at the gravel beneath his feet, forced his eyes back up to meet Farmer's. "It wasn't because of the suicide," he said.

Farmer smoothed a hand over his mustache but didn't say anything.

"That's not the reason I didn't go to Scott's funeral. It wasn't because it was a suicide, and it didn't have nothing to do with my father."

"I guess I hadn't thought about that part of it," Farmer said. "I just figured you had your reasons."

"Don't tell me you hadn't thought about it. You wouldn't be sitting outside my goddamned motel room for an hour if you didn't believe I was maybe spending too much time thinking about people killing themselves."

"If I was that worried, I wouldn't have waited around outside." He forged ahead. "But I was thinking. You shouldn't be wasting your money on this motel. Come stay at the house."

Wes wanted to say *No, hell no.* The days when such an invitation could be considered casual by either one of them were long gone. Fact was, though, Wes couldn't afford to say no right out. Literally couldn't afford it. He had just enough left in the envelope to get him to the hearing, sure, and probably enough gas to get back to Spokane. No more.

"There's the room upstairs," Farmer said. "I don't hardly ever go

up there. I wouldn't be in your business all the time, that's what's worrying you."

Wes blinked hard against the sting of the wind. "It'll get you in hot
water with Dennis."

"Dennis doesn't get to decide who my houseguests are."

Wes swallowed. Thought about the money. And the revolver, waiting. "Well, I tell you, Farmer, it'd be a help. Strapped with the medical
bills and all."

Farmer waved off the gratitude, like he didn't know exactly how
much it cost Wes to accept his offer. "Be good to have a little company,"
he said.

After church the next day, Wes left a twenty for the maid—Claire
had done that work once, before they met—and drove over to Farmer's place. Almost missed the turn, the way to his own house—Dennis's
house—was so ingrained. He left his fiddle downstairs in the living
room, in the corner beside Farmer's guitar and Lane's banjo. The room
upstairs had a single bed with whitewashed wrought iron at the head
and foot. A small dressing table next to it, a lamp and Bible resting on
a lace doily. A rocking chair beside the window, with a knitted afghan
folded neatly over the back. The room was painted a sunny yellow,
with white rabbits chasing each other around the perimeter, up near
the ceiling. Repurposed as a guest room, Wes realized, but intended
as a nursery. He looked again at the rabbits. Each had a green bow
painted around its neck.

"You settle in," Farmer said, lingering in the hall. "I was thinking
we'd eat at seven-thirty—that all right?"

"Sounds good."

The window faced west. Wes had been hoping it wouldn't, that
he'd be in the room across the hall instead, but it was crowded with
boxes and loose furniture. He heard Farmer moving downstairs, and
he went to the window and looked. The arena was on the far side of the
yard, the broodmare pastures beyond that. A half-dozen mares grazing, their coats gone dull and fluffy with the coarse winter hair grow-

ing in. And past them was a fence, and three more animals. They were far enough off that Wes could pick out the mule only by color; the long ears and sparse tail were details lost to distance. He could see the back of the workshop, and a bit of the house, a patch of white through the trees. He'd see Dennis if he caught him walking to his truck or checking on the horses.

Dinner was hamburgers—Farmer was careful; no more steaks—and afterward they went to the living room. Farmer switched on the television, and they watched a cop show set somewhere sunny and colorful. The characters all had lengthy backstories, and Farmer dutifully explained them all to Wes. It satisfied Wes to know that Farmer watched television often enough to know all these details. Seemed a little bit of a flaw in his character, and it made him easier to like. When the show was over, the local news came on; they were still talking about Scott. *No new developments,* the anchorwoman said.

"What 'new developments' they expect?" Wes asked. "The kid's dead."

Farmer turned the television off. "It's just a slow news time," he said. "They'll be on to something else soon enough."

The riot had dominated the news for weeks. So many reporters called the house that Claire had started leaving the phone off the hook.

"You can play your guitar if you want," Wes said. "I'm guessing that's what you usually do about this time."

Farmer watched him closely for a minute, but didn't ask was he sure, and Wes was grateful. Wasn't sure how convincing he could sound if he had to insist. The old Martin was already out of its case, resting on a guitar stand within reach of Farmer's easy chair. He took it up and tuned it, and even that was devastatingly familiar, the sequence and timing of the plucks, the little ten-note melody Farmer played once he thought he'd tuned right.

He'd gotten better. Of course he had, twenty years gone by, twenty years of daily practice. Farmer had always been a solid rhythm guitarist. It was an underappreciated skill, and vital to the band, but not especially showy. The breaks Farmer had taken on the bluegrass numbers had been competent but fairly simple, anything more than basic fingerpicking beyond his reach. Now he played quickly and clearly, and though there was still a hint of the rote about his playing—Wes would bet good money that Farmer always played a given tune exactly the same way—his fingers were fast and clean on the strings. Even now, he couldn't hold a candle to the way Lane or Wes had played back in the day, but he'd come into his own as a musician. He seemed proud of it, though he was careful to check the pride so it showed only in the slightest satisfied upturn of one corner of his mouth.

Wes didn't recognize the first tune he played, or the second. "Play something I know," he said.

Farmer glanced sideways, and Wes saw he was right; Farmer had been avoiding the old tunes on purpose. He laid his palm flat over the strings, drummed his fingertips against the wood for a minute, then started in on "Blackberry Blossom." It was a bluegrass standard, one they'd played at almost every show. Wes knew it forward, backward, upside down and sideways, but he'd never heard it like this. If he was honest, Wes had never thought much of the guitar. Though he'd only ever loved the fiddle, he could appreciate the allure of the banjo and the mandolin; the guitar, on the other hand, had seemed almost dull. No more. Farmer brought his attention to notes in such a way it was like Wes had never heard them before, and he kept a driving rhythm all the while. Lord, what Wes wouldn't have given to play this onstage again. He could hear where Lane would start in on one of his crazy-fast licks, rolls all up and down the strings, slides and hammer-ons and pull-offs, and then Farmer would come back in, yeah, and do what he was doing right now, and then it would be his turn, Wes's turn, and this is where he'd quit chopping and pull out all his slides and double-stops and slurs, and here came the shift from G to E minor, then the line he'd play so fast he'd snap a couple horsehairs, and he'd finish his break with a flourish and then blend back into the group, so easy, all together then, all three of them.

"Right nice," Wes said, when Farmer was done. The words choked a little coming out, and they weren't even his; they were Lane's, the understated praise he'd offer after an especially strong practice or performance.

Farmer nodded his thanks, set the guitar back on its stand. "Wish you could play with me." He said it simple, quiet, and despite the fact that Wes sometimes had a hard time with Farmer, Wes was glad to be with someone who knew him as he had been. Without Claire, he realized, there would be no one left back in Spokane who had ever heard him play. No one who knew he'd ever touched wood and horsehair.

"That's really why I got to go to this hearing, you know." Wes crossed one boot over his knee. Thought for a minute. "Those folks on the board, they read the reports and think the riot was a couple days of hard times, bad enough, maybe, but over and done with. They don't know what-all he took."

Farmer looked toward the window, but it was dark and Wes knew he wasn't seeing anything but the reflection of the lights inside the living room. "Try not to take this the wrong way, Wesley," he said, "but I'm gonna call bullshit on that."

Wes set his teeth against each other. "Why's that, exactly?"

"You weren't so hell-bent on going to this hearing till you heard about Williams getting religion. You hadn't done that, I think I'd probably been able to talk you out of going."

"You saying I don't care that my goddamn hands look like this?" Wes held them up, palms toward his face, the fingers so far from parallel they'd have looked comical if not so grotesque.

"No," Farmer said. "I'm saying if the question of faith hadn't gotten all mixed up in this, you might've talked yourself into not giving a shit about Williams. I mean, where's he from, Wesley? Dawson County? The hell kind of life you think an ex-con's gonna have out there? He ain't winning anything here, no matter what the parole board decides."

"He's got to be faking," Wes said. "The born-again thing. Guys like that are always faking."

Farmer raised an eyebrow.

"Don't give me that, Farmer!" Wes slammed his hand down on the arm of the chair. The cushion gave, and it wasn't the sharp blow he'd been hoping for. "I walked the tiers for twenty-one years. You think I don't know there are some halfway decent inmates? Sure, some of 'em move forward while they're inside. They study for their GED, they make toys for other inmates' kids at Christmas, they get sober and mean to stay that way, whatever. But I cringe every time I hear some-one say one of 'em is a different person. They ain't different. They're still exactly the same person who did whatever the hell landed them in a cell."

"You telling me you ain't ever seen a sincere conversion? I think I have, now and then."

Wes stood, paced across the room one way and then the other, ended up near the corner with the instruments. He nudged his fiddle case with the toe of his boot. "Do you remember how I played, Farmer? I mean, really remember?"

"Yes," he said softly. "I do."

Wes knelt, pushed up the snaps on the case, lifted the lid. "What I had with this fiddle," Wes said, "came from somewhere. My father taught me to play, okay, tunes and where to put my fingers and so on. But I had something else he couldn't teach me. The first day I touched my first fiddle, I had something, under all that beginner's awfulness, something my father never had and was never gonna have, no matter how many hours he put in."

"I know."

Wes took the fiddle in his hand and stood, and with the same ges-ture, the same rising, he brought it to his collarbone and lifted his chin and looked down along the varnished body to where Farmer sat. And with that single motion, he recalled the fine details of hundreds of days and evenings with this fiddle in this room, with this other man and a ghost. Days and evenings long past, still so close he could almost enter into them. "Whenever I picked up my fiddle, that something was there. All my life. I felt it, and anyone listening heard it. And whether you call it talent or a gift or magic or whatever else, that came from some-where, right? Had to come from somewhere." Farmer was staring, and it wasn't until Wes brought the fiddle back down to his side and let it dangle alongside his leg that the other man nodded, once, slow. "What I felt when I played," Wes said, "was the only thing that ever made me believe there was something else. Something more than just folks going through the motions day after day until there weren't no more days to come."

"God," Farmer said.

"Guess so."

Farmer rose and crossed the room to Wes. He took the fiddle from Wes's hand, gently, and knelt to lay it back in its velvet. "You know what the biggest test of my faith has been? Biggest in my life?"

Wes waited, but Farmer kept a knee on the floor, hands working the ribbons over the fiddle's slender neck, and Wes realized he expected a response. "Madeline," he offered. "The accident."

Farmer closed the lid, snapped it shut. He rose, turned. "You," he said. Wes looked down at the fiddle case. Maybe he ought to leave it here, with Lane's Gibson. A shrine to what used to be. "I know it's been a long time since we were close, Wesley. And I know you think I'm a meddlesome old man—don't argue. Some truth to that, I know. But I'm also your brother-in-law, and I think I'm still your friend. So I hope you won't see it as overstepping if I say it's plain to me that all your life you been looking for something you ain't found." He looked Wes in the eye, and Wes saw a flicker of doubt that was stark as it was slight, there in the eyes of a man Wes had always assumed to be nothing less than assured in all things. "It's made me question, Wesley. I don't know why a good man like you can search and search and still not find what he's looking for. I don't know why the one thing that seemed to be leading you toward it got torn away from you like it did. I'm ashamed for all the times I told folks in the Bible study it was easy, that faith was just there for the taking, 'cause I see now it's not always like that." He stopped suddenly, ran a hand over his mustache once, twice.

Wes said, "Feels like you're still working up to the moral of the story."

Farmer stepped closer, dropped his voice. "Don't go to this hearing, Wesley."

Wes glanced at the floor, felt his jaw clench. "You ain't the first to tell me that."

"That's because it ain't gonna do you any good. Whether Williams walks or doesn't, whether he's really found God or hasn't, none of that has anything to do with you, Wesley. None of it's gonna get you any closer to what you're looking for. And just . . . don't quit looking for it, all right? Don't give up. I don't know why you ain't found what you need yet, but it's out there, and I do believe it's gonna come to you in time."

Wes's first impulse was to say time was starting to get short, but he looked again into Farmer's eyes and saw the confusion there, and he felt his own features gentle a little. "I appreciate what you're saying," he said. "I do. But one thing I can tell you for certain is that someone else's faith just ain't much comfort."

—

Tuesday morning he woke early, before Farmer. He'd set the alarm but didn't need it; he'd slept only fitfully, never certain whether the images loitering half hidden at the edges of his consciousness were dream or memory. He took his time dressing. No tie today—it mattered, for some reason, that he offer something casual in his appearance—but he wore his suit coat over a crisp white shirt. Liked the idea of two sets of sleeves. He'd taken to wearing his hair a little ruffled these past few years—Claire combed it loose with her fingers if he didn't—but today he put a hard part in it, the way he had when he was younger. He looked at himself for a long time in the mirror, meeting his own gaze until he was satisfied he still knew how to control every feature, even his eyes. He set them steady and cold. Might be better to let something show through, give the board easier access to a sympathetic victim, but if he yielded even the slightest bit, he wasn't sure he could keep the emotion burning in his heart from spilling onto his face. All or nothing. It'd gotten him through twenty-one years inside the gate. Surely it could get him through a couple hours more.

He hadn't heard Farmer rise, but he was in the kitchen when Wes went downstairs, listening to the final percolations of the coffeemaker.

Farmer filled a mug almost to the brim and slid it across the counter toward Wes, who nodded his thanks and drank without waiting for it to cool. "I'll go with you if you want," Farmer said quietly.

"I ain't an old woman," Wes said. "You don't got to hold my hand." He closed his eyes, passed a hand over his face. More on edge than he knew. "Sorry. I didn't aim to take your head off like that."

Farmer accepted the apology without acknowledging it, offered a slight, hesitant smile. "Didn't really expect you to take me up on it," he said. "Wouldn't feel right not putting it out there, though." They drank in silence for a few minutes. Wes could hear an early freight passing through the canyon, its whistle sounding more clearly in the cool morning air than it did during the height of the day. "You remember Jamie Lowell?"

"Worked evening watch on Lane's tier, didn't he?"

Farmer nodded. "He's a sergeant now, in Max. Good officer. I gave him a call yesterday, and he's gonna meet you inside. I know you don't like me sticking my nose in, Wesley, but I figured you'd rather deal with someone you don't have to explain yourself to." He scratched his bald spot absently. "He'll let you stay after. Let you know what the board decides." Wes heard a hint of dubiousness in his last words.

"I know they might parole him, Farmer." Wes leaned back against the counter, tightened his hands against its edge. "I ain't gonna lose it, that's what you're thinking." He glanced at the clock. It was one of those cartoon-cat types, with the swinging tail and shifty eyes. Must've been Madeline's. "Well," he said, "guess I better get going."

He made himself meet Farmer's eyes, and waited for the platitudes and words of wisdom he figured Farmer had been saving up for this moment. But Farmer just gazed back, nodded once and said, "Guess so."

He stopped at the gas station on Main Street to use the head. Should've skipped the coffee; he was plenty alert, and it made him need to piss. And nerves. Nerves did that, too.

There were things he'd never told Claire, never told the folks who came to interview him and write down every word he said. During the riot, Williams had pissed in the corner of the control room—no toilet, of course, but he didn't even use the wastebasket. Pissed right down the side of the wall, a stream that soaked into the concrete where wall met floor, golden drops clinging to the thick industrial paint on the cinderblocks. The acid odor had made Wes suck his breath in through his teeth for a few minutes, but he'd already been smelling blood and his own burned flesh and the horrible sick scent that carried into the room on the smoke from the fires on the tiers. Wasn't like the prison smelled nice even on a good day. But hours into the riot, Wes had to go, too. Held it long as he could. He didn't want to ask Williams and risk setting him off, but finally the need was stronger than the fear, and he asked. Asked again. Begged, in the end. Still Williams denied him, and finally, without really making the decision, Wes pissed himself. Fought all the shame and anger and despair deep down into the depths of his heart and tried not to notice his own urine flowing warm down his leg, pooling in the chair and wetting the inside of one boot, puddling between his bound feet. His trousers had still been damp when he was rescued.

Wes smoked a cigarette in the parking lot, ground it out beneath his boot and lit another. Got in the truck and pulled back onto the road.

Clouds were beginning to come in over the mountains from the southwest when Wes turned onto the prison grounds, and the walls of the three main buildings—Low Side, High Side and Max—were silhouetted against the empty expanse of land in which they sat. Nothing like the old prison in town, this facility was bland and utilitarian, the three nearly identical structures set way back against the hills, a collection of smaller buildings scattered around them like unwanted offspring. From the road, Wes could just make out a figure moving at the top of the nearest tower. The sun was high in the sky, but inside the fences the metal-halide lights were all ablaze. The place was huge and imposing, yet impossibly dwarfed by its surroundings. The canyon opened up here, meadow stretching back toward foothills that gave way to the mountains that rose above the walls and towers. Ludicrous, in a way, to set a piece of this land off with concertina wire and electrified fences, even for the purpose of locking away the Bobby Williamses of the world.

The visitors' lot was mostly empty, just a half-dozen other cars and trucks bunched up at the near end. It was oddly silent as Wes walked the long, fenced outdoor corridor leading to the visitors' entrance. At the old prison, the yard had bound itself so tight around the buildings that sound leaked from inside the cellblocks, through the broken panes of glass high up on the walls, through the very bricks, it seemed. Once inside the gate, it had been impossible to pretend there weren't hundreds of inmates in there with you. Here, though . . . if he could've ignored the razor wire and the watchtowers, the place might've been an especially ugly school campus or business park.

At the check-in counter, Wes set himself to the paperwork. His name. Inmate's name. Driver's license number. Reason for entry. By the time he signed his name for the final time, his right hand was throbbing. Good. Feel it.

"Sergeant Lowell should be just another minute, sir," the CO told him, pulling the clipboard and its chained pen back into his booth.

Wes nodded.

"Um . . . I'm sure they'll deny parole," the officer said. Wes glanced back at him. Kid hardly looked any older than Scott, but of course he had to be. Light brown hair, forehead pocked with acne scars. Strong set to his jaw, though. "We study the, the . . . what happened in 'ninety-two. At the academy."

Wes looked at him for a long moment. He wondered what the kid saw when he looked at him. Something like a ghost, he supposed. A story to tell the other young COs at the bar tonight. *Carver. You know, from the riot . . .* "Well," he said, "can't say I share your confidence, but I hope you're right." It was good to talk like this. Good to practice being calm and collected, to make the fine adjustments to his voice so it would carry him when it was his turn to speak his piece.

He turned at the sound of sharp and purposeful footsteps. Jamie Lowell was well into middle age now, but he still looked like the man

Wes remembered, if more solid, more confident. "Wes Carver," he said. "Good to see you, even if under shitty circumstances."

Wes nodded, hoped he could forestall a handshake. "Sergeant."

Lowell winced a little, laughed. "Hell, don't call me that. I'd like to think we always got along all right."

Wes forced a smile to match Lowell's. "Jamie it is."

They walked together down corridors that were new to Wes, but familiar nonetheless. Lines on the floor, painted silhouettes of footprints next to doorways, signs warning inmates to stay quiet, stay in line, stay away from the CO desks. Something important seemed absent, and it took Wes a few minutes to realize it was because of the relative silence with which Lowell moved. No keys. In Wes's day, they'd all carried great rings of keys on their belts, and the jangling announced their approach to fellow officer and inmate alike. The inmates probably missed that. Used to be, the keys gave them a few seconds' warning to hide their contraband or gather spit in their mouths. For his part, Wes was acutely aware of the lightness at his waist, of the absence of the equipment he'd always carried inside the prison. He missed his uniform, the authority and purpose that came with it.

It was slow going through the prison, doors and gates every couple dozen yards, and Wes tried not to notice his heartbeat starting to become palpable inside his ribcage. All these locks didn't mean he was gonna get stuck in here. Just meant folks stayed where they were supposed to be. It was a good thing. "Farmer said you work Max these days," he said, as they navigated another beige corridor.

Lowell nodded once. "Going on ten years now."

"So you know Williams. Presently, I mean."

"I do."

Wes slowed. Wanted to get his answer before they hit the next gate. "This born-again business," he said. "It true?"

Lowell sighed. He stopped, looked first at the floor, then up at Wes. "I seen no proof to the contrary."

"So you think he's a new man." The words came out short, bitten off a little too soon.

"Wes, it don't matter what I think." Something pleading in Lowell's tone. "No one here's forgotten what he did, least of all me. That riot started an hour later, I'd have been right in the middle of it." He broke eye contact. "But I gotta tell you, Williams is one of the easiest inmates I've got over there."

They walked the rest of the way in silence. The hearing room was at the end of a long corridor of administrative offices. "You'll be the only one making a statement," Lowell said.

"Williams ain't got anyone speaking for him?"

"Williams ain't had one single visitor," Lowell told him. "Not ever." He unlocked the door, pushed it open. "You want me to stay?"

Wes shook his head.

"I'll meet you after, then. Good luck."

Wes was alone in the room. It smelled like new carpet, an unpleasant, industrial chemical odor. There was a long table at the front of the room, the kind found in schools, folding legs and a Formica top. A computer set up on one end. Four chairs pushed neatly beneath the table, a single chair a few yards away, facing the others. Another door behind it. And here, where Wes stood, twelve chairs perpendicular to the rest, two rows of six. Wes stood in the narrow center aisle for a moment. Made sense to sit on the same side of the room as the parole board, but in the end he took a seat in the front row nearest the single chair. Even that closest seat would put more space between him and Williams than there'd been during the whole of the riot.

Wasn't too late to leave. Might lose a little face, yeah, but folks would only talk behind his back, and even then they'd probably claim to understand. Maybe he shouldn't be so damn stubborn; maybe he ought to listen to the folks telling him this was a bad idea. But he sat. He waited.

Wes knew better than to expect the hearing to start on time, and he wasn't disappointed. There was a clock on the opposite wall, ensconced behind a metal cage; the red second hand moved in a single fluid motion, no ticking. Ten minutes past the scheduled start, the door he'd come through opened again and two men and a woman entered. They'd been speaking, but fell silent when they saw Wes. He watched them settle themselves behind the long table. He knew their names. He'd gone online at Dennis's house and looked up all seven parole board members. Wasn't hard to find out almost everything about them, photos included. He wondered if that ever worried them. The man nearest him, the balding one, was named Simon Frank and was a lawyer from Helena. The woman, who wore glasses on a beaded chain, was named Diane Copeland and was a businesswoman, also from Helena. The second man, who knelt in front of the table and fussed with the computer screen, was named Ernest Pike and was a retired police chief from Great Falls. There would be two other board members participating in the hearing via the Internet.

The computer gave the police chief some trouble, but soon he had it running, and Wes heard tinny voices through the speakers, saw blurred images on the screen. Another lawyer, a retired game warden. Twenty-three minutes past the scheduled start. He needed to piss again. The board members had thick binders in front of them. The woman leafed absently through hers; the two men sat and looked at the wall. Thirty minutes past, and the retired cop looked up and asked, "Wesley J. Carver?" and Wes said, "Yeah."

Thirty-eight minutes past the scheduled start, the door behind the single chair opened and Bobby Williams walked in. The two COs that followed him were strangers to Wes—he was grateful for it—and Williams waited with one officer's hand on his elbow while the other closed the door behind them. At the officer's prompting, he shuffled toward the single chair, each step slow and careful because he wore leg irons. His cuffed hands were fixed to the wide belt around his waist, and he held them in loose fists. One of the COs put his hand on Williams's shoulder and Williams sat, the chain between his legs sliding with a metallic jingle against the edge of the chair.

He looked first at the parole board, a scanning glance that didn't settle on any one face, and only then did he look at Wes. It wasn't a straight stare—more a sidelong look—but it lingered. Wes held Williams's gaze, steady, steady, steady, but even this felt like a risk, a real chance he'd bring his false confidence on too strong, reveal his fear in striving too stridently to hide it. The man Wes saw looked almost nothing like the one who haunted his memory. Williams wore the beige scrubs that served as the inmate uniform now, and they matched almost exactly the sallow shade of his skin. His hair was a bland brown shot through with gray; he wore it slightly longer than he had years ago. He seemed sturdier than Wes remembered, taller and wider both, and his face had become fleshier, though the new weight hung oddly over his bones. His eyes were the palest blue, and this troubled Wes. He had been so certain they were dark.

"Parole hearing for inmate Robert F. Williams commences at . . . eleven-ten a.m.," the lawyer announced. Williams turned his attention to the board, and Wes felt himself exhale for the first time since the man had come into the room. Despite his years as a CO, he didn't know that much about parole hearings, but he wasn't surprised by the tedium. A recitation of Williams's crimes. The first litany, the one Wes had nothing to do with, the old farmer and his doomed wife. And then the second, his own. *Participation in a riot. Possession of a deadly weapon by a prisoner in a facility. Aggravated assault. Assault against a peace officer. Unlawful restraint. Aggravated kidnapping.* Wes listened to the convictions. Marveled that the state would even consider letting a man who'd done these things—and done most of them not once, but twice—back into the world. He thought, too, of the things Williams hadn't been charged with, because no such charges existed. *Harboring vile thoughts toward my wife. Finding amusement in my suffering. Mocking my terror. Destroying my talent.* Williams listened mutely, offering no indication that he felt any involvement in the proceedings. Looked like he was listening to the goddamned weather report.

The board members mentioned the many statements and letters they apparently held tucked away in those binders, the testimonials and assurances that Williams was a changed man, had turned over a new leaf, et cetera.

"You converted to Christianity in 2001?"

"Yes, sir."

"You participate in the prison ministry?"

"Yes, ma'am."

"If released, do you intend to continue to participate in church activities?"

"Yes, sir, I surely do."

"It says here you've had no citations for misconduct since your conversion."

"That's right, sir."

It went on this way. An unchallenging catechism to which Williams offered nothing more than the barest answers. Wes tried to read truth or falsehood in Williams's voice, but there was nothing there for him to hold to one way or another. He realized he'd never heard Williams speak in a normal tone; during the riot it had always been that insidious whisper, occasionally a half-crazed bark or yell.

Finally the businesswoman turned a couple of pages in her binder and said, "These are horrific crimes." Wes didn't take his eyes off Williams, but in his peripheral vision he saw the woman glance at him over her glasses. "How do you explain them?"

Yes, Wes thought, barely keeping the words behind his teeth, *how do you fucking explain what you did to me?* Williams dropped his head to stare at his shackled hands; after a long moment he raised his eyes to the board members. "I can't explain them," he said, in that same unfamiliar straightforward tone. "The things I did were inexcusable." *The things.* Didn't so much as glance at Wes. Didn't even acknowledge he was in the room. "I wish I could undo them. Every day I wish it. But I can't. All I can do is choose to be someone different. Someone who would never do those things." The board waited, silent, but Williams offered nothing more.

The woman took another stab. "And you say you have, in fact, become someone different."

"Yes, ma'am. Through the merciful grace of the Lord and with His help."

Wes couldn't make heads or tails of what Williams was saying. It was the same bland bullshit any inmate might spout. Nothing there to say he'd really changed. (Nothing to say he hadn't.) The board members weren't asking the right questions. Nothing that might prompt an illuminating answer, nothing that might let Wes know whether this professed faith was real or a hoax. God, he wished he could say for certain, even if that meant knowing Williams was still an evil, lying bastard, or even if it meant knowing that his only real enemy had found the grace he himself had never been granted. All Wes wanted was to *know*.

The former police chief ended it. "Is there anything else you'd like to say?"

Here, maybe. Here Williams might reveal more than he intended, might go off-script. Williams looked down again. He clasped his hands together, and the links of the short chain between the cuffs sounded against themselves, a brief series of fine notes. And then he looked at Wes again, sidelong, still not straight on. He looked at him for a long moment, and seemed ready to speak—Wes could almost see Williams tasting the words on his tongue—but then he straightened and turned back to the board. "No, sir."

Wes's turn. The board acknowledged him, and he stood, though he wasn't required to. Had to get out of that chair. Too much to sit in a chair inside a room inside a prison with Bobby Williams not ten feet away. He opened and closed his fists several times—he'd been clenching them tightly these last minutes, and every poorly healed joint was making itself known. He wished he could pace. Had to find the words, the right words, the exact words that would make these people understand. Williams had held his own words to a minimum, mitigated the horror of what he'd done with silence and omissions. Wes had to bring that horror out of the past and into this room. And he had no idea how to do that.

"I got so much running through my head right now I don't hardly know where to start," he said, looking at the board members. He forced himself to meet each of their eyes, though he'd rather have let his gaze linger in the space between or above their heads. "I know you've all read reports about the riot. You have a pretty good idea of what happened in that control room, in a nuts-and-bolts kind of way. Ain't no need for me to go into all that. What I don't imagine those reports can tell you is how it feels to be that much at the mercy of someone who don't got a lot of mercy to offer." The words were coming hard. It was like they weren't quite familiar, like he'd learned them either too recently or too long ago. "Robert Williams and I didn't have no conflict before that riot. I hadn't hardly laid eyes on him before that day. Wasn't on my tier. I hadn't ever written him up, or canceled his yard time, or done anything else that might've begun to validate what he did, not even in his own head. I didn't even know his name till he carved it into my flesh." He was careful not to look at Williams. Let his vision go a little soft until that figure in the single chair blurred.

"I don't know if you know this," Wes said, then stopped. He looked at Williams—the other man met his eyes—and dropped his voice, real soft. "I don't even know if *you* know this." Wes forced himself to turn his attention back to the board. "I was a fiddler. I was good, real good. Better than you're probably thinking," he said, "and I don't say that out of arrogance; I say it so maybe you can better appreciate the fact that I ain't played my fiddle one single time since that riot. Can't. My hands don't work good enough anymore." He held them up, palms out. Beyond the crooked lines of his fingers, he saw the lawyer work his jaw, saw the businesswoman pass one of her own hands over the other.

"My wife," Wes said, and he hated to mention her here, to let even the barest idea of her enter Williams's mind, "passed on recently. She was real sick at the end. Not entirely herself." The grief turned sharp, suddenly, and he stopped, let a silence unfurl while he collected himself. "The day she died, she wanted me to play my fiddle for her. Last thing she ever asked of me. She'd forgotten, see, what'd happened. Thought we were still living in Black River, that we were younger, I guess. Or somehow her mind just erased the riot." Wes heard his own voice turning husky, and the more he tried to drive the rasp out of it, the more pronounced it became. His throat was tight, and he felt a flush forcing its way up his neck. He was angry—of all the moments for his voice to betray him!—but even as he cursed himself, even as he fought it, a smaller thought insistently pressed its way into his head. Hadn't he made the decision to lay it all bare? Didn't he believe it would take no less to keep Williams inside these walls?

"I can't stop thinking about the fact that I couldn't play for her. That my wife died waiting for me to play my music for her, and I didn't." He was shaking now, not hard, a tremor so slight he doubted anyone else could see it. Might even have been contained entirely within his body, starting right at the center with his grieving, trembling heart, carrying forth from his chest and mixing with rage and fear and hate and love and a lot of other things Wes neither could nor desired to name. "I suppose I ought to be grateful we had the last twenty years together, that Robert Williams stopped short of killing me and held himself to"— Wes steeled himself, said it—"to torture. But I couldn't save my wife. I couldn't make her treatments work, couldn't slow the disease, couldn't even do much to ease her pain." His voice was all but broken now, each word sparse and stripped. "And she knew that. She didn't ask me to do none of those things. But the one thing I could've done for her, the one thing she did ask—Robert Williams took that away from us in that control room. Now he says he's chosen to become someone different. Someone new. I have a hard time believing it's as simple as that, just a choice. But whatever you make of that, what he did to me has consequences. I know it seems like a long way in the past, but twenty years on, it still has consequences. It ain't over. Ain't over," Wes repeated, and then he was out of words. He looked at each member of the board once more and sat down.

Williams was watching him. He kept his head bowed, just a little, and Wes wondered if that was meant to look nonthreatening. Looked furtive, instead. His expression was still carefully guarded, but there was a slight crease between his brows, a suggestion in those pale eyes that he was troubled by what he'd heard. Whether that troubledness was due to the stirrings of newfound conscience or for fear of the effect Wes's words might have on the parole board's decision, Wes couldn't have said.

"We'll take this under advisement," the lawyer said, and the COs by the door crossed the room to Williams, who stood obediently. He shuffled back to the door, his chains sounding with each step. He did not look at Wes again. Wes watched him go. Watched the door shut behind him. Watched the place where he had been. After a minute Wes realized the board members were staring, waiting for him to go out his own door.

"You all right, Mr. Carver?" the former police chief asked. Wes glanced distractedly back at the man, and instead of answering, he stood and left the room.

Lowell was right outside. The corridor was marginally warmer than the hearing room had been, the fluorescent lights a touch brighter. The air seemed somehow clearer, too, no longer molasses in his lungs, and Wes felt instantly more alert, more himself. His heart quieted in his chest. He wondered whether Lowell had been out here the whole time, whether he'd been able to hear. If so, he appeared willing to do Wes the service of pretending he hadn't. "Well?"

"Under advisement," Wes said.

Lowell nodded tersely, went past him into the hearing room. He kept one hand on the side of the door but let it almost shut, and Wes winced at the unbidden thought that a single firm pull on the doorknob could shatter half a dozen bones at once. Lowell came back into the hall. "They're going to make a decision in a few minutes," he said. "I think it's a good sign they didn't rule at the end of the hearing. Means your statement carried some weight."

Wes walked with Lowell to the control booth at the end of the hall. It was large enough for three or four officers—though only one sat inside now—and had electronic locks and wired glass windows. A hell of a lot more secure than the chain link and iron of his control room back in the old prison. That had been little more than a space to do paperwork and radio the administrative offices without having to watch his back every second; this, on the other hand, was a true control room, with electronic mastery of all the gates and doors in this wing of the building. Lights and color-coded labels marked a map of the nearby area, and a computer screen on one end of the desk stuttered real-time updates of which inmates and staff were where. Wes let Lowell and the CO in the booth show him how it all worked, and he and Lowell halfheartedly reminisced about the medieval technology at the old prison. He felt a little like the children he had sometimes seen at the hospital during Claire's illness, kids with grave expressions who seemed to pretend interest in toys and games for the sake of the adults trying desperately to distract them from their families' crises.

After a short while Lowell slipped out of the room with a baldly casual "I'll be just a minute." Wes nodded dutifully and listened to the young CO explain the gating system. He was more confident about the hearing now that he was feeling like himself again. Williams had hardly made a case for his parole at all. He had volunteered nothing, made no effort to show the board the changes he claimed had taken place within him, hadn't offered any formal apology for his actions or made any conciliatory gestures toward Wes. Hell, he'd behaved almost like a sullen teenager, answering reluctantly and in monotone. Wes knew he himself had fallen far short of the articulateness he'd aimed for, but at least there'd been some passion behind his words. He'd laid it all out there, and it'd cost him, yeah — the shame of exposing his scars and sorrows still burned within him, a small but searing flame — but it was gonna be worth it. He had come. Faced the man. Said what needed to be said. He was suddenly sure of the board's decision, so sure he wondered whether he'd somehow heard it from this far down the hall, through these solid walls; he could almost taste the strong corners of the word, the way it closed with the same sharp certainty with which it opened: *denied.*

The door's magnetic lock sounded, and Lowell came back into the room. The young officer at the desk fell silent, and Wes looked up. Lowell knew how to guard his expressions as surely as Wes did, so there was no way to read the decision on his features, but Wes heard it again inside his own head: *denied.* Then Lowell's Adam's apple bobbed, and the word was coming up in his throat, but his lips were still pressed together and there was no glint of teeth, and the word vanished from Wes's mind and Lowell spoke.

"Paroled."

~

That night Wes tipped a handful of bullets from his box of ammunition and loaded the revolver. Went downstairs carrying his boots under one arm. Waited till he was on the porch before tugging them on and shrugging his chore coat over his shoulders, the revolver heavy in one pocket. He walked briskly through Farmer's yard, skirting the silent tractor and the empty arena. A horse whickered from the darkness as Wes passed the shuttered barns. Autumn was still hanging on during the day, but night had given itself over to winter, and the air burned cold in Wes's nostrils and lungs. A waning moon idled high in the sky, veiled in cloud, and it cast just enough light for him to see the immediate exhalation of his breath before it dissipated into the dark. He heard the Wounded Elk before he saw it, a gentle sound for an entity of such power. The moonlight dipped into the hollows between the rises and swells of the water, but save for those slight flashes of silver, it was the blackest of rivers.

The bank eased into the shallows here, and Wes stood at the edge of the rocks and let the water lick at the toes of his boots. He couldn't see across the river, but he knew this to be one of the narrow places, no more than twenty yards from one side to the other. There was no bank opposite, no beach. Just the straight jut of the mountain, the land rising right from the water.

Wes took the revolver from his pocket and shaped his left hand around it, maneuvering his index finger into place inside the trigger guard. He knew his own frailty well; even with this much pain, he'd be able to manage a single shot. He turned the revolver so the tip of its barrel rested against his breast; moonlight glinted once off the bluing. He stood unmoving, feeling the trigger beneath his finger, the gentle press of metal against his chest. He thought his heart ought to be racing, but he felt no rush in his veins, no rise of his pulse against the revolver's steel, as though he'd stilled his heart already. Made sense, maybe. *Hard for a man to fight his own blood,* he always said, and whatever else this was—cowardly, selfish, desperate—whatever else, this was in his blood.

Wes could think of no reason not to do it. None. But his hand remained steady, his trigger finger still. This was a moment for prayer, but Wes knew too well that any words he dared speak would wisp away into the night air, unheard, unanswered. So instead he swung the revolver away from his heart, set his feet the way his father had taught him, and fired at the great rising earth across the river. Two rounds, *one-two,* and the pain ripped a growl from his throat and he let his hand drop. No way to know where the bullets had homed to, and for a moment Wes felt a flash of his old self and thought of the rules he'd broken by firing into the dark, the safeties and cautions he'd ignored. Then the mountains behind him sounded a mimicry of his shots, and their brothers across the river echoed more gently, and finally he stood alone in the deep silence, breathing cordite and cold.

—

The next day Farmer stayed close. Still had to take care of his horses, though, and when he went out to the barn for the evening feeding, Wes found Farmer's address book and turned the pages until he found Jamie Lowell's name.

"I don't know if I ought to talk about that with you," Lowell said, when Wes had asked his question.

Wes leaned back against the kitchen counter, moved a ceramic saltshaker along the edge of the sink. "Bus station's right down on Main, Jamie. Can't really avoid it if I go into town." The saltshaker nearly tipped over; Wes caught it in a loose fist. "Look," he said, "I ain't exactly proud of feeling anxious as I do, but I figured you'd understand. You really gonna make me explain why I don't want to chance running into Williams?"

Lowell was silent for a long moment, and Wes knew he'd get his answer. He squinted through the window, didn't see Farmer. He could hear Dennis hammering across the pasture, the slightest of sounds at this distance, slight enough Wes ought to've been able to ignore it. "Friday," Lowell said finally. "He'll be released late morning. The bus comes at two."

"Appreciate it," Wes said. He hung up the phone, put the address book back just where he'd found it.

～

"You seem like a good man," Williams had said. No more than an hour before rescue. "Do you believe in God? You must. Most good men do." Williams crouched behind him, a faceless voice. "Are you praying now, Wesley? Right now?" The shank at his throat, suddenly. The flat of the blade sticky against his flesh, warmed with his own blood. "I think you should."

"God." A word wrenched from between clenched teeth, a word spoken through the grimace of pain and terror. Prayer or worse. "God." Better. Say it right. Make it worthy. "Help me," Wes had whispered, "survive this." The blade pulled tight below his jaw, arching his face up. He closed his eyes. "And if I can't—" he said "—survive—" the words coming faster, without thought, coming without his calling them, the way his music always had and never would again "—then ease my way home to You." Eyes open now, sight blurred by tears that wouldn't fall. "And please, God, above all else, watch over my wife and my son. Shelter them in Your love." No more. The blade was still there at his throat, his life moments—millimeters—from ending. If there were ever a moment in which to find faith, to be struck with the certainty of God's presence, Wes was enduring it, but he felt no comfort, no peace.

And then long seconds in which death did not come, in which no new pain was visited upon him. His breath, Williams's breath, audible, steady, matched. Finally: "You finished?" A nod—the slightest—

even that minute movement a risk with the blade at his throat, but Wes wanted to say nothing else, wanted no lesser words to come between his prayer—even if unheard—and his death, if that was what came next. But then the shank was gone. Reprieve. Williams's lips beside his ear. "You're supposed to say 'Amen' when you're done."

~

What Wes needed was to speak to Bobby Williams. To hear Williams—the real Williams—speak to him. Society's justice had failed, far as Wes was concerned, and there was nothing he could do to stop Williams walking through that gate today. But he might still have the chance to find the truth, to know for certain what lay in the heart of this man about to be loosed upon the world, if only he could really speak to him. The parole hearing had been all wrong, and Wes ought to have known it would be. The hearing was a production, a performance, every man playing his part, Wes included. Hadn't he dressed for it? The suit coat, the polished shoes, the part in his hair. Done himself up the way he thought they'd expect him to. So Friday Wes dressed as he did on any other day. He chose his darkest jeans, his green chamois shirt, his square-toed roper boots with the leather soles scuffed almost through. He combed his wet hair with his fingers and let it dry fanned over his forehead. His father's pocketwatch was hard against his hipbone in his right front jeans pocket, and his wedding ring—the replacement he'd bought after the riot, the one Williams stole missing to this day—was on his finger, below a joint so swollen Wes didn't know that he could've taken the ring off if he'd wanted to.

Farmer watched him closely all morning, something untrusting in his eyes, but Wes looked as he did any other day, behaved—he was careful of this—as he did any other day. He sat at the kitchen table and drank his coffee and read the local section of the Elk Fork paper. (There'd been a fatal car wreck up on the Flathead reservation yesterday. A hunter from Ovando had bagged a record-setting elk. The animal shelter was waiving adoption fees for cats through the end of the month.) Wes read and Farmer, who'd had his own breakfast hours before, turned the pages of the sports section and watched Wes.

"You're worrying me a little here," Farmer said after a while.

Wes flipped a sheet over. (One of the newly elected city councilmen had vowed to increase funding for snowplowing.) "You worry a lot," he said. "Ain't good for your blood pressure."

Farmer rapped the fingers of his right hand on the tabletop—ring-middle-index, ring-middle-index—and then stopped abruptly. Sensitive even in his nervous habits. "Jamie called for you yesterday," he said. "Wanted you to know he double-checked the bus schedule and it comes at one, not two."

Wes didn't stop his eyes going to the clock, and Farmer saw him look.

"He explained that you wanted to know so you could be elsewhere." Farmer waited, having offered the challenge, but Wes looked at him and locked down anything dangerous behind his eyes, and soon enough it became clear to both of them that Farmer didn't have it in him to call Wes a liar.

Wes took his mug to the sink, rinsed it and went back upstairs. He was careful of his hands as he loaded the revolver, taking light hold of the weapon and its bullets, reserving what strength he could. He sat for a time in the rocking chair beside the window, watching the mountains and sky. It was thickly overcast, the space above the peaks clotted with heavy white clouds. Claire had once told him that white clouds piled atop one another like these meant snow.

At a quarter past noon, Wes stood up. His coat was downstairs on the rack beside the front door, so he put the revolver inside the waistband of his jeans, against the small of his back, and untucked his shirt so it hid the grip. Felt a little like a two-bit gangster in a movie, but Farmer was still waiting downstairs. Wes descended the staircase as quickly as he could without seeming to hurry, and when Farmer looked up from the kitchen table and asked where he was going, Wes said, "Out." Like he was Dennis as a teenager, sullenly monosyllabic. Dennis or Scott.

It was cold enough the truck didn't want to start, and Wes had to turn the key three times before the engine turned over. He rubbed his right hand with his left while he waited for the rumbling to steady and for the defroster to make headway against the lattice of ice hugging the windshield. As the ice began its retreat, he saw Farmer's truck parked ahead, and Wes stepped out of his own truck and went to Farmer's and sank the blade of his pocketknife deep into both driver's side tires. It hurt him, but he used his right hand and spared the left. He spotted the telephone line snaking from beneath the eave of the house down the clapboard to the foundation, and he ran his blade through that, too.

He got back in his truck and put it into gear and was almost to the woods when Farmer slapped the hood and put himself in front of the truck. Wes shifted into neutral but didn't kill the engine. He began to roll down the window, but it was stiff with ice and stopped after a few inches, so when Farmer came up beside it he couldn't put his elbows on the sill and lean into the cab the way Wes knew he wanted to.

"Wesley," Farmer said, and his breath was a little weak. "Don't do this."

The air from outside was the sharp sort of cold, and Wes felt it on one side of his face while the other was hot with the air blowing from the dash vents. "How far are you gonna go to keep me here, Farmer? You willing to lay hands on me and use whatever strength you got to stop me? 'Cause I'm warning you now, it won't take no less."

Farmer hesitated only a moment, and then he hauled open the driver's side door and moved toward Wes and then he stopped because he saw the revolver. It was resting on Wes's thigh, almost casual-like, except Wes had gone to the trouble of working his finger through the trigger guard and the end of the barrel was staring right out at Farmer. Wes said nothing and Farmer said nothing and after a minute Farmer took one step back and hooked his arm over the open door. Something shifted in his face, and Wes couldn't have said what changed, exactly, the eyes or the mouth or something else, but his expression closed. "Well," Farmer said, "I guess now we know where we both stand."

Wes waited, but Farmer said nothing else. After a minute Wes took his hand off the steering wheel and reached for the door handle, and

Farmer stepped back and took his arm off the door, and Wes pulled it shut and shifted gears and drove into the woods, and he didn't look in the rearview, not even once.

—

The bus station was just a single wooden bench, thickly coated with blue paint and set against the outside wall of the gas station, and the empty gravel lot beside the pumps, bare save for a scattering of hardy weeds and, for ten minutes twice a day, a lumbering Greyhound bus that didn't even stop long enough to halt its engines' shuddering. The old prison occupied the opposite side of the street, the top of the red cellblock just visible above the gray wall. Bobby Williams was looking at it when Wes pulled into the lot at a quarter to one. He sat alone on the bench, a large paper bag beside him, its top rolled shut. He wore a new blue shirt and dark dungarees, the fabric so stiff it looked liable to crease and split like cardboard if he moved.

Wes had the revolver back in his coat pocket, and he put his hand in with it, settled the grip against his palm and found the trigger guard with his crooked index finger. It was a heavy coat, the canvas rough even after years of washing, and no one would be able to say for sure whether there was anything but his hands in the pockets. He glanced outside. One truck at the pumps. Its owner inside, talking to the kid behind the register. Wes set his face and held it, then got out of his truck before he could decide it wasn't a good idea. He took three steps toward the gas station and stopped. Waited.

Williams watched him for several seconds before rising. He left the paper bag on the bench and crossed the gravel slow, walking like someone still learning how, each step a hair shorter or longer than the one before. He stopped a couple yards away, hooked his thumbs into his belt loops. "I been inside so long I don't hardly know what to do without lines on the floor and COs telling me what to do," he said. "I don't even know how close I ought to stand to you."

"You're plenty close," Wes said, and Williams looked over Wes's shoulder and let one side of his mouth pull into a brief smile. Wes saw now that Williams wasn't really bigger than he remembered, as he'd thought at the hearing, but merely filled out, healthy flesh gentling bones that had been more pronounced twenty years ago. He still exhibited hints of the nerviness and restlessness Wes remembered, looked at Wes only in flickering glances: a few seconds on his face, away; a moment meeting his eyes, away.

"I guess all inmates think about the day they get out," Williams said. The first snowflakes had begun to fall between them, singly, each somehow shameful in its solitude, like a note mistakenly played before the beat. "I always thought it'd be sunny when my day came."

"Things don't always turn out the way we think they ought."

Williams turned his gaze on him outright then, and inside his pocket Wes let his finger slide inside the trigger guard. "I didn't know you were a fiddler," Williams told him. "When we were in the control room."

"Would it've made a difference if you had?"

Williams didn't hesitate. "I'd have skipped the cigarettes and the shank and gone for your hands right off."

Wes held his features where he'd put them. "That's about how I figured it," he said. He thought Williams might try to tell him it'd be different now, that he was real sorry for what he'd done, but he didn't. Just let his eyes drift away from Wes's face and into the air, following one flake and then another in its descent toward the ground.

The man with the truck came out of the gas station and put the pump back in its cradle but forgot to close the gas door before getting back into the cab. He drove away with the gas door standing open, the flap of metal jouncing with each jolt of the tires over the potholed gravel.

"I should say it was you that led me to Christ." It seemed to Wes that Williams was standing closer now, but he hadn't heard him move, and he'd taken his eyes off him for only an instant. "You said this gorgeous prayer during the riot, you remember that? I guess I didn't think much of it at the time, but I kept hearing it in my head afterward. Those things you said. The way you said them. I don't expect you to be much concerned by the fact, but I didn't know any kind of churching or, or, spiritual sort of matters in my upbringing. Your prayer was the first time I ever been witness to faith of that kind. And it changed my life; it truly did. So I thank you for that."

For a long moment Wes stood silent, heart warring between incredulity and fury, and finally he had to do something and that revolver was ready in his hand but he kept it still and laughed instead. A bitter sound even to his ears. "Lord," he said, "if that ain't a load of bull you just spouted off, you got it so wrong I don't hardly know where to start. Yeah, I remember what I said; I remember every second of that riot and will till the day I die. And what you heard wasn't *faith,* Williams. You heard terror. Desperation. Maybe a little bit of yearning. But you didn't hear faith." A snowflake alighted on Wes's eye, and he blinked it away. Williams watched him impassively, only the slightest, almost imperceptible shake of his head suggesting he'd even heard Wes's words. "Hell, you say *you* remember this so well," Wes said, his voice rising more than he meant to let it. "You remember the part where the only reason I was praying at all was you put a goddamned blade to my throat and told me you thought I *should?*"

Williams looked Wes in the eye again, and what Wes saw there wasn't exactly the familiar malice but was still sharper than he'd expected. "Wesley," he said, "did you ever think maybe that blade made the things you said to God more true, not less?"

Wes knew then he could do it. He could take his father's revolver out of his coat pocket and he could aim it and let it loose its bullets to taste flesh for the first time. He would watch the blood bloom on this man's chest and he would watch him fall, and then he would let the consequences come as they may. He could do it. He wanted to. "I came here because I thought talking to you would clear some things up," Wes said, his voice low but even. "I don't got to tell you what happened in there," he jerked his head in the direction of the old prison, "so I also don't got to tell you why I was sort of taken aback to hear you supposedly found Jesus and all. It's been bothering me something fierce, wondering whether that was possible for you, of all people. What it means if you're lying, and what it means if you ain't. You and me, I guess in our own way we know each other pretty well. So I thought if I came today and talked to you, just the two of us like it was back then, I'd know for sure one way or another whether you really were a changed man or born-again or however you want to say it. That's all I really wanted, to know for sure. But now I'm here and I've talked to you and I know I don't like you and I wish more than anything you were still locked up, but I don't know a whole lot more than that. All I got's your word that you are what you say you are."

Williams watched Wes steadily, but if there was something to see in those eyes, some truth there for him to read, Wes couldn't find it. Slowly Williams's gaze slid toward Wes's coat pocket, and a downward twitch at the corner of his mouth gave Wes his first hint that Williams might know what waited for him there. "So," Williams said, glancing back up at Wes's face. "What are you going to do?"

Wes gave himself one moment more to imagine the satisfaction that would come with blood. Then he took a deep breath. Closed his eyes. And let the revolver slip from his wounded grip. "I'm going to believe you."

~

Wes sent the truck hard down the gravel drive, the wipers scraping starbursts of melted snowflakes from the windshield. Trees reached for him as he steered sharply around the curves, branches grazing metal more than once. Then he was parked outside the house and Dennis was sitting on the porch steps, holding Rio's lead in one hand. His head was bowed and the black horse's muzzle rested almost in his hair. Wes got out of the truck and walked toward the porch. He was aware of moving too fast, and he forced himself to slow, loitered there below the first step. The horse flicked one ear toward him, but Dennis didn't lift his head. After a minute Wes lowered himself onto the top step beside him. Kept his face out of the snow, but flakes dusted the toes of his boots.

"Arthur seems to think you might've done something stupid," Dennis said finally.

"Yeah?" Wes took the revolver out of his pocket, set it carefully on the warp of the wooden boards between them. "What do you think?"

Dennis glanced at it, but his expression didn't change. "I think there's still six rounds in that gun."

Wes's hands stung with the cold, the burn of his skin joining with the ache of his joints, but he didn't put them in his pockets. Hard to look at Dennis—not ready to meet his eyes—so he stared toward the river, squinting against the snow. It was falling harder now, the mountains ghosted outlines only.

"I got the vet coming in a couple hours," Dennis said. "Rio can't handle another winter and it wouldn't be right to ask him to try." He touched the revolver with the very tips of his fingers. "I had an idea I might do it myself, but it seems I don't have it in me."

Wes wanted to lay a comforting hand on Dennis, but he couldn't say how the man would react. He ran his palm over Rio's mane instead; the white flakes that had caught in the hairs melted beneath his touch and left glittering wet beads behind. "I could be there with you," Wes offered. "When the vet comes. If you want."

Dennis didn't say *Yes* or *Thanks* or even *Hell no,* didn't even seem to have heard. Wes thought it was good that he'd offered anyway.

They sat silent for a time. That winter quiet Wes knew so well had come down on the canyon. The noises of man—the trains, the interstate—were muted, and the sounds of the land, almost too subtle to hear—the descent of the snow, the journeying river, the breath of animals—had woven together in a gentle hush. Wes had come here without much thought. He knew there were things to say, about Williams and Claire and his fiddle and most of all about him and Dennis, the past and the future, but those words escaped him now, and that was all right. The silence would lift. It was early yet, a melt still ahead, warmer days before winter truly settled.

"I know I shouldn't be so torn up over this," Dennis said. He laid his palm on Rio's face, gingerly, as though the horse might already be gone. Mirage. "Especially not after everything that's happened. He's just a horse," he said. "An old horse. But . . ."

Wes looked out across the land. Mountains gone. White from heaven to earth. "Tell me," he said.

And Dennis spoke, the words tumbling from his lips, each as fragile and hushed as a snowflake. They came unsteadily at first, then stronger, and they built upon each other, settling and burying what lay between father and son.

Wes listened.

ACKNOWLEDGMENTS

I am grateful to the Wisconsin Institute for Creative Writing for their generous support during the writing of this book. Thanks also to the faculty, staff and graduate students whose time at the University of Oregon Creative Writing Program overlapped mine; I am especially appreciative of David Bradley, Laurie Lynn Drummond, Cai Emmons and Ehud Havazelet.

Many thanks to fiddlers Chip Cohen and Brian O'Donnell for teaching me to play many of the tunes that appear in these pages, and to farrier Michael Waldorf for letting me watch him shoe horses.

Thank you to Lorin Rees for being everything I could have hoped for in an agent, and to Nicole LaBombard for her careful reading and thoughtful feedback.

I am thankful to everyone at Houghton Mifflin Harcourt for their enthusiasm and dedication. Special thanks to Jenna Johnson for her insightful suggestions and for being my guide through this process, to Nina Barnett for having all the answers, and to Larry Cooper for his sharp eye.

Finally, and most of all, I am immensely grateful to my parents for their unwavering love and support.